CONTENTS

EDITOR'S PREFACE

This book is part of a series of commentaries seeking to interpret the books of the Bible from a Wesleyan perspective. It is designed primarily for laypeople, especially teachers of Sunday school and leaders of Bible studies. Pastors also will find this series very helpful. In addition, this series is for people who want to read and study on their own for spiritual edification.

Each book of the Bible will be explained paragraph by paragraph. This "wide-angle lens" approach helps the reader to follow the primary flow of thought in each passage. This, in turn, will help the reader to avoid "missing the forest because of the trees," a problem many people encounter when reading commentaries.

At the same time, the authors slow down often to examine particular details and concepts that are important for understanding the bigger picture. Where there are alternative understandings of key passages, the authors acknowledge these so the reader will experience a broader knowledge of the various theological traditions and how the Wesleyan perspective relates to them.

These commentaries follow the New International Version and are intended to be read with your Bible open. With this in mind, the biblical text is not reproduced in full, but appears in bold type throughout the discussion of each passage. Greater insight will be gained by reading along in your Bible as you read the commentaries.

These volumes do not replace the valuable technical commentaries that offer in-depth grammatical and textual analysis. What they do offer is an interpretation of the Bible that we hope will lead to a greater understanding of what the Bible says, its significance for our lives today, and further transformation into the image of Christ.

David A. Higle
Senior Editor

AUTHOR'S PREFACE

S aint Athanasius, a leader of the church in the early 300s A.D., considered himself "devoted to the Psalms." They provide, he wrote, a picture of the human soul. Whatever your particular trouble, in Psalms you will find words to address your need and the way to "remedy your ill." Through Psalms, you will come to know God and are shown how to worship Him. This commentary is written to help you become more "devoted to the Psalms." As the psalms are illuminated, may you see yourself, see God, and learn of His will for you.

Special thanks are due to those who have instructed me in the beauty and enigmas of the Psalter, especially Dr. David Dorsey of the Evangelical School of Theology and Dr. Paul Riemann of Drew University. I am grateful to Dr. Keith Drury and David Higle for their contributions to the commentary series. Thanks to Dr. Bud Bence and Indiana Wesleyan University for their encouragement, and thanks to my tremendously insightful Sunday school class at College Wesleyan Church.

A special word of thanks is due to my wife, Eileen, and my children, Abigail and Ethan, for their love, support, and patience. In particular, this book is dedicated to my wife, whose companionship, whether in "the valley of the shadow of death" (Psalm 23:4) or "the courts of our God" (Psalm 92:13), has been irreplaceable.

Stephen J. Lennox
Marion, Indiana
March 1999

INTRODUCTION

T here is probably no Old Testament book more familiar to Christians than Psalms. We catch snatches of the psalms in the New Testament, we sing them in choruses and hymns, and we recite them in worship. Instinctively, we turn to them for comfort, confidence, and penitence. With good reason Martin Luther called this the "book of all the saints." Everyone, in whatever situation he or she may be, can find words and psalms that fit the situation as if they were put there just for his or her sake.[1]

If we are honest, however, most of us would have to admit that we use a few psalms a great deal but others not at all. When we do read the psalms, we hear strange things: the psalmist cursing his enemy, scolding and complaining to God, claiming to be righteous. Then there is the difficulty of trying to understand what life was like in the ancient Near East about three millennia ago. This commentary is written to make the familiar more familiar and the unfamiliar less so. My prayer is that it will help to remove whatever obstacles prevent the reader from fully understanding the God of the psalmist and of us.[2]

COMPILATION OF THE PSALMS

The collection of Hebrew poems we know as the Book of Psalms (or Psalter) is actually a collection of collections. We can discern anthologies attributed to David (see Psalm 72:20; 86), to Asaph (Psalms 73–83), and to the Sons of Korah (Psalms 42–49, 84–85, 87–88). Evidence exists for smaller collections used in Israel's worship, such as the Songs of Ascent (Psalms 120–134).

New psalms were added to older ones and different collections compiled before the psalms were set in their present order, with appropriate selections placed at the beginning and end. The psalms are divided into five books (Psalms 1–41, 42–72, 73–89, 90–106, and 107–150), each of which ends with a brief call to praise. Those who created the five-book structure almost certainly did so on the basis of existing divisions and earlier collections and in a way consistent with the overall formation of the Psalter.

13

No one knows when this five-book division was instituted. Rabbinic tradition puts it in the days of David, but this is entirely too early to account for some of the later psalms (like Psalm 137). The division could not have been done later than the writing of 1 and 2 Chronicles (about 400 B.C.), which quote Psalm 106:47-48, including the doxology (see 1 Chronicles 16:35-36).

Although early tradition has suggested that the five-book division was intended to parallel the five books of Moses (the Pentateuch), there seems to be little or no evidence within the psalms to support this. Nor was the division based on common themes within the books. More likely, the divisions were made for liturgical purposes.

About the only noticeable distinction between the books is the use of the names of God and the presence of smaller collections. "Yahweh" is the preferred name for God in certain books (Books 1, 4, and 5), while other books (Books 2 and 3) prefer "Elohim." Psalms attributed to David are found primarily in Book 1, with additional, smaller clusters found in Books 2 and 5. A collection of eleven psalms of Asaph is found in Book 3, while the eleven psalms of the Sons of Korah are split unevenly between Books 2 and 3.[3]

This collection of collections probably reached its finished form during the post-exilic period, that is, after Israel returned from exile in Babylon. Songs are included which could not have been written earlier (see Psalm 126). Chronicles, composed about the same time, seems to know the Psalter in its final form (1 Chronicles 16:35-36).

Titles indicating the type of psalm, musical and liturgical instructions, ascriptions of authorship, and historical notes were probably added at this time.[4] Scholars remain uncertain about many of these terms, including the meaning of *Selah,* which occurs seventy-one times in the psalms. It is almost certainly some kind of instruction, but for what is unclear. It may have indicated a musical interlude during which silent prayer or meditation would ensue. It may have cued the singers to repeat what they had just sung or to sing it louder.

The titles, as well as the content of the psalms, demonstrate the use of the Psalter as Israel's hymnbook in worship. As with our modern hymnals, some selections were more appropriate for specific Holy Days, some for liturgical or sacramental acts, some as corporate expressions of praise, and others for individual use.

AUTHORSHIP

Traditionally, David is regarded as the author of many of the psalms. Almost half contain the phrase "Of David" in the title; thirteen titles contain historical notes linked to David's life. The New Testament, in several places, calls him the author of Psalms (see Mark 12:36-37; Romans 4:6-8; 11:9-10). Other Old Testament passages identify David as a musician and poet (1 Samuel 16:17-23; 18:10; 2 Samuel 1:17-27; 23:1-7; Amos 6:5) and credit him with organizing Israel's worship (2 Chronicles 29:25-27, 30).

David's authorship has been challenged on several grounds.

First, "Of David" is vague and could also be translated "dedicated to David," "inspired by David," or "about David." It is certain that preceding a name with "of" did not *always* mean authorship, since this style appears twice in one title referring to two different people (see Psalm 88—"of the Sons of the Korah. . . . of Heman the Ezrahite").

Second, the psalms which bear David's name exhibit only general resemblance to David's experiences, even when the title contains a historical reference. By contrast, David's psalm on the death of Saul and Jonathan mentions them by name and contains details of their death (see 2 Samuel 1:17-27). At times, the content of the Davidic psalms seems too late, such as when he speaks of the Temple, which was not built until after his death (Psalms 122, 138).

Although these arguments merit attention, they do not rule out the possibility of Davidic authorship. Specific references, which may originally have been included in these psalms, could have gradually eroded away in the centuries of use prior to assuming their final form. Israel felt free to modify existing psalms for new purposes; therefore, some Davidic psalms were probably altered and even supplemented with later elements.

When the title mentions David, his authorship should be considered, but not automatically assumed. The study of particular psalms may suggest that David is the subject rather than the author, that David is receiving credit for his material reused by a later author (possibly Psalm 53), or that some psalms are credited to him as the Father of psalmody (see 72:20). The evidence on Davidic authorship is too ambiguous to make this a test of orthodoxy. The psalms are God's inspired Word, whether written by David or not.

Twelve psalms are attributed to the Sons of Korah (Psalms 42–49, 84–85, 87–88), a family of Temple singers (see 1 Chronicles 6:31-47;

2 Chronicles 20:19) which probably lasted into post-exilic times. Asaph, associated with 12 psalms (Psalms 50, 73–83), was a Levitical musician of David's day (see 1 Chronicles 15:17-19; 16:4-5; 2 Chronicles 29:30). A post-exilic choir bearing his name (Ezra 3:10) could be responsible for some of these psalms, especially those which deal with later events (Psalms 74, 79).

King Solomon is linked with Psalms 72 and 127 and Moses with Psalm 90. Psalm 88 is connected with Heman the Ezrahite, known from David's day (see 1 Chronicles 15:17, 19; 25:5) and Solomon's reign (1 Kings 4:31). Another Ezrahite, Ethan, is associated with Psalm 89 (1 Kings 4:31; 1 Chronicles 15:17, 19). Some identify him as Jeduthun, one of David's chief musicians and founder of three choirs (1 Chronicles 9:16; 16:38, 41-42; 25:1, 3, 6; 2 Chronicles 5:12) and add Psalms 39, 62, and 77 to Psalm 89.

HEBREW POETRY

Parallelism

Although the psalms are poems, they do not depend heavily on meter and rhyming words, hallmarks of English poetry. The chief characteristic of Hebrew poetry is parallelism, the rhyming of thoughts. In the basic pattern, called *synonymous parallelism,* the thought of the first line is reproduced in the second using different but synonymous words. For example,

Lord, who may dwell in your sanctuary?
Who may live on your holy hill? (Psalm 15:1).

Dwell and **live** correspond to one another, as do **sanctuary** and **holy hill.** Or consider Psalm 19:1—

The heavens declare the glory of God;
the skies proclaim the work of his hands.

Heavens is synonymous with **skies, declare** with **proclaim,** and **glory of God** with **work of his hands.**

The Hebrew poet turns this basic pattern into an almost infinite variety of forms, each variation adding emphasis to his point. *Antithetic parallelism* reinforces a single truth using two contrasting thoughts. This type, which occurs frequently in Proverbs, is found to a lesser degree in Psalms.

**For the LORD watches over the way of the righteous,
but the way of the wicked will perish** (Ps. 1:6).

The single truth here—that God rewards people according to their actions—emerges from the contrast between how He treats the righteous and the wicked (see Psalm 90:6).

The poet may express this parallelism using *analogy,* as when he compares the psalmist's longing to a panting deer (see 42:1) or the enemy to a snake and slug (58:4, 8). Sometimes the poet will *reverse the order* of elements in two lines, as in 92:2 (translated literally):

> To tell in the morning your steadfast love
> and your faithfulness in the nights.

The order of phrases is deliberately reversed. The same can be done with four lines, where a parallel is drawn between the first and fourth and between the second and third. Note 51:1:

**Have mercy on me, O God,
according to your unfailing love;
according to your great compassion
blot out my transgressions.**

Another variation resembles a staircase with a thought stated, then repeated and built upon to the climax. Note the progression in 29:1-2:

**Ascribe to the LORD, O mighty ones,
ascribe to the LORD glory and strength.
Ascribe to the LORD the glory due his name;
worship the LORD in the splendor of his holiness.**

Other examples of *staircase parallelism* can be found in 24:8; 93:1, 3; 97:5; 98:4-6; and 113:8. In yet another variation, the psalmist leaves a phrase *unparalleled.* In 24:1, **is the LORD's** is left out of the second line:

**The earth is the LORD's, and everything in it,
the world, and all who live in it.**

(For other examples, see 91:5-6, 9; 96:3; 98:9b.)

At times, two phrases are constructed to revolve around a

common word or clause, called a *pivot.* In 72:1, the imperative verb **endow** is meant to accompany both lines. Translated literally, this verse would read,

> O God, your justice to the king endow
> and your righteousness to the king's son.

(See 98:2, where **made his salvation known** and **revealed his righteousness** pivot on **to the nations,** and see 114:7, where **at the presence of the** LORD and **at the presence of the God of Jacob** pivot on **Tremble, O earth.**) Many of these have been lost in the translation from Hebrew to English.

The psalmist could even make the *stanzas of entire psalms parallel* using repeated words and themes. This appears to be the case with Psalm 36, which can be outlined as follows:

> A. The behavior of the wicked (36:1-4)
>   B. The Lord's lovingkindness (36:5-9)
>   B'. Prayer for lovingkindness (36:10)
> A'. Prayer for protection from the wicked (36:11-12)[5]

Why did the Hebrew poet rely so heavily on parallelism? The remains of the poetry of Israel's neighbors indicate that this was a common poetic device at that time. Writer A. Cohen suggests that the antiphonal use of the psalms (where one person or group reads one part and is answered by another person or group) helped to foster this technique.[6] Parallelism also made the psalms easier to memorize, an important quality in Israelite culture.

Repetition, such as parallelism, is an essential component in all artistic expression. Music and art employ it commonly when they state and develop a theme. English poetry repeats with rhyming words and meter. Repetition through Hebrew parallelism satisfies the reader's need for unity (enabling a quicker grasp of the truth) and variety (sustaining interest).

In parallelism, the second line does not always just repeat the first, but often *intensifies, expands, elaborates,* or *reaffirms* it. Note the intensification in Psalm 44:2:

> **With your hand you drove out the nations**
> **and planted our fathers;**

**you crushed the peoples
and made our fathers flourish.**

Stronger than **you drove out** in line one is its parallel element in line three, **you crushed.** Only **planted** in the second line, the fathers **flourish** in the fourth (see 37:6; 79:5).

Pay attention to parallelism when studying the psalms. Some who have not been alert have made distinctions between two elements which the psalmist used as synonyms. For example, **son of man** in 8:4b should be understood as synonymous with **man,** not as a reference to the Messiah. Parallelism can help make sense of a difficult phrase as in 78:51, where what is meant by **tents of Ham** is clarified by its parallel, **Egypt.**

Imagery

Like the English variety, Hebrew poetry evokes powerful feelings. No one with a fear of drowning should read Psalm 69:1-3, and there may be no literature as comforting as Psalm 23. Part of what makes this material so evocative is its terseness. It can say a whole sentence in one word. If "poetry packs the biggest thoughts into the least amount of words,"[7] then Hebrew poetry wraps the final package even tighter.

The Hebrew language often expresses abstract concepts using concrete terms. To come into a person's presence is to literally come before his face. The same word translated *road* can also be rendered *lifestyle.* What the New International Version translates as **to the nations** in Psalm 98:2 is, literally, "to the eyes of the nations." Concrete terms hit harder than abstract.

Other Literary Elements in Hebrew Poetry

The Hebrew poet also used literary devices such as a *refrain* (see Psalm 42:5, 11; 43:5; 46:7, 11) and *alliteration* (the repetition of particular sounds). Note the occurrence of the *sh* and *l* sounds in this transliteration (Hebrew words in English letters) of Psalm 122:6-7:

> sha'alu shelom yerushalayim
> yishlayui ohavayik
> yehi shalom bechelek
> shalvah be'armenotayik

In an alphabet *acrostic,* the first letter of each line or lines begins with the succeeding letters of the Hebrew alphabet. Psalms 9, 10, 25, 34, 37, 111, 112, 119, and 145 are alphabet acrostics, with Psalm 119 as the most developed.   Acrostics functioned as memory aids for purposes of instruction.   They also served to emphasize the orderliness of God's world and His sovereignty over every aspect of it.

PSALM TYPES

There are basically two types of psalms—praise and lament.   The predominance of praise is indicated in the Hebrew title for the Psalter, "Book of Praises."   Some praise psalms celebrate God as Creator or Redeemer.   These hymns often begin and end with a call to worship; reasons for praise are provided in between (see Psalm 103).   Other psalms praise God by celebrating His city, Jerusalem (Psalms 46, 122, 125), or His appointed representative, the king (Psalms 2, 45).   Some psalms praise God by celebrating His law and the good effects of obeying it (Psalms 1, 19, 119).

In many psalms, praise is offered for some specific act of deliverance. These songs of thanksgiving, often addressed directly to God, usually contain an account of the psalmist's trouble, a vow to praise God if delivered, and an account of God's deliverance.   Very likely, they were sung in the Temple courts after a thank-offering sacrifice and during a communal meal held in appreciation to God (see Psalms 66, 116; Leviticus 7:16; Deuteronomy 12:7-19).   The invitation to praise with which these psalms sometimes conclude would be directed to the guests at that meal.

About one-third of the psalms are of the second type, the lament or complaint, sung as an appeal for God's help in personal or national difficulty.   These psalms usually contain an account of the distress, a plea for help, and reasons why God should answer.   Often these psalms will suddenly change their tone and end with a statement of confidence (Psalms 17, 35), the promise of praise (Psalm 79), or praise itself (Psalm 22).   This change may have resulted from a prophetic oracle to the psalmist (see 2 Kings 19:20-36; 2 Chronicles 20:14-30).

Only a handful of psalms suggest that the psalmist's distress was brought about by his own sin.[8]   Instead, his trouble was usually caused by a person or group of persons.   Some are identified (Cush the Benjamite, Psalm 7; Doeg the Edomite, Psalm 52; the Edomites and Babylonians, Psalm 137), but most are unnamed.   Immoral and proud of it, the goal of the enemy is the destruction of the psalmist. The enemy's weapon of choice? A deceitful and slanderous tongue.

THEOLOGY OF THE PSALMS

Although the psalms are quite diverse, one theme pervades them all: God is King. His dominion extends throughout the universe because He created and sustained it. This reign will never end because He is eternal and all-powerful.

In His sovereignty, this Great King chose Israel to be His people. He revealed himself to them by a special name, Yahweh, and linked Israel with himself by a covenant. Initiated with Abraham (see Genesis 12, 15, 17), God expanded this covenant with Moses (Exodus-Deuteronomy). In essence, Yahweh promised to serve as a faithful king over Israel in return for its worship and obedience. With such a promise and such a King, it is no wonder praise predominates in the psalms.

The Great King chose Jerusalem for His royal city and the Temple for His palace. In the covenant, He revealed His will for His subjects. Those psalms which praise Jerusalem, the Temple, and the Law, in reality, praise the God who chose them.

"The primary function of an earthly king is to administer justice within his realm, protect the weak from exploitation, and ensure security to his subjects. Precisely so is it with God, the King of the earth."[9] Confident of God's rule, Israel went to Him for justice, asking Him to vindicate Israel's cause and punish the wicked. Because the Israelites knew He was a compassionate and good King, they pled for protection from their enemies.

At that time, only Israel acknowledged God's sovereignty. This would change, however, and ultimately all the earth would worship Yahweh as King (Psalm 22:27-28); Israel would become the premiere nation. The gods of the surrounding nations (which the psalmist knew were not gods at all) would have to admit that Yahweh ruled. What prevents this from being merely propaganda is the nature of Israel's mission. This nation was chosen by God, not merely to serve Him, but to serve as a light to the nations, bringing them to God (see Genesis 12:3; Isaiah 49:6). Israel's victory (Psalm 2) meant that purpose was closer to being accomplished.

Although God was King, He chose to appoint, as His earthly representative, Israel's king (see Psalm 2), specifically David and his descendants (2 Samuel 7; Psalm 89). The earthly king was to be righteous and obedient to God's Law (Deuteronomy 17:18-20). He should act like God, administering justice, protecting the weak, and ensuring security and blessing to his subjects. Thus, some of the descriptions of the king's rule picture him in terms larger than life (see Psalm 45:2-5; 72).

After the Babylonian exile terminated the monarchy, Israel read these royal psalms in a more idealistic way. They came to expect from God another king, an Anointed One in the line of David who would lead Israel to the victory God had promised. Such passages informed and fueled the Jewish hope for the Messiah. Jesus' coming was understood by many as the fulfillment of this hope. Consider Zechariah's description of Him as "a horn of salvation for us in the house of his servant David" (Luke 1:69).

The question, "Can Jesus be found in the Psalms?" would have to be answered, "Yes and no." When the psalmist wrote about the Anointed One, he was not thinking of Jesus but of the earthly king. Although "son of man" is a messianic term in the Gospels,[10] it does not carry this connotation in the psalms. Larger-than-life descriptions of the king originally reflected the ancient Near Eastern tendency to exaggerate rather than a prophecy of the Messiah. Although situations may seem to describe events from Jesus' life (see Psalm 22; 69:3-9), they are primarily intended to depict circumstances contemporary with the psalmist. No, the psalms do not speak of Jesus.

Although the psalmist may not have envisioned Jesus, God—the ultimate Author of the Psalms—certainly did. For this reason, the New Testament authors were right to claim that passages from the Psalms spoke of Jesus (see Acts 2:29-36). That God could make the experiences of the psalmist resemble those of Jesus "is an arrangement of divine power, mercy, and wisdom."[11]

STRANGENESS OF THE PSALMS

The Righteousness of the Psalmist

There is surprisingly little mention of penitence in the Psalms. In fact, it is more common for the psalmist to deny guilt than admit it (see Psalm 7:3-5; 17:1-5; 44:17; 59:3-4). This has proven so troubling that some have "found" guilt between the lines. They see it "implied" as the reason for the psalmist's distress and for God's anger. More likely, the psalmist does not express guilt because he does not feel guilty. Sometimes his claims of innocence are specific to a particular situation (see 7:3-5; 59:3). At other times, however, his claims are general and sweeping (17:3-5; 26:1-8).

It is ironic that the Old Testament believer could feel such freedom before God. We tend to imagine that life under the "law" meant inescapable guilt, while life for us under "grace" means unbounded freedom and full access to God. Compare the prayers of the psalmist with those of many Christians, and you will find that the opposite is true.

The psalmist's example demonstrates that guilt is not a spiritual virtue. Guilt, like pain, is an important clue in diagnosing illness and should be "treated" immediately. But, like pain, guilt is a symptom of illness, not of health. Too many Christians are spiritual hypochondriacs, imagining guilt where there is none, because we cannot imagine God could be happy with us unless we were unhappy with ourselves.

The psalmist's claims to righteousness are just one measure of his confidence before God. He accuses God of neglect (see 7:6; 10:1; 35:17, 22; 44:23). He bargains with God, reminds Him that others will observe the outcome (74:22; 143:11), declares he cannot praise if he dies (6:4-5; 88:10), and promises to praise if delivered (35:18; 144:7-9). He places significant requests before God and expects God to answer (144:5-8). He makes plans and asks God to bless them (20:4). After making requests, he does not say, "Thy will be done."

How can the psalmist be so confident before God? The answer lies in his covenant relationship with Yahweh. He knew that the all-powerful God had freely and lovingly committed himself to Israel. He knew that, as a member of this people, he was a party to that agreement. He knew what that agreement required: loyalty on his part and loving protection and provision on God's. He knew that God would keep His part of the bargain; His goodness, love *(chesed),* and faithfulness guaranteed it. The boldness that strikes us as presumption was merely confidence—covenant confidence— the product of knowing who he was, whose he was, and what was promised.

Again, it is ironic that many Christians seem to lack such confidence before God. The same all-powerful, loving God has entered into a relationship with us, a covenant with terms no less abundant. He has given His Holy Spirit to seal that agreement and to assure us of our rights, what John Wesley called the "witness of the Spirit." To know who we are, *whose* we are, and what was promised provides more than sufficient grounds for "covenant confidence."

Imprecatory Psalms

Another strange thing about the psalms is the presence of imprecations, or curses against the enemy. Eighteen psalms contain some element of imprecation; three contain a significant amount (see Psalm 35:4-6; 69:22-

28; 109:6-15). Against his godless, vicious, and slanderous enemies, the psalmist prays that God's anger would bring on them precisely what they have tried to do to him (7:14-17; 28:4-5; 109:17-20).

This seems to contradict Jesus' teaching (and example) to "bless those who curse you." Because we regard the Bible as God's word, we can neither ignore these curses nor deny they are inspired ("These are man's words rather than God's"). We cannot claim an inferior code of ethics for the Old Testament unless we also ignore the Old Testament commands to love one's neighbor and forgive one's enemy (see Exodus 23:4-5; Leviticus 19:18). We also cannot see these as only prophetic of the final conflict between God and evil, for this denies the historical setting in which the psalmist spoke them.

These imprecations are not as bloodthirsty as they sound. The psalmist has skillfully woven them into his poetry; they are literary expressions, not angry outbursts (see Psalm 69). As is characteristic of poetry, exaggeration should be assumed. Passages such as Psalm 35:12-14 and 109:4-5 show that the one cursing also knew how to be kind to his enemies. If David wrote these curses, his treatment of Saul assures us that he understood compassion.

When the psalmist asks that the enemy endure what he has inflicted on others, such a request is more than fair—it is essential. God cannot vindicate the righteous (which everyone applauds) without also judging the wicked (see 143:12). Furthermore, the covenant God swore with Israel contained His promise to bring justice. God's reputation depended on keeping that promise.

These imprecations reflect the psalmist's last resort. He spoke these words out of his feelings of powerlessness and desperation. Death was approaching and he was helpless to prevent it (see 69:1-3; 109:22-24). He was powerless to neutralize the slander which threatened his reputation. His only remaining recourse was to appeal his case to the Heavenly Judge in language appropriate to the need (see 58:11; 109:27-28).

The more desperate the problem, the more aggressive the treatment must be. Even in his desperation, the psalmist knew that the enemy's threat was not primarily against him but against God. By attacking God's covenant partner, the enemy was rebelling against God (see 5:10; 28:4-5; 69:7; 139:20). The psalmist reacts with righteous indignation, knowing that such rebellion threatens the security of society. Either God puts down the rebels or anarchy will result.

The suggestion that such imprecations violate the New Testament standard betrays a one-sided view of the New Testament that ignores passages like Acts 23:3; 2 Thessalonians 1:6-9; 1 Timothy 1:19-20; 2 Timothy 4:14; James 5:1-6; and much of Revelation (especially 6:9-10). The righteous indignation which motivated the psalmist to curse his enemies motivated Jesus to cleanse the Temple and sharply criticize the Pharisees (see Matthew 21:13; 23:13-35). The New Testament's use of these imprecations[12] betrays an awareness of the same struggle between God and evil.

While Jesus' experience showed how unjust suffering could be transformed into something redemptive, it did not make unjust suffering any more just. That God can bring good from it should not prevent us from being angry at injustice. That retribution is not God's only word on the subject does not mean He has nothing to say about it.

Of what use can such psalms be to us today? They can remind us of the need for righteous indignation. Injustice will not disappear if ignored. If it disappears at all, it does so only when someone becomes sufficiently angered to take a stand against it. The inability to become indignant at sin is not a sign of spiritual health but of paralysis.

The problem, of course, is that self-righteous indignation can look and feel so much like righteous indignation. History is full of examples where people have taken up arms against others in God's name. Perhaps we would be wise to avoid using these imprecations, not because they are sub-Christian, but because "they are too lofty for most of us to imitate without danger."[13]

These psalms also remind us that God is just and hates wickedness. One day He will make the wrongs right again, including those wrongs that lay outside our reach like the suffering of the innocent. He will punish sin and, where necessary, the sinner. There is comfort here . . . and a warning.

HOW TO USE THIS COMMENTARY

Two final words of instruction remain, the first procedural and the second foundational.

First, begin your study by reading the psalm in your Bible, writing down your own observations. Then read the commentary on that psalm, comparing frequently with the verses in the passage. In this way, my words will become a servant, rather than a master, of your own study and of the text.

The second word of instruction will help you apply what you discover. Applying the Bible causes many to struggle, especially when it comes to the Old Testament. Some look for Christ there, and at times may "read

Him" where He does not appear. Others take the Old Testament figures as heroes, ignoring the fact that none provides a flawless example. Many look for principles to live by, a selective process which fails to do justice to the differences between Old Testament society and today. Some hope to bypass application entirely and read the Old Testament like they take their medicine. They swallow the passage, trusting it will do some good but without understanding how. Sadly, many have given up hope and avoid the Old Testament altogether.

My suggestion is embarrassingly simple: As you read, ask, "What does this passage say about God?" Since the Bible is God's revelation of himself, we should expect that its primary benefit would be to show us what He is like. We can learn about Him from what He says about himself, from what others say about Him, or from what He does or does not do. For example, Psalm 1:2 says that God has revealed himself through the Law; therefore, He must want to be both known and obeyed. He will bless those who make it their obsession to know and obey Him (1:2-3), but those who disregard Him will be punished (1:4). Because God knows the ways of the righteous and wicked (1:6), He must be able to see inside the heart.

A fact about the nature of God is a fact that is always true in every situation and one which can be put to use with immediate results. Since God wants to be known and will bless the person who desires to know Him, I should make this my goal. God's knowledge of the heart challenges me to keep my motives pure. It also assures me that He will bring justice out of injustice. By asking the simple question, "What does this passage tell me about God?" the book of Psalms becomes a wonderful treasury of insights into the character of God.

ENDNOTES

[1]Martin Luther, *Works,* vol. 35, E. Helmut Lehmann and Theodore Bachmann, eds. (Philadelphia: Muhlenberg, 1960), p. 256.

[2]An excellent introduction to the Psalms is *How to Read the Psalms* by Tremper Longman, III (Downers Grove, Illinois: InterVarsity Press, 1988).

[3]For more on the division of the Psalter into five books, see *How to Read the Psalms* by Tremper Longman (Downers Grove, Illinois: InterVarsity Press, 1988) and "The Division and Order of the Psalms" by R. Dean Anderson, *Westminster Theological Journal,* 1994, vol. 56, issue 2, pp. 219–41.

[4]For a very helpful explanation of these titles, see *Psalms 1–72* by Derek Kidner, Tyndale Old Testament Commentaries, D. J. Wiseman, ed. (Downer's Grove, Illinois: InterVarsity Press, 1973), pp. 32–46.

[5]Peter C. Craigie, *Psalms 1–50,* Word Biblical Commentary, vol. 19, David A. Hubbard and Glenn W. Barker, eds. (Waco, Texas: Word Books, 1983), p. 291. This is called a chiastic structure because it resembles the Greek letter *chi,* which is shaped like an X.

[6]A. Cohen, *The Psalms,* Soncino Books of the Bible, A. Cohen, ed. (London: Soncino, 1950), p. xv.

[7]Barry L. Bandstra, *Reading the Old Testament: An Introduction to the Hebrew Bible* (Belmont, California: Wadsworth Publishing Company, 1995), p. 407.

[8]The church has identified seven penitential psalms (Psalms 6, 32, 38, 51, 102, 130, 143), but of these, only Psalms 38, 51, and 130 express penitence.

[9]Cohen, p. xiv.

[10]The Gospels include the New Testament books of Matthew, Mark, Luke, and John.

[11]F. Delitzsch, *Psalms,* Commentary on the Old Testament, vol. V, translated by James Martin (reprint, Grand Rapids, Michigan: Wm. B. Eerdmans Publishing Co., 1978), p. 306.

[12]John 15:25 uses Psalm 35:19 and 69:4; John 2:17 uses Psalm 69:9; Acts 1:20 uses Psalm 69:25 and 109:8; Romans 15:3 uses Psalm 69:9; Romans 11:9-10 uses Psalm 69:22-23.

[13]J. L. McKenzie, "The Imprecations of the Psalter," *American Ecclesiastical Review,* vol. 111 (1944), pp. 81–96, as cited by Leslie C. Allen, *Psalms 101–150,* Word Biblical Commentary, vol. 21, David A. Hubbard and Glenn W. Barker, eds. (Waco, Texas: Word Books, 1983), p. 75.

PSALMS OUTLINE

I. BOOK 1 (1:1–41:13)
    A.   The Happiness of the Righteous (1:1-6)
    B.   Kiss the Son (2:1-12)
    C.   Sleep in Heavenly Peace (3:1-8)
    D.   Who Can Show Us Any Good? (4:1-8)
    E.   Waiting in Expectation (5:1-12)
    F.   But You, O Lord, How Long? (6:1-10)
    G.   Court Is in Session (7:1-17)
    H.   What a Name! (8:1-9)
    I.   But You, O God, Do See (9:1–10:18)
    J.   When the Foundations Are Being Destroyed (11:1-7)
    K.   Human Words and God's (12:1-8)
    L.   "How Long?" (13:1-6)
    M.   What a Fool! (14:1-7)
    N.   "Who May Dwell in Your Sanctuary?" (15:1-5)
    O.   "In Pleasant Places" (16:1-11)
    P.   The Wonder of God's Love (17:1-15)
    Q.   Celebration of Victory (18:1-50)
    R.   Join the Heavens in Praise (19:1-14)
    S.   Confidence in Battle (20:1-9)
    T.   Celebration in Victory (21:1-13)
    U.   "Proclaim His Righteousness" (22:1-31)
    V.   "The Lord Is My Shepherd" (23:1-6)
    W.   Worship the Glorious King (24:1-10)
    X.   A Conversation About Life (25:1-22)
    Y.   God Is Just (26:1-12)
    Z.   Wait for the Lord (27:1-14)
    AA. Help for the Helpless (28:1-9)
    BB. The Sound of Glory (29:1-11)
    CC. Joy Comes in the Morning (30:1-12)
    DD. Take Refuge in God (31:1-24)
    EE. The Sweetness of Sins Forgiven (32:1-11)
    FF. "The Earth Is Full of His Unfailing Love" (33:1-22)
    GG. "Taste and See That the Lord Is Good" (34:1-22)
    HH. Divine Legal Aid (35:1-28)
    II.   The Limitless Love of God (36:1-12)

F. Blessing on the Righteous (112:1-10)
G. "Who Stoops Down to Look" (113:1-9)
H. The Presence of the Lord (114:1-8)
I. "Our God Is in Heaven" (115:1-18)
J. Call Upon the Lord (116:1-19)
K. "All Peoples on Earth Will Be Blessed Through You" (117:1-2)
L. A Procession of Praise (118:1-29)
M. In Praise of the Law (119:1-176)
N. Eager to Return Home (120:1-7)
O. Israel's Watchman (121:1-8)
P. Coming Home (122:1-9)
Q. An Appeal to the Judge (123:1-4)
R. We Have Escaped (124:1-8)
S. As Solid As Jerusalem (125:1-5)
T. A Song of Restoration (126:1-6)
U. "Unless the LORD Builds the House" (127:1-5)
V. A Blessing on the Pilgrims (128:1-6)
W. Bowed but Not Broken (129:1-8)
X. A Prayer From the Depths (130:1-8)
Y. Content in His Arms (131:1-3)
Z. Remembering David (132:1-18)
AA. Life Forevermore (133:1-3)
BB. A Farewell Blessing (134:1-3)
CC. The Ever-Powerful Name of Israel's God (135:1-21)
DD. His Love Endures Forever (136:1-26)
EE. By the Rivers of Babylon (137:1-9)
FF. Better Than Promised (138:1-8)
GG. "You Know Me" (139:1-24)
HH. The Faithful and Righteous God (140:1-13)
II. An Ascending Appeal (141:1-10)
JJ. Friend to the Friendless (142:1-7)
KK. A Loyal Servant in Need (143:1-12)
LL. "Blessed Are the People Whose God Is the LORD" (144:1-15)
MM. Let the Earth Hear His Voice (145:1-21)
NN. "The LORD Reigns Forever" (146:1-10)
OO. His Powerful Word (147:1-20)
PP. Praise From Heaven and Earth (148:1-14)
QQ. A Song of Final Victory (149:1-9)
RR. Hallelujah (150:1-6)

Part One

BOOK 1

Psalm 1:1–41:13

All but four of the psalms in Book 1 are attributed to David. Of those that are not, two (Psalms 1–2) are thought to have been written later to introduce the entire Psalter. Psalm 10 is thought to have originally been combined with Psalm 9 (see comments on Psalm 9), and some wonder if Psalm 33 was at one time connected with Psalm 32. The psalms in Book 1 show a clear preference for the use of the name of Yahweh (272 times) over Elohim (15 times) when speaking of God.[1] Assuming that psalms attributed to David were written by him, Yahweh was the name David preferred in referring to God. Book 1 concludes with this doxology: "Praise be to the LORD, the God of Israel, from everlasting to everlasting. Amen and Amen" (Ps. 41:13).

ENDNOTE

[1]Tremper Longman III, *How to Read the Psalms* (Downers Grove, Illinois: InterVarsity Press, 1988), p. 44.

THE HAPPINESS OF THE RIGHTEOUS

Psalm 1:1-6

laced first in this "Book of Praises" is not a call to praise, as one might expect, but a call to righteousness. Since devotion must always precede true praise, here is where the psalmist begins. These verses reveal two paths (righteousness and wickedness) and where those paths lead (happiness and destruction). The righteous traveler completely avoids even the slightest detour from the proper path. Though sin might appear harmless—just listening to the "advice of the wicked" (NJB)—the righteous person knows where this path leads: to a sinful character (**counsel of the wicked**) and a cynical, anti-God attitude (**seat of mockers** [Ps. 1:1]).

Instead of being preoccupied with sin, the righteous person is preoccupied with God's Law. The word **law** used in 1:2—*torah*—can describe the Law revealed to Israel on Sinai (see 1 Kings 2:3) or, more broadly, all of God's words to His people, of which the Law of Moses is the chief and defining component (Isaiah 1:10).

It is probably this broader meaning that the psalmist has in mind here: The righteous person is delighted with God's Word. Valued like a precious jewel, the Word is jealously guarded and continually contemplated.[1] Day and night the righteous one meditates upon it, examining its every facet and relishing each insight it gives into God's character.

The person so preoccupied with God's Word is **like a tree** that is green, fruitful, and rooted (Ps. 1:3). The tree never lacks for moisture because it is planted by an ever-flowing stream. Every season, it bears **fruit** and continually provides nourishment and enjoyment. Every year, its roots reach deeper and deeper into the soil, and it becomes more permanent.

The sharp contrast with the wicked person is emphasized by the psalmist's abrupt turn in 1:4, which is well translated by the New International Version: **Not so the wicked! Chaff** is the husk of grain separated from the kernel by threshing. Both the chaff and kernel are then scooped and tossed into the air, leaving the weightless chaff to blow away. Dead, useless, and temporary, chaff provides a striking contrast with the living, fruitful, permanent tree.

To show the destiny of these "lightweights," the psalmist pictures a gathering place (see 1:5). Whether it is the Temple or the city gate where court cases would be heard,[2] this place is a "no standing zone" for the wicked. The righteous person, however, firmly planted on an impeccable character and devoted to God's Word, will stand.

In 1:6 is the heart of happiness for **the righteous,** the affectionate attention of God. The verb translated **watches over** means more than supervision or protection; it is more like what we find in the New Jewish Publication Society version: "God cherishes the way of the righteous."

This suggests another reason why the Psalter begins with a call to righteousness: God has designed a world where the right choices are ultimately the best choices. This God, whose praises will be sung by those who love Him, loves them, rewarding obedience and devotion with His loving care.

ENDNOTES

[1] In Isaiah 54:12, the word for "delight" is translated "precious" and modifies stones.

[2] See Ruth 4:1; 2 Samuel 15:2; and 1 Kings 22:10 for references to the city gate as the site for civil court.

2

KISS THE SON

Psalm 2:1-12

The Israelites lived in a difficult place. Located on a land bridge between the great military powers of the South and the North, they were constantly on the "hot seat." The temptation to find security in international treaties or a strong military was great. God promised safety, however, only to those, according to the psalmist, **who take refuge in him** (2:12).

Psalm 2 begins with word of a conspiracy—probably by nations in subjection to Israel—against Yahweh and His earthly representative, the king (see 2:2-3). In the ancient Near East, such conspiracies were common at the coronation of a new king, the occasion for which this psalm was probably composed.[1]

The rhetorical question preceding these words of sedition (see 2:1) and God's laughter which follows (2:4) demonstrate that rebellion is futile. God does not fear insurrection; He only mocks the foolishness and futility of such attempts (2:4).

He does more than laugh, however; He rises up in indignation, rebuking and terrifying His enemies (see 2:5). Because their rebellion is not only directed at God but also at His designated ruler, God reaffirms His blessing: **I have installed my King** (2:6; **I** is emphatic in the Hebrew). Because God is his father, the king need only **ask** in order to be given worldwide domination (2:7-9).[2]

Instead of rebellion, the wise posture is reverent and humble service (see 2:10-12), for, as commentator Derek Kidner has written, ". . . there is no refuge from Him, only in Him."[3] Kissing the king (see Psalm 2:12) meant acknowledging him as rightful ruler and implied voluntary submission and a promise of obedience. One translation counsels, "Do homage in purity."[4]

Such service, far from groveling servitude, is instead a reason to rejoice (see 2:11). To be aligned with the sovereign Lord—the **One**

enthroned in heaven (2:4)—is to be assured of victory in the end. This is why the one who takes refuge in God—who freely submits to His authority—is **blessed** (2:12).

Psalm 2 ends as Psalm 1 began, emphasizing the path to blessedness (one reason why some believe the two psalms were originally one psalm). Psalm 1 spoke of the blessedness of the righteous person; Psalm 2 of the blessedness of the righteous nation. It is, however, the same path: By meditating on God's law or kissing His feet, one demonstrates absolute loyalty to and dependence upon Him.

ENDNOTES

[1]Many commentators, Jewish and Christian, have taken references to the son of God (see Psalm 2:7, 12) and **Anointed One** *(mashiach)* as referring to the Messiah. In the eyes of the early church, such passages found their ultimate fulfillment in Jesus of Nazareth. At each of the many times this psalm is quoted or alluded to in the New Testament (see Acts 4:25; 13:33; Hebrews 1:5; 5:5; Revelation 12:5; 19:15), the authority of Jesus Christ is emphasized.

[2]Pottery broken with a rod of iron speaks of stern and complete punishment.

[3]Derek Kidner, *Psalms 1–72,* Tyndale Old Testament Commentaries, D. J. Wiseman, ed. (Downer's Grove, Illinois: InterVarsity Press, 1973), p. 53.

[4]A. Cohen, *The Psalms,* Soncino Books of the Bible, A. Cohen, ed. (London: Soncino, 1950), p. 5.

3

SLEEP IN HEAVENLY PEACE

Psalm 3:1-8

P salm 3, the first of many psalms which seeks to elicit God's help in a difficult time, alternates between heart-wrenching cries for help and bold statements of confidence. What is clear is that no matter how difficult life became, David knew God would help him.

This is also the first psalm which contains a historical reference in the title: **When he fled from his son Absalom.**[1] During those dark days, David was opposed by many foes; the original Hebrew of 3:1 suggests that enemy reinforcements continued to arrive even as he spoke. Such a description fits the time when David was told, "The hearts of the men of Israel are with Absalom" (2 Samuel 15:13; see 17:11).

As David fled Jerusalem during Absalom's revolt, he was accosted by Shimei, who cursed David and explained David's troubles as divine judgment (see 2 Samuel 16:7-8). Shimei's words may lie behind the taunt of the enemy in Psalm 3:2: **God will not deliver him,** words meant to impugn David's reputation and shake his faith.

David remained confident, however, and described God as a surrounding shield capable of protection from the vast enemy army (see 3:3). David was sure God would restore the glory known prior to this attack and would fully vindicate him. To have one's head lifted up meant a divinely ordered turn from despair to hope. When David fled Jerusalem, his head was covered in grief (see 2 Samuel 15:30), but his return brought a lifting of the head (2 Samuel 22:48-49).

The key verse in Psalm 3 is verse 4 where the whole matter is concisely and clearly stated: "I cried to God and He answered me." David was confident that he could fall peacefully to sleep (see 3:5-6) in spite of the danger surrounding him (see 2 Samuel 17:1, 16). The

Hebrew of Psalm 3:5 is emphatic: "As for me, I shall lie down and sleep."[2]

Because David was so confident in God, he did not attempt to take matters into his own hands. Instead, he repeatedly lifted his concerns to Yahweh in prayer, asking God to arise, deliver him, and disable his enemies (see 3:7). The victory is described either as an accomplished fact (see 2 Samuel 19:1-2) or as a claim by faith (see 3:8).

David maintained his faith through difficulty because he knew that, as part of God's covenant people (see 3:8), he would be protected by Yahweh. Circumstances could not shake David's conviction that God was still in charge (see 2 Samuel 16:12). Christians, God's new covenant community, can also claim this surety. We can call out to God, sure that our cries are heard (see Psalm 3:4) and can fall asleep in the Father's sustaining arms (3:5). While the unaided eye sees only the surrounding army, divinely assisted sight sees the "hills full of horses and chariots of fire" belonging to the army of God (see 2 Kings 6:15-17).

ENDNOTES

[1] For a concise comparison between this psalm and the experience of David in 2 Samuel 15 through 19, see *Psalms 1–50* by Peter C. Craigie, Word Biblical Commentary, vol. 19, eds. David A. Hubbard and Glenn W. Barker (Waco, Texas: Word Books, 1983), p. 73. See the discussion of authorship in the introduction to this commentary.

[2] See Acts 12:6—Peter sleeping in Herod's prison.

4

WHO CAN SHOW US ANY GOOD?

Psalm 4:1-8

Although founded on Yahweh's laws, Israelite society was not perfect. External and internal opposition caused the righteous no small amount of trouble. That Psalm 4 arises from such challenges is made clear by the cry for help with which it begins (see 4:1).

Specifically, David is challenging the idolatry that was so much a part of the ancient Near East and which plagued Israel throughout her history. To look for good to the gods of the neighboring nations was foolish and a move that dishonored the glory (see 4:2) of the one true God (implied in 4:1). Such "gods" were, after all, nothing but delusions, and false in every respect. Jeremiah 10:5, one of the most scathing condemnations of idolatry found in the Old Testament, compares an idol to "a scarecrow in a melon patch," unable to speak, walk, or do either harm or good.

Instead of such folly, David commands that one acknowledge Yahweh's ability to do great things like choosing the godly and attending to their needs (see Psalm 4:3). The three imperatives in 4:4 require a humble heart that opts for God's way over one's own. This thought continues with the demand for right sacrifices (as opposed to those to idols) and trust in the Lord, rather than anyone or anything else.

The question that the psalmist has been considering in this psalm is finally expressed in verse 6: **Who can show us any good?** David already knows the answer, however, for what follows is unadulterated confidence (see 4:6-8). He asks for **the light** of God's face to **shine upon us** (4:6b), thus echoing the priestly blessing of Numbers 6:25.

Such illumination would bring greater joy than that brought by a bumper crop (see Psalm 4:7). For an agricultural society, an abundant harvest meant more than food on the table. It meant a well-fed family

41

in the leaner months and seed for the next year's planting. While the harvest was an indication of God's power and a gauge of how that nation stood in God's eyes, abundant yields meant divine blessing and a guarantee of God's power.[1] Only the light of God's face could bring greater joy than this.

To seek good from God also brings **peace** (4:8), another element of the priestly blessing (see Numbers 6:26). The Hebrew word used in Psalm 4:8 *(shalom)* means more than the absence of conflict; it is a positive term indicating a well-ordered, wholesome existence as evidenced by the smile of God. This is a peace that conquers insomnia. The Hebrew phrase translated **lie down and sleep in peace** implies that the psalmist wishes to sleep and at once is able to do so.[2]

Some feel peace because they do not know of the present dangers; others because they imagine they can handle them. Our peace, however, is grounded in the knowledge that our God is greater than whatever dangers there might be. It does not depend on the strength we have, for it is the Lord "alone" who keeps us safe (see 4:8). "Who can show us any good?" Only God can.

ENDNOTES

[1]This is especially true in light of the fact that the gods most tempting to Israel were the fertility gods of Canaan, such as Baal.

[2]See Psalm 3:5. Several commentators note that this is an "evening psalm" and a sequel to Psalm 3, a morning psalm.

5

WAITING IN EXPECTATION

Psalm 5:1-12

ife as God's covenant people was not always easy. The psalms reveal a rough world, complete with suffering, danger, and disappointments. Psalm 5 refers to one problem found frequently in the Psalter: evil enemies with words for weapons.

David's response to this predicament is instructive. He did not throw up his hands in panicked surrender, switch his loyalties (see 5:2), or abandon his trust in God's protection (5:3). Nor did he overestimate his ability to handle these enemies and take matters into his own hands. Instead he turned to God. With words and sighs he prayed for God to intervene (see 5:1-3).

Having taken his problems to God, David left them there: **In the morning I lay my requests before you and wait in expectation** (5:3). David could be so expectant because he knew God's character demanded that God would intervene on the side of the righteous (see 5:4-6). Because God is holy, all that is unholy awaits judgment. Because David was righteous and showed it by coming into God's house, bowing before Him and following His ways (see 5:7-8), he could anticipate God's rescue.

Waiting is no easy task, especially when we are surrounded by vicious enemies (see 5:9-10). Rotten to the very core, all their words are deceptive and destructive. To be trapped by those words leads one stumbling into the **grave** (5:9). David could wait because he knew that while his enemies were powerful and vicious, they were no match for God, who would pronounce their guilt and punish them for it (see 5:10).

David knew God would act on his behalf (see 5:11-12). God's protection is described in 5:11 as a canopy and in 5:12 as a **shield** of favor that will **surround** and cover the whole body from head to toe.[1] Above me, before me, and behind me, from my head to my toe, God's favor envelopes me and I can forever sing for joy. David did not know when or how God would intervene. What he knew was that God would **surely . . . bless the righteous** (5:12), and convinced of that, David knew enough to wait.

ENDNOTE

[1]A. Cohen, *The Psalms,* Soncino Books of the Bible, ed. A. Cohen (London: Soncino, 1950), p. 12.

6

BUT YOU, O LORD, HOW LONG?

Psalm 6:1-10

Psalm 6 immediately draws us into David's experience. We sense his deep anguish as he calls out to God for mercy, healing, and help. From his words in 6:1, many assume he had sinned.[1] It should be noted, however, that in this psalm David neither confesses sin nor asks forgiveness as he does elsewhere (see Psalm 32). Like Job, another righteous sufferer, David cries out to God for rescue from undeserved suffering.

David describes his physical anguish as faintness (see 6:2); he is shriveling up like a withering plant. While his **bones are in agony** (6:2), his **soul** is excessively so (6:3).[2] A cry bursts from his breaking heart: **How long, O LORD, how long?**

David's suffering soul[3] stands in need of deliverance; it is for this that David pleads in 6:4-5. He appeals first on the basis of God's **unfailing love** (*chesed;* 6:4). This rich word suggests God's permanent, loyal devotion to His chosen people. Because David knew God cared about him, he makes his appeal (see 6:1-3) and waits for mercy (6:2).

Out of this covenant relationship, David found the confidence to bargain with God in 6:5: "If I die, there will be one less person to praise you." Sheol (**grave**) is not a place of punishment but a shadowy and silent realm where the rich and powerful are humbled (see Job 3:13-19). Slanderers are silenced (see Psalm 31:17), but so too are worshipers (see Psalm 6:5). Sheol is not outside the reach of God, but God and all that is good in life lie outside the reach of those in Sheol.

David, exhausted from his agony, yet unable to sleep, weeps so much that he claims his tears **drench my couch** (or "melt" *[tanakh]* his couch; 6:6).[4] His eyes **grow weak with sorrow.** Although "weak eyes" would

45

certainly follow a night of such weeping, David meant more than this. Since in the Old Testament physical health could be described in terms of weak or strong eyes,[5] this seems to be another reference to David's illness.

At its lowest point, the psalm takes a dramatic upward turn as David experiences victory over those oppressing him (see 6:8-10). He dismisses **all you who do evil,** proclaims his prayer answered, and pronounces doom on his foes. The thought of God's faithfulness may have filled him with hope or perhaps he received a prophetic message of future victory (see 2 Samuel 7:17). Either way, David's newly found confidence arose from faith in God's word, whether spoken in the past or at that moment by a prophet. Such faith pleases God. Although our difficulties may prompt us to ask, "How long, O Lord?" confidence in the reliability of God's Word provides a safe place to wait until God brings the answer.

ENDNOTES

[1]For this reason, Psalm 6 was numbered among the penitential psalms, along with Psalms 32, 38, 51, 102, 130, and 143.

[2]The same verb, **agony,** which means to be disturbed, dismayed, or terrified (Francis Brown, *The New Brown-Driver-Briggs-Gesenius Hebrew and English Lexicon* [Peabody, Massachusetts: Hendrickson Publishers, 1979], p. 96), is used to describe the suffering of both bones and soul. An additional word in the Hebrew indicates that the suffering of David's soul has reached the highest degree. The psalms commonly use a part of the body (**bones,** for instance) for the whole.

[3]The word for **soul** (Ps. 6:3) appears again here, translated **me.**

[4]Such a description not only continues the reference to night and morning found in the previous three psalms but contrasts with the experience of the psalmist in Psalm 4:8.

[5]The reference to Moses' eyesight at his death (see Deuteronomy 34:7) alludes to his health, not just his vision. When Jonathan's physical strength returned after tasting the honey, 1 Samuel 14:27 says, "his eyes brightened."

7

COURT IS IN SESSION

Psalm 7:1-17

O nce again David faces a ferocious enemy; the psalm's title reveals his foe—**Cush, a Benjamite**—about whom the Old Testament is otherwise silent. Since King Saul was from the tribe of Benjamin, fellow Benjamites resented the popularity of this upstart, David, from the tribe of Judah. Their slander may have prompted Saul to try to kill David. After Saul's death, Saul's family, outraged at David's claim to the throne, fought David for it and continued their slander for years (see 2 Samuel 16:5-8).[1]

Cush's attack against David was fierce (see Psalm 7:1-2), like a lion against its prey. David's protest of innocence in 7:3-5 suggests that Cush's attack relied on slander and probably reflects the very accusations made against David. The reference to wronging an innocent person (see 7:4) may imply a charge of disloyalty to the anointed king, Saul.

The last line of 7:4, **without cause have robbed my foe,** is difficult to translate. Some propose "if I have rescued my ally's adversary empty-handed," suggesting that David is accused of violating the cultural prohibition of helping the enemy of one's friend.[2] If such were true, says David, "**Let my enemy pursue and overtake me,** let him trample me as if by horses' hooves, and leave me in death and dishonor" (7:5).

While running from Saul, David tried to defend himself from such accusations. In one dramatic incident, when he had the chance to kill Saul, he refused, choosing instead to take only a piece of the king's robe (see 1 Samuel 24). From a distance David then tried to convince Saul of his innocence by showing Saul the fragment. David may have had this incident in mind since the word translated **robbed** (Ps. 7:4) can also refer to stripping an enemy corpse, which David could have done to Saul in the cave.

Arise, O LORD, David calls to the righteous judge in the first of four imperatives in 7:6. David asks God to let His anger rouse Him to action. Since the silence makes it seem like God is asleep, David pleads with God to **Awake . . . decree justice,** knowing that until God takes His seat on the bench, the psalmist and all the righteous must endure injustice (7:7-8). Only God can judge justly, for only He knows **minds and hearts,** the source of all actions (7:9).

That God does intervene is made clear by 7:10. The verse could be translated, "My shield is upon God," suggesting that God himself carries the psalmist's shield to protect him from attack.[3] For the wicked, God's intervention means punishment (see 7:11-13). The execution of God's judgment, although delayed, is imminent, for God stands ready with strung and bent bow, prepared weapons, and arrows already dipped in oil or pitch and set afire. God will punish the wicked by bringing on them the disaster they had intended for others.[4] The psalm closes with a promise of **praise** for the Righteous Judge who will take His place on the bench and gavel His court to order.

ENDNOTES

[1] Early Jewish commentary identifies Cush as King Saul (A. Cohen, *The Psalms,* Soncino Books of the Bible, ed. A. Cohen [London: Soncino, 1950], p. 15).

[2] See Peter C. Craigie, *Psalms 1–50,* Word Biblical Commentary, vol. 19, eds. David A. Hubbard and Glenn W. Barker (Waco, Texas: Word Books, 1983), pp. 100–101.

[3] Craigie, p. 98.

[4] The Jews living in Esther's day witnessed an example of this when Haman's heinous plot came down on his own head. This may be why Psalm 7 is read on Purim, which commemorates this event.

8

WHAT A NAME!

Psalm 8:1-9

To stand outside on a dark, clear night and look up into a star-studded sky fills one with a sense of God's splendor. Such an experience may have prompted David to write Psalm 8. He begins, however, by praising God not for natural wonders, but for God's name.

David knew that God's name (see 8:1) was more than the title given Him; it describes His nature. Yahweh (**LORD**), meaning "I am who I am" or "I will be who I will be" (see Exodus 3:14), is a name worth praising, for it points out the eternal nature of God and had been revealed to Israel by God. By making His name known, Yahweh gave Israel privileged access to His ear and heart. To think that this eternal God, who created the heavens with His word, had linked himself with Israel filled David with praise (see Genesis 1:14-19).

Psalm 8:2 declares that God's power is so great He can use even the weakness of the weak—**the lips of children and infants**—to bring victory.[1] The faculty of speech in small children is limited and undeveloped. God is so powerful that He can silence the speech of enemies with a toddler's babbling.

Contemplation of God's majesty leads one naturally to ask, What is humanity by comparison? There is a measure of despair in this question, for how can one look up into the night sky without feeling small and insignificant, a tiny speck on a tiny planet in a very big universe? Despair is all one could know if God had not stooped to our level and informed us that we are, in fact, the gem of His creation.

This is what is implied in the description of humankind in 8:5, which literally reads, "You have made him a little lower than God" (see the New International Version footnote). These staggering words echo God's own: "Let us make man in our image" (Gen. 1:26). Because only humanity was made in the image of God, only we, of all creation, can ask the question, **What is man . . . ?** And only we have the opportunity to ask it of God himself. Humanity's worth cannot be measured in comparison to the universe but as the object of God's loving care (see Psalm 8:4).

In describing our dominion over the created order (see 8:6-8), David continues to allude to Genesis 1:26. Far from puny and insignificant, we have been made in God's image, crowned with His glory, and set enthroned over our own kingdom. Some object to this description. They warn against putting too much emphasis on human ability and observe that whatever glory humanity had at the beginning was lost in the Fall. While sin has considerably hampered progress, the description given in Psalm 8 describes not pre-Fall Adam but the **son of man** (or "Son of Adam" [Ps. 8:4]), a term that refers to humankind *outside* the Garden of Eden.[2]

That Psalm 8 ends exactly as it began (see 8:1, 9) suggests that the greatness of humanity is never more fully realized than when it returns to a God who is greater still. Only when we can say, "O Lord, our sovereign" (literal translation of 8:1, 9), can we truly experience the glory that is ours.

ENDNOTES

[1]"To bring victory" is preferred over **ordained praise** (Ps. 8:2). For a New Testament illustration, see Matthew 21:16.

[2]New Testament authors used Psalm 8 to point to the Son of Man who died and rose again, is now "crowned with glory and honor," and is bringing "many sons to glory" (Hebrews 2:6-10; 1 Corinthians 15:27).

9

BUT YOU, O GOD, DO SEE

Psalms 9:1–10:18

salms 9 and 10 were probably written as one psalm. The Septuagint treats them as one psalm, and together they represent an alphabet acrostic,[1] although an incomplete one. This would explain why Psalm 10 is the only psalm from Psalm 3 to Psalm 32 to be without a title. These psalms share a common theme (justice for the oppressed) and common words (the only Old Testament uses of the phrase **times of trouble** are in Psalm 9:9 and 10:1).

Taken together, these psalms present an informative structure. The first section (9:1-12) shares with the last (10:16-18) an emphasis on God's rescuing the oppressed and defeating His enemies. The second and fourth sections (9:13-14; 9:19–10:15) describe the oppression of the enemies. The central section (9:15-18), the place of emphasis in such a structure, affirms that God will bring about justice.

Not only has God brought justice to the psalmist (see 9:4), but He will set up **his throne** and judge the entire world **in righteousness** (9:7-8). What else would be expected from a God who is **known by his justice** (9:16)? The wicked will be utterly destroyed (see 9:3-6, 19-20; 10:15-16) and sent back to **the grave** (*Sheol* in Hebrew) from which they have come (9:17). God will **break the arm of the wicked**—that is, render them harmless (10:15). Punishment will come, at least in part, from **the work of *their* hands** (my emphasis): the **pit they have dug** and the **net they have hidden** (9:15-16). God's judgment also will mean rescue for the oppressed. He will show himself **the helper of the fatherless** (10:14) and the avenger of blood (see 9:12).

It is evident from these psalms that God's judgment has not yet come. As the psalmist speaks, the wicked abuse the weak, mock God, and prosper (see 10:1-13). The oppressed feel helpless and forgotten, as if God were hiding himself when they need Him most (10:1, 12). To all appearances, for both oppressors and oppressed, God is not a righteous judge; He does not even see what is happening.

Yet to this point David returns again and again in Psalms 9 and 10. God *does* see what is happening, even when others think He is blind. In 10:14, the original Hebrew is emphatic: **But *you*, O God, do see trouble and grief; you consider it to take it in hand** (my emphasis). God does remember all that has happened, even when others imagine He has forgotten (see 9:12, 18). With striking irony, the psalmist predicts that the wicked, who have forgotten God (9:17; 10:4) and who imagine that God has forgotten all their evil deeds (10:11, 13, 15), will themselves be forgotten (9:5-6) and sent to **the grave** *(Sheol)* where one's identity is lost (9:17).

Even in those times when it seems that God is not watching and will never intervene, His people must continue to **trust** Him (9:10; 10:14). Aware of our circumstances (10:14) and attentive to our cries (10:17), He will strengthen our hearts (10:17) until He judges the world in righteousness (9:8).

ENDNOTE

[1]The Septuagint is the Greek translation of the Old Testament prepared between 200 and 300 B.C. For more on acrostics, see the discussion of literary elements in Hebrew poetry in the introduction to this commentary.

10

WHEN THE FOUNDATIONS ARE BEING DESTROYED

Psalm 11:1-7

In the face of an imminent and serious crisis, the psalmist must make a decision. Will he continue to stand his ground, trusting in God, or will he escape and hide as counseled (see Psalm 11:1)? He is told to escape because the attackers are right now bending their bows and stringing their arrows to kill him. They have planned an ambush, to secretly shoot from the shadows and catch him unaware (see 11:2). **The foundations are being destroyed** (11:3)—society is on the verge of collapse—so do not look for justice to be done.

The question raised in 11:3 can be translated either **What can the righteous do?** or "What is the Righteous One doing?" (see the New International Version footnote). While the former would fit, the latter is preferred since this is the question that 11:4 answers. It also fits the description of God in 11:7.

Where is God when the foundations are crumbling? Just where we need Him to be, **in His holy temple** (11:4). The Tabernacle and Temple were constructed by the Israelites, at God's direction, to represent the dwelling place of God. Although His presence was depicted in various ways, the Hebrews knew that God did not dwell in the Temple, but was present everywhere (see Solomon's prayer in 1 Kings 8). In spite of how the circumstances might appear (Psalm 11:1-3), God was still among them. They remained His chosen people, and God would come to their aid. God, seated **on his heavenly throne** (11:4), is the holy Sovereign of the universe and the One able to intervene on behalf of the righteous. From these two pictures of God—in His Temple and on His throne—the Israelites could draw confidence.

Contrary to appearances, the compassionate King has been watching all the time (see 11:4). His eyes pierce the darkness and see all, even what the enemy does in secret (11:2). His eyes not only see but carefully inspect what is happening since **examine** (11:4) implies the testing of metals through fire. The **righteous** undergo this scrutiny (11:5), but for them testing only brings greater purity. When the wicked pass through the fire, however, it will be like Sodom and Gomorrah revisited (11:6; see Genesis 19).

With a righteous God on the throne—one who loves righteousness— no other possibilities exist. The wicked will be punished, but the upright will gain access to God. The metaphor is drawn from the throne room, which only the privileged could enter (see Esther 1:14; 4:10-11).

There is, throughout Psalm 11, a recurring motif: the hidden and the revealed. The enemy seeks to remain hidden (they **shoot from the shadows** [11:2]), but the righteous are fully visible to God (11:4). In the midst of difficulties, God seems to be invisible (11:3) but will become visible to the righteous (they will **see his face** [11:7]). Because God is still on His throne, "There is nothing concealed that will not be disclosed, or hidden that will not be made known" (Matthew 10:26).

11

HUMAN WORDS AND GOD'S

Psalm 12:1-8

I n many of the psalms, the righteous complain to God of the slander of the enemy. Psalm 12 not only provides such a complaint, but presents the differences between human speech and divine speech. In so doing, it reveals the profound difference between God and humanity and summons all to a faith in Him.

Verses 1 through 4 present the dark side of human speech. The psalmist has found himself completely surrounded by deception. Not a single word he hears can be trusted, for **everyone lies to his neighbor** (12:2a). The falsehoods spoken are particularly troublesome because they come couched in supposed praise. Verse 2b speaks of "lips of smoothness," an expression well-translated as **flattering.** Only kind words are spoken to the psalmist's face, but they are spoken only for self-centered manipulation. Little wonder the psalmist refers to such speech as flowing from **deception** or "double-heartedness" (12:2b). Such speech is meant not only to profit the flatterers but to destroy the righteous. This would explain the plea for help in 12:1 and the reference to **oppression** and **groaning** in 12:5.

A more serious problem with human speech is described in 12:3-4. Human beings, created in God's image as capable of speech, proclaim themselves independent of God's authority: **We own our lips—who is our master?** (12:4b). Deceptive words flow from the heart that sets itself up as its own authority and turns the powerful, God-given tool of communication against its Maker and His creation in order to serve its own selfish purposes. At its worst, human speech stands opposed to the sovereignty of God, and for that reason it will be silenced (see 12:3).

Psalm 12 knows another type of human speech, however, for in the words of the psalmist there is humility rather than pride, and confident dependence rather than rebellion. Words can express confidence in God (see 12:7), cry out to God for help (12:1), and appeal to God with reason (12:7-8). Having requested God's intervention and spoken of God's willingness to act, the psalmist concludes with a final appeal: a reminder to God that unless He intervenes, the wicked will continue in their pride.

Rather than feeling offended by such bold speech, God—who knows the heart and sees that such words flow from faith and not pride— answers! He rises to intervene (12:5) **because of the ... groaning of the needy.** His promised protection uses the same root verb as the cry for **help** in 12:1.

It is not the eloquence of words that persuades God to help. Instead, He responds to even the simplest, heartfelt cry. The final phrase in 12:5 should probably be translated "I will protect those who pant after it." The panting of a thirsty, exhausted animal is eloquent, but not for its words. It is the cry for help and the **groaning of the needy** that moves God (see 12:5). Ironically, God silences the smooth and manipulative speech of the self-assured but rises to save those who can only moan from a humble, dependent heart.

God's words are everything that the words of the proud are not. The proud speak to deceive, to manipulate, and to destroy, but God's speech is **flawless** (12:6). God's words are always honest, always spoken for good, always intended for ultimate happiness and never designed to twist one's will. They are as free from deception as silver that has been passed through the furnace is free from impurity. For this reason, God's word can always be trusted (see 12:7a).

12

"HOW LONG?"[1]

Psalm 13:1-6

F our times in the opening two verses of Psalm 13, the psalmist asks God the plaintive and familiar question, **How long?** God's expected coming was delayed, leaving the psalmist struggling in God's absence. Psalm 13 also demonstrates how the psalmist was able to cope with God's delay.

It seems as if the psalmist and his difficulties had slipped God's mind. **Forever** could refer to time: **Will you forget me forever?** (13:1) or "How long . . . will you forget me? For ever?" (JB). Or it could refer to the completeness of the forgetfulness: "Wilt thou quite forget me?" (NEB). God's face, symbolizing the source of all good gifts, was hidden from the psalmist. Left feeling desolate and alone, the psalmist pleads that God would again look at him (see 13:3).

The psalmist provides no reason for God's rejection, making God's absence all the more puzzling and raising the question of divine justice. Feeling abandoned, and not sure why, the psalmist knew the unbearable loneliness of being alone and unsupervised in a vast universe.

Such feelings left the psalmist emotionally distraught (see 13:2) and in a "turmoil of thought."[2] His distress prompted him to pray for **light to my eyes** (13:3), a Hebrew idiom indicating health (see Job 17:7). Dim eyes spoke of physical and emotional weakness. What the psalmist desired was the light of God's face to make his own eyes brighten (see 1 Samuel 14:27). More than one commentator has suggested that the turmoil of the psalmist went around the clock. During the night he tossed and turned wondering what to do and proposing solutions; during the day he despaired as he watched his solutions fail. The one who feels abandoned by God not only knows unspeakable loneliness and emotional turmoil but also must endure the gloating of the enemy (see Psalm 13:2b, 4).

The discussion of the imprecatory (cursing) psalms in the introduction of this commentary notes that the psalmists were concerned not only for

57

themselves but also for their society. If David is the author of Psalm 13, such a concern would be especially warranted, since the king was ultimately responsible for the preservation of justice.

The psalm does not end with the question "How long?" but with a word of confidence and song of joy (see 13:5-6). How the psalmist moved from the one to the other is worth noting. Verse 5 begins with an emphatic **I**. It is as if, with his enemy's taunts and God's silence ringing in his ears, he bursts out, "In spite of these, **I** will trust God." He had already demonstrated this trust by appealing to God for help (see 13:1-3), but now that trust is reaffirmed in a bold way.

Two reasons are stated for the psalmist's trust, the most important being God's **unfailing love** (*chesed;* 13:5). This expression, emphasized in the Hebrew, speaks of the continual and unending love of God, which is based on the relationship already established between Him and His people.

If the psalmist needed any proof that God took this commitment seriously, he could find it in a review of past blessings (13:6), **for [God] has been good to me,** the second reason for the psalmist's trust. Whether these blessings are specific acts of kindness or the spirit of generosity that provide such, they result in the clear demonstration of the unending love of God. The psalm moves from the turmoil of 13:1-2 to the trust and joy of 13:5-6. "In the storm-tossed soul of the suppliant all has now become calm. Though it rage without as much now as ever—peace reigns in the depth of his heart."[3]

ENDNOTES

[1]See Psalm 13:1-2.

[2]Derek Kidner, *Psalms 1–72,* Tyndale Old Testament Commentaries, ed. D.J. Wiseman (Downer's Grove, Illinois: InterVarsity Press, 1973), p. 77.

[3]F. Delitzsch, *Psalms,* Commentary on the Old Testament, vol. V, translated by James Martin (reprint, Grand Rapids, Michigan: Wm. B. Eerdmans Publishing Co., 1978), p. 201.

13

WHAT A FOOL!

Psalm 14:1-7

P salm 14, repeated almost verbatim in Psalm 53, provides a revealing look at foolishness, a motif which figures prominently in the book of Proverbs. To us a fool is either harmlessly silly (like the "class clown") or hopelessly stupid. To the Hebrew, a **fool** was morally deficient, having chosen to live "without the direction or acknowledgment of God."[1]

David encountered such a person whose name, Nabal, befitted his character as a fool. When the opportunity came to repay David and his men for the protection they had provided to Nabal's flocks and shepherds, this fool rudely refused. He violated the customs of the day in an attitude of "aggressive perversity."[2]

The fool's words, **There is no God** (14:1), are far from a philosophical assertion by an honest seeker after truth, puzzling over the mysteries of the universe. Instead, this summarizes an attitude which chooses to deny God any place in one's life. God has revealed himself in His Word, but the fool refuses to seek God (14:2) or communicate with Him in prayer (14:4). Rather than submit to God's authority, the fool's corrupt and evil actions (14:1, 3) demonstrate defiance.

The psalmist is also troubled by the way the fool treats the righteous. The psalmist speaks of economic oppression (14:4) as well as countless daily humiliations (14:6). Still worse, fools feel no remorse for their destructive behavior. They disregard the needs of their fellow humankind out of disregard for the will of their common Creator. In both ways, they show contempt for God.

Verses 4 through 6 contain God's answer to the fool, beginning with a rhetorical question which points out the folly of the fool: **Will evildoers never learn . . . ?** (14:4). They fail to see the obvious consequences of disregarding God. God will come, and when He does the fool will be **overwhelmed with dread** (14:5). The original Hebrew suggests that they will be more than just frightened; they will be terrified by the arrival of the God they have denied as He comes to defend the very ones the fool has oppressed (see 14:6). The psalm concludes with longing for God's arrival to restore **the fortunes** of the oppressed and unmask the fools for who they really are (14:7).

For the fool, here is a warning: The God whom you deny will come and bring His judgment with Him. There is also comfort here for the faithful servant of the Lord. God will restore **the fortunes of his people.** Today's suffering saint can join in prayer with the psalmist: **Oh, that salvation for Israel would come out of Zion!** (14:7a).

ENDNOTES

[1]Peter C. Craigie, *Psalms 1–50,* Word Biblical Commentary, vol. 19, eds. David A. Hubbard and Glenn W. Barker (Waco, Texas: Word Books, 1983), p. 147.

[2]Derek Kidner, *Psalms 1–72,* Tyndale Old Testament Commentaries, ed. D.J. Wiseman (Downer's Grove, Illinois: InterVarsity Press, 1973), p. 79.

14

"WHO MAY DWELL IN YOUR SANCTUARY?"[1]

Psalm 15:1-5

For the righteous Israelite, no place was more precious than the **sanctuary** of God. It was a place of peace and security. The thought of residing there and always enjoying the presence of God could make one envy the swallows that nested in the Temple (see Psalm 84:3).

But what characterizes the person so privileged? In a list that may have been designed to instruct children, the psalmist lists ten qualities. He begins with three general statements—stated positively—then proceeds to three negatives and adds two more specific positives and two very specific negatives. The number ten may have been chosen to remind the hearers of the Ten Commandments or as an aid to count off these qualities (one for each finger).

The first three qualities are general; the remaining seven are more like their application. **He whose walk is blameless** (Ps. 15:2) refers not to sinless perfection but to a way of life that is sound and wholehearted. God's favorites do **what is righteous**—deeds which are not only appropriate and suitable but are also morally proper (15:2). Further, they speak **truth** from the **heart.** More than just speaking what is true, their true words reflect what is in their hearts. They are people of integrity, genuine to the core.

In three negative statements, the psalmist provides more details about the life of such people. Bible commentator Peter Craigie's translation picturesquely captures their honest speech: "He has not tripped over his tongue."[2] The more common translation, **slander,** suggests that the righteous will avoid gossip. They will not harm their neighbors by their deeds or by public insults (see 15:3).

Instead, they show themselves to be stalwart in their loyalty to the truth, either God's or the truth of their own words (see 15:4). They avoid those who continually do evil and honor those who reverence God; by implication, they seek them out as companions (see 1:1). So important is the truth to them that they will fulfill their oaths, even at personal cost.

Two final qualities are stated negatively. First, the righteous person does not practice **usury,** lending money at exorbitant interest (15:5). The Old Testament does not condemn interest, but harshly condemns those who take advantage of their neighbors by exploiting them in this way (see Deuteronomy 23:19-20; 24:6). Second, the righteous person will not compromise the truth by taking a **bribe** (15:5; see Exodus 23:8; Deuteronomy 16:19).

Remarkable in this description of the righteous person is the prominent role given to relationships with others. No mention is made of sacrifices, pilgrimages to Jerusalem, and frequent reading of the Law. That these were important to the Israelites is evident from other passages. The psalmist knew, however, that while devotion to God can be demonstrated in religious acts, the truest test of piety is what is done to another human being, especially where money is concerned.

Clearly, if all these qualities were conditions for fellowship with God, no one would qualify. Instead, these indicate the kind of person with whom God desires fellowship and who can experience the wonderful security that Psalm 15:5 promises—the one who does these things **will never be shaken.**

ENDNOTES

[1]Psalm 15:1a.

[2]See *Psalms 1–50* by Peter C. Craigie, Word Biblical Commentary, vol. 19, eds. David A. Hubbard and Glenn W. Barker (Waco, Texas: Word Books, 1983).

15

"IN PLEASANT PLACES"[1]

Psalm 16:1-11

M any times, in the face of difficulty, the psalmist speaks of God as his refuge. In Psalm 16:1, he not only makes such a claim, but he develops, through the remaining verses, how to take refuge in God and what such refuge provides. For the psalmist, to take **refuge** in God means to rely on Him and acknowledge Him as one's sovereign (16:2). Clearly, such reliance implies an exclusive loyalty that will not be shared with another.

The New International Version understands 16:2-4 to say that the one who takes refuge in God (see 16:1) delights in what pleases God (**the saints who are in the land** [16:3]) and disdains what dishonors God (to **run after other gods**—in idolatrous practices, for example [16:4]). Verse 3 could also be understood, as indicated by the NIV footnote, to condemn pagan priests and nobles who worship false gods. By either reading, loyalty to God denies any possibility of syncretism (joining the worship of the true God with that of other gods).

Some pursue **other gods** (16:4), but the psalmist is joyfully settled in the territory God has given him (see 16:5-6). Others will worship their deities by pouring out **libations of blood** (blood offerings; 16:4), but God has given the psalmist the cup of blessing (see 16:5). The psalmist refuses to speak the names of these other gods (see 16:4) but he readily addresses Yahweh (16:5), his refuge: **You have made my lot secure.** The darkest **night** may come, but even then God will counsel him (16:7).[2] In trouble the psalmist need only reach to his right to steady himself in the hand of God. Such security fills his heart so full of joy that it overflows (see 16:9).

The early church found in 16:8-11 a reference to Jesus' resurrection from the dead (see Acts 2:25-28; 13:35). While this was not what the psalmist had in mind, God filled this passage so full of meaning that it could only be completely understood after the resurrection of Christ. Unlike the psalmist, Jesus was not spared death, but through death brought life to His followers. The psalmist faced and was released from fear of death, but Jesus, through His death and resurrection, removed the fear of death from us (see Hebrews 2:15).

With God as one's refuge (see Psalm 16:5-6), endless blessings come from His right hand (16:11). There one finds security, pleasant places, and a delightful and eternal inheritance. Even in the midst of problems, the presence of God brings joy.

ENDNOTES

[1]See Psalm 16:6.

[2]The Hebrew uses a more intensive form of the word for "night" in Psalm 16:7b.

16

THE WONDER OF GOD'S LOVE

Psalm 17:1-15

salm 17 presents a poignant plea for vindication. After the psalmist's opening cry for help (see 17:1a), he explains that God should listen and respond because the psalmist is righteous (17:1b-5).[1] The psalmist's is a **righteous plea** (17:1a), one which **does not rise from deceitful lips** (17:1d). This claim to righteousness falls short of a declaration of sinlessness but surpasses an assertion of innocence for these particular circumstances alone. The **night** (17:3) is a time of transparency when the hurry of the day yields to solitude. Let this refining process (**examine, test** [17:3]) continue even at the time when his conscience is most tender, and the result will be the same: innocence. He credits his innocence, both in word (see 17:3c) and deed (17:4-5), not to himself but to God (**the word of your lips** [17:4a]).

A new appeal begins in 17:6, based not on his righteousness, but on something more solid: God's love (see 17:6-9). The psalmist is certain that God will listen to him and respond because of God's wonderfully **great love** (*chesed;* 17:7). This love linked God to His people and assured them of His concern (see 17:6).[2] It promised deliverance by God's strong **right hand** (17:7b) and protection. His desire to be **the apple of your eye** (17:8a) refers to God's pupil. The psalmist prays to God, "Protect me as you would your very eyes" (TEV). The psalmist asks for sheltering care like that given by the eagles for their young (see 17:8b). Because both of these metaphors are drawn from Deuteronomy 32:10-11, David may have had that passage in mind.

Such sheltering is necessary, given the ferocity of his foes (see 17:10-12). Their hearts are **callous** (literally, "they have closed their fat"[3]) because they have rebelled against God. Like wild animals, they have pursued and pounced upon their prey (see 17:11-12). The need is urgent! **Rise up, O LORD,** the psalmist pleads (17:13-14a).

As if God immediately answered that prayer, the tone changes from urgency to confident praise (see 17:14b-15). As God's protection was described in terms drawn from Israel's wilderness wanderings (17:8), so too are the blessings God brings: food, children, and security (see 17:14c; also Deuteronomy 32:14).

Psalm 17:15 may refer to bodily resurrection, with **when I awake** coming after death (see Isaiah 26:19; Ezekiel 37:1-14; Daniel 12:2). Because the psalmist knew very little of such a view of resurrection, however, and because this view ignores the temporal allusions to evening (see Psalm 17:3) and morning (17:15), it seems better to understand this as a reference to the psalmist's struggle. His longing for God to reveal himself (17:2) is answered when God arrives (17:15).

Once again the psalmist may be thinking of Israel's wilderness experience. The Israelites were instructed to build the Tabernacle in the middle of their camp. Each morning upon awakening, all could turn toward that spot and behold their God (see Deuteronomy 12:7). **Show the wonder of your great love** (Ps. 17:7), cried the psalmist, "as You showed it to our fathers in the wilderness." "Just as they were able to behold You in the tabernacle, let us be filled with the vision of you" (17:15 NJB).

ENDNOTES

[1]See the discussion of the strangeness of the psalms in the introduction to this commentary for more on this bargaining.

[2]**I** is emphatic in Psalm 17:6a.

[3]Peter C. Craigie, *Psalms 1–50,* Word Biblical Commentary, vol. 19, eds. David A. Hubbard and Glenn W. Barker (Waco, Texas: Word Books, 1983), p. 160.

17

CELEBRATION OF VICTORY

Psalm 18:1-50

That this psalm is a hymn of celebration to God for the victory He has given to the psalmist is evident not only from the psalm itself but also from its title.[1] God's promise to insure David's dynasty—the foundation beneath this hymn—was good news for the rest of Israel since it meant God's ongoing favor to their nation. For this reason, Psalm 18 continued to encourage the Israelites long past David's death.

When Nathan informed David of God's covenant with him, the king's first question was, "Why would you do this for me?" (see 2 Samuel 7:18-19). The same question plays an important role in this psalm. God cares about His people and longs to help them. When He heard David's cry for help (see Psalm 18:4-6), the earth shook under the force of God's concern. He burst through the sky on His swiftest steed and exploded onto the scene with the force of a natural disaster (see 18:7-15).

All this eruption of divine energy was so that God could extend His hand and rescue the struggling psalmist (see 18:16-19). The contrast between His fury and His gentleness is striking. David exclaims that God **drew me out of deep waters** (18:16) and set him in a **spacious place** (18:19), free from the press of his enemies. All this display was because God loves him (18:19).

The psalmist knew he had been rescued because God's justice cannot permit the ongoing persecution of the righteous by the wicked. This is why the psalmist proclaims his innocence, not in legalistic self-righteousness, but in the firm belief that he has done nothing deserving such treatment from his enemies (see 18:20-24). Vindication, although not immediate, is as certain as the holy character of God himself. **To the faithful** He will show himself as faithful, but to the crooked He is as crafty as a fox (18:25-26).

While God's compassion and justice provide the motivation to rescue His people, God's power makes such rescue a certainty. This power has already been demonstrated in God's dramatic rescue (see 18:4-19); it is again displayed in 18:27-45. There is an interesting twist in these passages: In the former, the psalmist is passive and helpless until God intervenes; in the latter, the psalmist is enabled to accomplish the victory by God's help. So it is that "when I am weak, then I am strong" (2 Corinthians 12:10). The psalmist's feet are made firm (see Psalm 18:33) and his stride steady (18:36-37). Placed on strategic high ground (18:33), he is trained and empowered to use the strongest weapons (18:34). With God to support and shield him (18:35), victory is assured (18:38).

Near the center of the psalm (18:28-32), the poet combines God's love, justice, and power into an eloquent testimony of faith. God's love maintains the psalmist's flame; God's justice is revealed through His perfect, **flawless** Word (18:30; see 12:6); and God's power enables the psalmist to accomplish great feats (18:29, 32).

The conclusion of Psalm 18 echoes its introduction. The psalmist began (18:1) by expressing his deep love for God and ends by extolling God's love *(chesed)* for him (18:50). This celebration of victory is framed by a word of praise (18:1, 46) and offers reasons for praise (18:2, 47-48) and testimony to the faithfulness of God (18:3, 49-50).

As this psalm is enveloped in love and praise, so is the psalmist enveloped by a loving and praiseworthy God. And so are we enveloped in this God who remains **rock, fortress, refuge, shield,** and **stronghold** to His people (18:2).

ENDNOTE

[1]Psalm 18 is found in essentially the same form in 2 Samuel 22, where it is introduced in words very similar to the title given here.

18

JOIN THE HEAVENS IN PRAISE

Psalm 19:1-14

hristian writer C. S. Lewis considered Psalm 19 to be the finest poem in the Psalter and one of the finest poems in the world.[1] Drawing from the created world and the revealed Word, the psalmist extols God's greatness in a masterful way.

It begins with eyes turned upward to the **heavens** (Ps. 19:1). No specific celestial body is singled out, but the entire sky, including the sun, moon, stars, planets, and the backdrop in which they are set are mentioned in this poem. From these we learn of God's glory, for they are His creation. At a time when many of the surrounding nations worshiped the heavenly bodies, such a statement takes a bold stand for the supremacy of God. It is no less striking in our day when the sun, moon, and stars are regarded as nothing more than hot gas and cold matter. They are clearly more than this: They are visible and undeniable evidence of God's greatness. Their testimony would be no less eloquent were they given tongues to speak. In fact, although they are mute, they **pour forth speech,** speaking a universal and continual language, repeated day and night for all to hear (19:2-3).

The psalmist next concentrates his thoughts on the **sun** (19:4b-6) which he personifies but does not deify. Housed in **a tent** of God's making (perhaps a picturesque description of the horizon), the sun rises **like a bridegroom** coming from his **pavilion.** This is a reference to the groom's emergence from either the wedding tent after the ceremony or the bridal chamber on the next day. In either case, the groom, in the prime of his life, joyously and eagerly anticipates a new day.

After the sun's initial appearance, it moves through the sky with the graceful stride of a world-class marathon runner. No corner of the world is left untouched by its rays; no person, animal or object is unaffected by its light and heat. As with the heavens, it provides continual, undeniable proof of the greatness of God.

In 19:7, the psalmist turns to explore another reason to praise God: His teaching. The psalmist describes this in various ways: as God's **law** (19:7a), a comprehensive term for God's revelation, which included but was not limited to the Law of Moses; as **statutes** (19:7b), a term which emphasizes God's covenant with Israel; and as **precepts** and **commands** (19:8), which celebrate the precision and authority of God's law. **Fear of the Lord** (19:9a) is either a title for the Law or a description of how God wants us to receive it.[2] The **ordinances** (19:9b) may refer to the helpful way the Law was applied to different circumstances.

However described, the Law is of sterling quality. It is perfect, not only because it is without error, but also because it is directed toward human well-being. It is dependable (19:7b), the straight path (19:8a), illuminating (19:8b), pure (19:9a), and sure, righteous, precious, and temptingly sweet (19:9b-10). Like the sun, the Law renews life (19:7a), brings joy to the heart (19:8a), illuminates (19:8b), and remains day after day and year after year (19:9a). The Law, however, does much more than the heavens.

Only the Law can make **wise the simple** (19:7b) and can warn and reward (19:11). The sun cannot reveal **hidden faults;** only the Law can do that (19:12). Only God's Law can create the desire for purity, can lead one to confession, and can forgive (19:12-13). Creation can reveal God's glory, but only God's Word can make possible a personal knowledge of the Creator. This point is made subtly but unmistakably in the uses of God's name in the two sections of Psalm 19. The section which deals with creation uses the generic name for God only once. When speaking of the Law, God's holy name—Yahweh—is used seven times.

Only because God spoke can we speak to God in prayer (19:12-14) and praise (19:14). Only because God spoke can we speak personally of Creator God as **my Rock and my Redeemer** (19:14). Having come to know Him through His Word, we too can take our place with the mute heavens to declare the glory of God.

ENDNOTES

[1]C.S. Lewis, *Reflections on the Psalms* (New York: Harcourt, Brace and World, 1958), p. 63.
[2]Daniel G. Ashburn ("Creation and Torah in Psalm 19," *Jewish Bible*

Quarterly, vol. 22 [1994], pp. 241–48) embraces the former (p. 246; see Isaiah 11:3); and F. Delitzsch (*Psalms,* Commentary on the Old Testament, vol. V, translated by James Martin [reprint, Grand Rapids, Michigan: Wm. B. Eerdmans Publishing Co., 1978], p. 287) embraces the latter.

19

CONFIDENCE IN BATTLE

Psalm 20:1-9

Most scholars agree that Psalm 20 formed part of the liturgy which Israel observed when sending its army into battle. The psalm itself and evidence from 2 Chronicles 20 suggest that this occurred at the Temple and was accompanied by sacrifices and burnt offerings. Different speakers participate in this corporate expression of confidence and request for military victory.

A group of people, asking God to grant victory and promising celebration, speaks first (see Psalm 20:1-5). Then a solitary voice is heard—whether from a religious official or the king himself—confidently announcing imminent victory (20:6). A group, perhaps the army, answers, affirming their confidence in God to bring success (20:7-8). The psalm concludes with a final public appeal to God for victory in battle (20:9).

Shining clearly throughout this psalm is a bold confidence in God. Verse 6 begins with a Hebrew word used to indicate a dramatic turning point and contains other clues which imply that victory has already occurred, even though the battle remains in the future. Confidence laces the public speeches as well (see 20:7-8). The people will not trust in **chariots** or **horses**—the sophisticated weapons of that day—but in the God who is greater than all weapons. Their request to be raised and see the enemy **brought to their knees** (20:8) suggests the people sang these words even while oppressed. God can help because He is free from spatial limitations. Verse 2 speaks of help coming from the Temple (**the sanctuary**), but verse 6 describes that help as coming from heaven itself.

The people's confidence is based on two pillars: God's past action and His covenant relationship with Israel. In 20:1, He is described as **the**

God of Jacob, a title which recalls the great acts of God in the history of Israel, most particularly the Exodus and the granting of the Promised Land. This wonder-working God has graciously chosen to link himself with Israel in a covenant. He has made himself known to them by name (**the LORD** [20:6]) and even established His dwelling place among them (**support from Zion** [20:2]). The Tabernacle and the Temple were visible proofs of God's love for them. For these reasons, He could be trusted to know their needs (20:1-2) and desires (20:4-5) and to do what was best for Israel (20:6).

It is noteworthy that, in spite of their tremendous confidence in God, they did not hang up their weapons and let God fight the battle. They used those weapons and trusted God for His help. They offered **sacrifices** and **burnt offerings** (20:3) not as charms, but as symbols of their consecration to His cause.

Because struggle is not eliminated from the life of His followers, confidence in God is essential. When joined with prayer, consecration, and diligence, God's victory can be obtained and praise can follow (see 20:5).

20

CELEBRATION IN VICTORY

Psalm 21:1-13

salm 21 is evidently a companion to Psalm 20 since the prayer for victory expressed in the former has been answered and is being celebrated in the latter. While the king and his people enjoy this victory, it is evident that God, more than anyone else, is the true hero of the psalm.

That God possesses the power to grant victory over the king's enemies is clear from 21:1-6. The description of this triumph is rich. Victory comes in response to the king's **request** and his heart's **desire** (21:2; see 20:4). The king is, as it were, **welcomed** back from the battle by God (21:3), who places on his head **a crown of pure gold,** perhaps the crown taken from the conquered monarch (see 2 Samuel 12:30).

Some assume that Psalm 21:4 speaks of the king receiving eternal life. Since it was customary to greet kings with "May the king live forever" (see 1 Kings 1:31), this more likely expresses a wish that the king's reign may be long and prosperous. Victory has brought majesty and splendor to the king (see Psalm 21:5), but it is glory reflected from God, as the moon shines with reflected, not self-generated, light. Saved for last, perhaps because it is the most precious result of victory, **the joy** of God's **presence** is granted to the king as he returns to the Temple (21:6).

Not only is God's power stressed, but also the certainty of God's future victories (see 21:7-12). In the original Hebrew it is unclear whether God or the king is being addressed in 21:8-12. If spoken to the king, these words assure him that his future victories will come through God's power. If addressed to God, Israel's enemies are strikingly presented as God's enemies (see 21:8). To enter into covenant with another country automatically made their enemies your own enemies. Whether addressed to the king or God, it is the **Most High** (21:7) who will bring overwhelming victory.

There is good reason why the confidence expressed in verses 7 through 12 follows verses 1 through 6. Israel found its hope for the future in past experiences of God's victory. God's past actions, especially the Exodus, demonstrated His power. Psalm 21 is framed by reference to the strength of God in which the king rejoices (see 21:1) and for which God is praised (see 21:13). God's past actions, including the establishment of the covenant and the revelation of His name, Yahweh (**LORD** [21:1, 7, 9, 13]), also convinced them of His **unfailing love** (*chesed;* 21:7). Because Israel knew the power and love of God, trust was the only proper response.

21

"PROCLAIM HIS RIGHTEOUSNESS"[1]

Psalm 22:1-31

t is difficult to read Psalm 22 without imagining the Crucifixion, which fulfills it so completely. From the opening, **My God, my God, why have you forsaken me?** to the closing, **He has done it**—similar to Jesus' cry, "It is finished"—the Christian finds special meaning. Even prior to the New Testament, however, these words held meaning for the Israelites. By examining this psalm from the perspective of the Old Testament believer, the Cross will come to mean even more.

This psalm falls into two parts, sharply distinct in tone. In 22:1-21, we hear the psalmist crying for help in the midst of serious difficulty. His is the bitter distress of one abandoned by God. Three times in 22:1-2, he calls out to his God, asking why he has been forsaken. In 22:3-5, the psalmist appeals to God's sovereignty (22:3)[2] and past deliverance (22:4-5).

Being forsaken by a sovereign God leaves the psalmist feeling sub-human: **I am a worm and not a man** (22:6). Divine silence, in spite of the psalmist's lifelong commitment to God and his desperate circumstances (22:7-11), worsens his pain. Verbal abuse gives way to physical abuse (22:12-18). Violent attackers—described as **strong bulls of Bashan** (22:12; **Bashan** was a region known for strong livestock), ferocious **lions** (22:13, 21), a pack of **dogs** (22:16, 20), and **wild oxen** (22:21)—leave him in **the dust of death** (22:15). His reservoir of strength is as dry as a broken piece of pottery (see 22:14-15). His body is dehydrated (22:15), gaunt (22:17), and racked with pain (22:14). Lacking even a shred of courtesy, people stare at his naked, dying body and divide his clothes among them. The evidence suggests that 22:21 should be translated as follows:

> Save me from the mouth of the lion
> from the horns of the wild oxen,
> You have answered me![3]

God breaks into the psalmist's plea and answers midsentence.

From this abrupt beginning, the second part of Psalm 22 proceeds to universal praise. References to public thanksgiving (see 22:22, 25-26) suggest a thank offering in the Temple with an accompanying communal meal.[4] Praise will spread beyond those assembled to all ranks of people (22:29) and all nations (22:27). It will begin a never-ending cycle of praise to God, for **posterity will serve him** and the newly born will come to trust in God (22:30), just as the psalmist had (22:10).

Why would a sovereign God allow one of His faithful servants to endure so much before interceding? There are no good answers to this question; the suffering of the innocent is inexplicable. What Psalm 22 teaches, however, and what the Cross demonstrates to a far greater degree, is that God can turn the most unjust of circumstances into a reason for all the universe to **proclaim his righteousness** (22:31).

ENDNOTES

[1] See Psalm 22:31.

[2] **You** is emphatic, indicating the firmness of his belief.

[3] Peter C. Craigie, *Psalms 1–50,* Word Biblical Commentary, vol. 19, eds. David A. Hubbard and Glenn W. Barker (Waco, Texas: Word Books, 1983), p. 195.

[4] For more on songs of thanksgiving, see the discussion on psalm types in the introduction to this commentary.

22

"THE LORD IS MY SHEPHERD"[1]

Psalm 23:1-6

Psalm 23, perhaps the best-loved psalm, has delighted the child, rejoiced the faithful, emboldened the dying, and comforted the grieving. It is built on the metaphor of the shepherd, a common figure in Israel. Indispensable to the flock, he is its constant companion, its guide and source of provision, its physician, and its defender.

Although the term "shepherd" was commonly applied to rulers in the ancient Near East, God is not often called Shepherd (see Genesis 48:15; 49:24). Psalm 23:1a is therefore especially striking in its claim: **The Lord is my Shepherd.** The psalmist has claimed an intimate relationship (**The Lord is *my* shepherd** [my emphasis]) with Yahweh, Israel's covenant God.

The rest of 23:1 flows naturally from such an assertion. He who has Yahweh, "the possessor of all things, himself has all things."[2] With such a provider, this person cannot lack materially. Whether feeding on fresh and tender grass (see 23:2), drinking at **quiet waters** (23:2) or feasting at the **table** of his host (23:5), every material need is abundantly met. Also implied is Yahweh's ability to provide just what is needed. Sheep, who cannot drink by rushing waters, need to be led to those which are still. Perfect provision will continue, since it is given **for his name's sake** (23:3). God's giving is consistent with His character; since this does not change, neither will His habits of provision.

With God as his Shepherd, the psalmist can rest. **He restores my soul** (23:3a) does not refer to God's restoration of wayward sheep but to how He imparts new life to the sheep. It can rest in the shepherd's protection, comforted by the **rod** (23:4), a weapon used for defense. Restoration is also found at the **quiet waters** (23:2), literally, "waters of restfulness."

Although the metaphor changes from the pasture to God's table, the emphasis on rest continues. There is no further need to fear enemies, for as God's guest (see 23:5), the psalmist's protection is the concern of his host. The foes, unable to harass, must look on as the psalmist feasts (see 23:5).

Now, instead of being pursued by enemies, the psalmist is pursued by **goodness and love** (23:6). **Goodness** is the steady and faithful kindness for which God is known. **Love** refers to God's covenant kindness *(chesed)* which is unending and undeserved. **Follow** is too mild; these things *chase* the psalmist. What is more, he has nothing else to fear, since **surely** could be rendered "only."

The psalmist knows the rest which comes from joy. His head is anointed with perfumed oils (see 23:5b), an action that symbolizes festivity, honor, health, and blessing.[3] His **cup overflows,** symbolizing a life "overblessed" in every way by God.

With Yahweh as his Shepherd, the psalmist knows he will always be led in the "right paths," as **paths of righteousness** (23:3) should be translated. The psalmist need not find his own paths but only follow the staff of the Shepherd, taking direction from its gentle guidance (see 23:4). The Shepherd may lead into the **valley of the shadow of death** (23:4), but this too is one of His right paths.[4] In 23:1-3, the psalmist speaks *about* God; when the psalmist moves into this dark valley, he speaks *to* God (see 23:4). When he needed God the most, God was most truly present.

Of all that comes from having God as his Shepherd, the psalmist is most delighted with God's presence. The center of the psalm (see 23:4) resounds with this affirmation without which none of the good gifts would be possible. Without the shepherd, there is only a harassed and helpless flock (see Matthew 9:36). Without the host, there is no banquet. Of all the places where the psalmist might choose to be, he longs to stay in God's presence all his days (see Psalm 23:6). From the first verse of this psalm to the last, the focus has been on Yahweh. The search which has occupied humanity—for provision, rest, guidance, and fellowship with the divine—ends in God.

ENDNOTES

[1]Psalm 23:1a.

[2]F. Delitzsch, *Psalms,* Commentary on the Old Testament, vol. V, translated by James Martin (reprint, Grand Rapids, Michigan: Wm. B. Eerdmans Publishing Co., 1978), p. 329.

³*Theological Dictionary of the Old Testament,* vol. III, translated by John T. Willis and Geoffrey W. Bromiley (Grand Rapids, Michigan: Wm. B. Eerdmans Publishing Co., 1978), p. 310; Francis Brown, *The New Brown-Driver-Briggs-Gesenius Hebrew and English Lexicon* (Peabody, Massachusetts: Hendrickson Publishers, 1979), p. 206.

⁴This phrase literally means "very deep shadow" and suggests a black and threatening ravine.

23

WORSHIP THE GLORIOUS KING

Psalm 24:1-10

As Psalm 23 speaks of the comfort of having Yahweh as a Shepherd, Psalm 24 delights in having Him as King. It may originally have been used in a religious procession celebrating God's enthronement in Jerusalem (see 24:7-10; 2 Samuel 6:12-19).

Everything and everyone belongs to Yahweh (see Psalm 24:1) because He created them (see 24:2). Alluding to Genesis 1, the psalmist speaks of God's laying the earth's foundation on the water (see Psalm 24:2). It would surely sink down into those waters were it not "in itself upheld by the creative power of God."[1]

In Canaan, sea and rivers were thought to pose a threat to divine order. Baal, one of the Canaanite gods, established his kingship when he defeated the god of the sea. By portraying Yahweh as Creator and Controller of the waters, the psalmist rejects such idolatry and asserts God's status as the all-powerful King who has established His throne in Jerusalem.

"Who may go to meet with Him there?" is the important question raised in Psalm 24:3. Only those with **clean hands and a pure heart** (24:4) may enjoy His fellowship. These imply integrity; both actions and motives must be unsullied. God demands complete loyalty and will not tolerate those who worship idols or regard them as possessing any authority (see 24:4).

As a reward, the pure worshiper experiences God's **blessing** and **vindication** (24:5). God's **blessing** replaces the empty promise of fertility made by the Canaanite gods. His **vindication** banishes the chaotic effects of injustice and produces in the pious a peace reflecting God's orderly reign (see 24:2).

The pure worshipers of 24:4—those who seek God's presence (see 24:6)—are granted their wish, for their glorious King is, symbolically, in procession to the Temple. As Yahweh moves toward His house, the gates are told to **lift up your heads** (24:7)—that is, expand the entrance. As large as they might be, they are too small to accommodate the glorious King. **"Who is this king of glory** who is coming?"** inquire the **gates** (or gatekeepers). He is Yahweh—powerful, strong, and victorious in battle. For emphasis, the call to expand and the inquiry are repeated. This time, God is described as **LORD Almighty** (Yahweh Almighty), a term which portrays the power and universal sovereignty by which God subdues the forces of chaos and establishes a righteous and orderly world.

Although Christians no longer celebrate Yahweh's enthronement in Jerusalem with sacred processions, some things have not changed. God still rules the universe, and only those with **clean hands and a pure heart**—those undivided in loyalty who seek His face—may come into His presence.

ENDNOTE

[1]F. Delitzsch, *Psalms,* Commentary on the Old Testament, vol. V, translated by James Martin (reprint, Grand Rapids, Michigan: Wm. B. Eerdmans Publishing Co., 1978), p. 335.

24

A CONVERSATION ABOUT LIFE

Psalm 25:1-22

P salm 25 reads like a conversation, perhaps between the psalmist and himself. One party voices heartfelt concerns, while the other responds with words of confidence and direction. Addressing God, the psalmist begins by asserting his **trust** and asking not to be made **ashamed** (25:1-2). His counterpart reminds him that the one who trusts in God is never ashamed, unlike the faithless person (see 25:3). Not wanting to be faithless, the psalmist prays for God to guide and be merciful toward him (see 25:4-7). **Mercy** reflects the attitude of a mother toward her child, while **love** describes God's covenant compassion toward His people (*chesed;* 25:6).

The psalmist is answered with the affirmation that God hears the kind of prayer he has just prayed (see 25:8-10). A **good and upright** God whose ways are all loving and faithful not only hears but removes whatever obstacles remain, including sin. In humble and trusting response, the psalmist requests this forgiveness (see 25:11).

The verses that follow (25:12-15) tell of the blessings that come to the person who fears the Lord, as if to applaud the psalmist's penitence. The guidance that the psalmist sought earlier (25:4-5) will be granted; Yahweh will even disclose insight into His ways (25:14). Having been assured that God wants to reveal himself, the psalmist, struggling and lonely, asks God to do so (25:16-21).

This conversation reveals how important it is to remain faithful to God during times of concern. Because the psalmist knows God is listening and has helped in the past, he voices his present concerns to Him (25:6). As each level of the dialogue brings new revelation of truth, he responds with trust and obedience (25:8-11).

The psalmist has even employed the alphabet acrostic to highlight the connections between concern and confidence.[1] This device was used as a memory aid, assisting the young to learn God's Word. The psalmist wants even children to know how to face difficult times.

Acrostics also reveal the orderliness of the world and God's sovereignty over it. The psalmist wants to show that life occurs under the watchful and loving eye of a sovereign God. Even in those times of concern, **All the ways of the LORD are loving and faithful for those who keep the demands of his covenant** (25:10).

ENDNOTE

[1]For more on alphabet acrostics, see the discussion on other literary elements in Hebrew poetry in the introduction to this commentary.

25

GOD IS JUST

Psalm 26:1-12

P salm 26 finds the psalmist under some kind of accusation as his appeal for vindication (see 26:1-2) suggests. Others may consider him guilty, but he knows that God will find him innocent, so he willingly subjects his heart and mind to the refiner's furnace (**test, examine** [26:2]). He follows his appeal with reasons why God should come to His rescue, like a defendant offering evidence to establish innocence (see 26:3-8). The psalmist begins with God's **love** (26:3a), for it is only because of this covenant kindness *(chesed)* that he can make an appeal at all.

The claim to be **blameless** (26:1, 3b-6a) may sound strange, but it is a claim the psalmist often makes. He does not declare himself sinless but wholeheartedly devoted to God. He objects to the inaccurate and unfair judgment that lumps him with **sinners,** with whom he has resolved not to associate (26:9).

In language similar to Psalm 1, the psalmist denies association with those who are false and deceptive (see 26:4) and with the **assembly of evildoers** (26:5). Bible commentator Peter Craigie's translation demonstrates the psalmist's shift from past choices to future choices:

> I have not sat with men of falsehood,
> nor will I consort with dissemblers.
> I have hated the assembly of evildoers
> and I will not sit with the wicked.[1]

This same past and future commitment virtually frames the psalm, which begins with a claim to have walked blamelessly (see 26:1) and concludes with the promise to walk this way in the future (see 26:11).

The psalmist pledges a purity like the priests, those who were charged with a very high standard of holiness. As the priests would wash at the basin and sacrifice on the altar, the psalmist promises to wash his hands (whether figuratively or literally) and **go about your altar** (26:6). This last phrase is somewhat unclear. Because the Hebrew behind **go about** is used to mean a thorough traversing (such as when the wicked prowl around the city like dogs; see Psalm 55:10 and 59:6, 14), many translate it as the New International Version does. Less likely, but also possible, is to take this expression as the psalmist's complete commitment to keep God's law (see the ideas of shielding, guarding, and surrounding in Deuteronomy 32:10; Psalm 32:7, 10; Jeremiah 31:22). The psalmist continues to defend his right to God's vindication by pointing out how faithful a worshiper he has been (see Psalm 26:6b-8). This is not legalistic righteousness but a claim of faithfulness.

Once again the psalmist appeals to the just Judge for vindication (26:9-11). Because he has not associated with the wicked in life, to be condemned with them in death would not be fair. He appeals to God's mercy, not his own self-righteousness (26:11).

The psalm concludes on a note of confidence (26:12). The psalmist is certain he will not be swept away with the wicked but will stand. The place which has been his delight (26:8) will be the place where he publicly celebrates his vindication. The world may not be fair, but God is. He will listen to our cries for vindication and when the time is right, bring about perfect justice.

ENDNOTE

[1]Peter C. Craigie, *Psalms 1–50,* Word Biblical Commentary, vol. 19, eds. David A. Hubbard and Glenn W. Barker (Waco, Texas: Word Books, 1983), p. 223.

26

WAIT FOR
THE LORD

Psalm 27:1-14

From the very first verse, Psalm 27 reveals a confidence as profound as any in the Bible:

> **The Lord is my light and my salvation—**
> **whom shall I fear?**
> **The Lord is the stronghold of my life—**
> **of whom shall I be afraid?**

The psalmist does not fear his enemies, for he walks in God's light while **they** (emphatic in the Hebrew) stumble in the dark (27:2). No army can frighten him; with the Lord as his fortress, the psalmist has all the security he needs.

Because in God he has all he needs, God is all he wants (see 27:4-6). He asks to **dwell in the house of the Lord** all his life, not to escape from the world, but because **in the house of the Lord** there would be uninterrupted fellowship with God. There one could **gaze upon the beauty of the Lord** (27:4)—that is, really perceive and understand it. In the Temple, God could be sought. Verse 5 refers to the security provided by the host for his guest, one of the most significant social obligations of that day. The psalmist would joyfully acknowledge the source of his confidence by sacrificing and singing to Yahweh (see 27:6).

In 27:7, however, the tone changes dramatically from confidence to concern. The same one who would sing praises to the Lord (27:6) is now calling to Him for help (27:7). The one who felt secure in God's presence and who felt sure God would keep him safe in trouble now cannot find

Him (27:8-9). The enemy whose defeat had been predicted (27:2) now rises against the psalmist, **breathing out violence** (27:12).

Although the circumstances have clearly worsened and his earlier confidence has faded, the psalmist maintains his faith. In fact, whereas the first six verses were spoken *about* God, verses 7 through 12 are spoken *to* God. The psalmist feels separated from God but remembers that this is where his hope lies; thus he makes the seeking of God's face his first priority (27:7-9). He knows that, in spite of appearances, God's faithfulness is stronger than even the most permanent of human bonds, such as that of parent and child (27:10). Especially in perilous times like these, he knows he must find the right path (27:11). Perhaps his request should be understood as an orphan's plea for instruction from his adopted parent (27:10). His circumstances are all the more urgent, considering the hostility of his enemies (27:12).

As with many lament psalms, this one ends on a note of confidence (27:13-14). Circumstances may have changed, but God has revealed himself and will again reveal himself. The command to **wait for the LORD** that concludes the psalm (27:14) is important for all believers to obey. The God we serve is, after all, the slowest One who is always on time. Waiting is easier when we remember that **the LORD** is sovereign (27:1), has mercifully promised protection to His people (27:13), and has been faithful in the past (27:1, 9). God is at work as much in the delay as He is in the answer, so **wait for the LORD.**

27

HELP FOR THE HELPLESS

Psalm 28:1-9

P salm 28 falls neatly into two parts: the psalmist's cry for help (see 28:1-5) and his response to God's answer (28:6-9). Through both sections, the psalmist seems intent on emphasizing his dependence on God. He makes it clear that he is helpless before his enemies (28:3-5)—those who flatter to his face but hate him in their hearts (28:3). Although he fears for his reputation, the psalmist cannot vindicate himself. He longs to work justice, repaying evildoers for their deeds, but his hands are tied (28:4). Still worse, if no one intervenes, the psalmist will become like one who goes down into **the pit** *(bor)*—that is, the grave (28:1), with nothing he can do to prevent it. The evildoers' rejection of God (see 28:5) prepares us for the judgment assumed in 28:6-9.

While the psalmist wants to reveal his own inadequacy in the face of trouble, he also wants the reader to know that God is able to do what he cannot. The psalmist accomplishes this, in part, by repeating the words of his **cry** for help (28:2) in the answer in 28:6.

Although the psalmist is helpless before his enemies, God can defend his cause, vindicate his name, and work justice (see 28:5). The psalmist feels helpless and in danger of death, but God is able to protect and rescue him (28:7). Even the king needs God's help, so God takes on the role of eternal Shepherd over His own inheritance (28:9).

While the psalmist may be helpless, he is not passive. He trusts God to work on his behalf (28:7), cries out to God for help (28:6), refuses to take matters into his own hands (28:4), and remains a person of integrity (28:3). Once the answer comes, he lifts his voice in praise to God (28:6-8).

The feeling of helplessness is familiar to all. How comforting to know that though we cannot accomplish our own rescue, protection, or vindication, God can. For those overwhelmed by the burden of leadership, God is capable of bearing that heavy load in their place. In our helplessness, we must trust, pray, obey, and remain humble. Then, when God's help arrives—as it will—ours must be the song of praise.

28

THE SOUND OF GLORY

Psalm 29:1-11

Psalm 29 sings God's glory to the accompaniment of a violent thunderstorm. It is crafted to move the reader beyond marvel at the power of the storm to praise for the God who sent it. Yahweh's name appears four times each in the introduction (see 29:1-2) and conclusion (29:10-11) and ten times in the body of the psalm. The numbers four and ten are significant in Hebrew.

To Israel's neighbors, most natural phenomena, such as thunderstorms, were thought to have supernatural causes. The Canaanites thought Baal, the storm god, rode on the clouds and hurled lightning as his weapon.[1] Psalm 29 not only celebrates the glory of God as seen in the storm but also declares Yahweh's superiority over all other gods.

The psalm opens with a formal, measured call to praise God for His glory (see 29:1-2). It is addressed to **mighty ones** (29:1a), which could mean angels (see 89:5-7), but probably refers to the gods worshiped by Israel's neighbors (see 97:7). It is difficult to know how to translate the final phrase of 29:2: **in the splendor of his holiness.** Rendered, literally, "in holy splendor," it could refer either to God's holiness or to the holiness of His worshipers. To read it as a quality of God ("worship the Lord as one possessing holy splendor") makes good sense of the original Hebrew and fits the rest of the psalm (see 29:4b, where the same Hebrew word is used to describe God's acts).

Seven times (seven is often considered the perfect number) in 29:3-9, God's **voice** is mentioned. Since the word translated **voice** can also be rendered "thunder" (see 18:13; also Jeremiah 10:13), the psalmist seems to be saying that every thunderbolt testifies of God. God's **voice** also suggests His word, a powerful force which created the universe out of nothing and spoke God's law to Israel.

The **mighty waters** over which His voice **thunders** (Ps. 29:3) may refer to the rain clouds, to the Great Sea (Mediterranean Sea) from which many storms enter Palestine, or to the Canaanite sea god over which God rules. God's voice is so mighty and **majestic** (29:4) that it **breaks the cedars** (29:5) and causes the mountains to jump like frightened animals. The psalmist mentions cedars and mountains because these are symbols of strength. Against Yahweh's voice and lightning bolt, however, they are powerless (see 29:7).

It is unclear which **Kadesh** is meant in 29:8. It could be the city near the Orontes River in the northern part of Palestine, near Mount Lebanon and Mount Hermon (referred to as Sirion in 29:6). If it refers to the better-known Kadesh Barnea, located in the southern wilderness (see Numbers 20:1, 16), the storm is described as sweeping from north to south with such power that it **twists the oaks and strips the forest bare** (Ps. 29:9). To the worshiper of Yahweh, this storm is more than an act of nature; it is an act of God. Therefore, all in His Temple should cry **"Glory!"** (29:9).

Not only worship, but submission should follow the recognition of God's glory (see 29:10). Yahweh rules **over the waters** (or flood), possibly a reference to His defeat of the sea god (see 29:3). This could instead refer to the flood from which God saved Noah, since that is the only other context where the Hebrew word for "flood" appears (see Genesis 7:17-24).

In Psalm 29:10b, the thought expands from God's rule in the natural realm to His universal rule as King forever. As a result of God's rule, His subjects will know **strength** (29:11). This is quite a promise considering what God's power has been shown to do (29:1 uses the same Hebrew word). Equally surprising is the promise of **peace** (*shalom;* 29:11b). Such peace shines like a rainbow after the fury of the storm. God is a God of power whose word can wreak havoc in heaven and earth. He is also a God who cares enough for His people to provide them with a share of His strength and bless them with His peace.

ENDNOTE

[1]Robert M. Good, "Baal," *Harper's Bible Dictionary,* gen. ed. Paul J. Achtemeier (San Francisco: Harper, 1985), pp. 84–85.

29

JOY COMES
IN THE MORNING

Psalm 30:1-12

I n the Hebrew language, the first word of Psalm 30 is a verb translated
"praise." Indeed, this is a psalm which begins and ends with adoration,
taking joy as its theme. The title mentions that the psalm was used **for
the dedication of the temple.** If David is the author, the title could refer
to his dedication of the Tabernacle (see 2 Samuel 6) or of the Temple
building materials, or it could refer to a song written by David for use when
the Temple was dedicated. Since the Hebrew word for **temple** could also
be translated "house," it may have been used at the dedication of the king's
palace. It is also possible that the title refers to a later use for one of
David's psalms.

The first three verses of Psalm 30 thank God for rescuing the psalmist.
Lifted me (30:1) is used elsewhere to describe the lifting of water from
a well. As God had lifted the psalmist, so he "lifts up" God in praise.
Having been rescued, the psalmist will not experience the ridicule of his
enemies who would gladly assume that his suffering was a judgment
from God.

You healed me in 30:2 could be either physical or metaphorical.
Either would fit the psalmist's description of being lifted up from the
grave *(sheol)* and **pit** *(bor;* 30:3). *Sheol* refers to the shadowy realm
where the dead are thought to reside. **Pit** could refer either to the grave
or to a well (see the "lifting up" in 30:1).

Deliverance is followed in 30:4-5 with a call to God's people to
praise. The phrase **you saints of his** suggests that this psalm
accompanied a thank offering and meal at which public testimony to
God's faithfulness would be given.[1] The reason for praise comes in 30:5:
God may become angry, but only temporarily, only **for a night,** as a

95

lodger who is just passing through. God's **favor,** on the other hand, comes like the dawn and lasts all life long. When one is lying deep within difficulties, the night seems so long. But morning is on the way, and with it, joy. How comforting to know that God's favor is as regular as the sunrise and lasts throughout each day, all life long.

Verses 6 through 12 provide a more complete description of the psalmist's difficulties, his cry for help, and God's solution. He addresses these verses to God rather than the audience of verses 4 and 5; he publicly acknowledges to God his need for divine aid, allowing the "eavesdroppers" to obtain a greater appreciation for God's compassion and might.

When God smiled on the psalmist, the psalmist **felt secure** (30:6) and elevated to safety (30:7). His confidence led, as it often does, to self-confidence; the **I** is emphatic in **I will never be shaken** (30:6). His precarious position became obvious when God hid His face, prompting the psalmist to turn to God for help (30:7). Verses 8 through 10 reflect his honest cry. He not only asks for God's mercy but reminds God, with covenant confidence, that if he dies, there will be one less person to praise God.

God's rescue, arriving in response to the psalmist's cry, prompts the psalmist to break out into praise (see 30:11-12). Tears and **wailing** have given way to dancing; **sackcloth** has been replaced with a garment of joy. **Sackcloth** was dark cloth made of goat or camel hair. While not necessarily uncomfortable, its dark color and low quality symbolized mourning. The second part of 30:11 contains a play on words, for the word for **joy** is the same word used to described the enemy's response to his defeat (30:1). Such a complete reversal is reason enough to thank God **forever** (30:12).

ENDNOTE

[1]For more on songs of thanksgiving, see the discussion on psalm types in the introduction to this commentary.

30

TAKE REFUGE IN GOD

Psalm 31:1-24

While we do not know the circumstances which prompted the writing of Psalm 31, it is clear that the psalmist, David, struggled with enemies too strong for him. Having put his trust in God and finding Him a secure hiding place, the psalmist summons his readers to do the same.

Frequently in the first five verses, David speaks of God as his refuge, fortress, and rock—metaphors of permanence and safety. The basis for such security, however, was not the absence of trouble but a recognition of the character of God; it is to this that the psalmist appeals. God will deliver because He is righteous (see 31:1) and because He is **the God of truth**—One who stands for and defends truth (31:5). Security comes because God will always act consistently with His nature—**for the sake of your name** (31:3). Jesus, knowing this security even at death's door, quoted 31:5 from the cross: **Into your hands I commit my spirit** (see Luke 23:46).

David had come to know God's nature through earlier experiences of rescue, to which he refers in Psalm 31:6-8. Assured that his God was true and powerful, he absolutely refused to trust in what was false and impotent (the last phrase in 31:6 is emphatic). Because of God's steadfast **love** (*chesed*) and past help (31:7), and because he knew he had not been abandoned (31:8), David anticipates a joyous deliverance (31:7).

Given the distress described in 31:9-13, deliverance needs to be soon. David appeals for help in 31:9a, echoing the affirmation made in 31:7b (**distress** and **anguish** translate the same Hebrew word). The physical effects of his distress are described first in 31:9b-10, beginning and ending in Hebrew with the word meaning "waste away."[1] Everything is being consumed: his **eyes, soul, body, life, years, strength,** and **bones.**

David then describes his emotional distress (see 31:11-13). He has become alienated from his friends due to the slander of his enemies. Alienation is always painful but especially in a society like Israel's, where so much importance was attached to the community. His alienation was complete; there was terror on every side.[2]

In spite of all this, David emphatically affirms his trust in God. His future rests not in the hands of the enemy, but in the hands of God to whom he has committed himself (see 31:5). Because these are loving hands (*chesed;* 31:16), the psalmist prays for the light of God's face (31:16), and the silence of his enemies (31:17-18).

His answer seems to come between verses 18 and 19, for the tone changes sharply. God has proven that He protects those who take refuge in Him, echoing the psalmist's cry in verse 1. Like any host of that day, God provides full assurance of protection when one was within His dwelling (see 31:20).

Earlier the psalmist felt abandoned (31:2) and surrounded by terror (31:13) as if in a **besieged city** (31:21). The second part of 31:22 begins with a word intended to emphasize a strong contrast, much stronger than the New International Version's **yet** (31:22b). The psalmist felt cut off and out of God's sight (see 31:1-6), but in fact God was watching in love (*chesed*) all along.

The psalmist concludes by calling others to trust God (see 31:23-24). He had experienced God's love, so he calls others to love God. He had known God's protection, so he calls others to trust. Keep on hoping in God, he says, for He loves us too much to turn away.

ENDNOTES

[1]Some have suggested that the word could imply "moth-eaten" since it comes from the word for moth. The New International Version adds **with grief** for clarity.

[2]"Terror on every side" is used several times by Jeremiah (see 6:25; 20:4, 10; 46:5; 49:29; also Lamentations 2:22).

31

THE SWEETNESS OF SINS FORGIVEN

Psalm 32:1-11

Counted among the seven penitential psalms, Psalm 32 represents a testimony of forgiveness and a call to experience God's love. Twice in 32:1-2, the forgiven person is pronounced happy, a term more exuberant than **blessed.**[1] There is good reason for this happiness, for sin is not only **forgiven** (literally, "lifted") but pardoned (literally, "covered"). The combination of these verbs affirms that sin is completely removed, leaving no trace.

When sins are not confessed, serious consequences result. Just as an untreated infection can spread and quickly destroy large amounts of tissue, so sin, if kept hidden, will devour soul and body. The psalmist's self-imposed silence was broken by moans which his silence produced (see 32:3) while his suffering was unrelenting (32:4). The ultimate cause of his suffering was spiritual—it came from God's hand (32:4), draining his strength like a tree withering in a summer drought.[2]

Sapped and suffering, the psalmist decides to face his sin and confess it. As soon as he announces his intention to uncover his sins—**I will confess** (32:5b)—God's forgiveness follows (32:5b; see 32:1). The arrangement of the psalmist's words and the emphatic **you** in 32:5b shows that God is so eager to forgive that He does so at the first sign of contrition.[3]

Having experienced God's forgiveness, the psalmist invites others to call on God (note the word **therefore** which begins 32:6). David summons the **godly** (32:6), those whose piety is evidenced not by the absence of sin from their lives, but by their promptness to confess it when it is discovered. They should call on God when He may be found, a reminder that not all times are times of repentance.

Verse 1 pronounced a blessing on those who have been forgiven; verses 6 through 10 detail these blessings. There is the blessing of protection (see 32:6-7), for those who call on God find a refuge **when the mighty waters rise.** Protection from floods was a great comfort in the ancient Near East, where the sea was viewed as a destructive force. Instead of being surrounded by rising waters, those God protects are surrounded by **songs of deliverance** (32:7).

Those who call on God also know the blessing of God's instruction: **I will instruct you and teach you** (32:8). As if to highlight this privilege, God himself (the Hebrew for **you** is singular) promises to teach the right way to go. His is compassionate counsel, for God promises: "I shall not take my eyes off of you" (32:8b NJB; see 33:18). As 32:3-5 makes clear, God can only guide those willing to obey.

The blessings of protection and guidance spring from the soil of God's **unfailing love** *(chesed)* for His people (32:10). The love which forgave the tormented sinner now surrounds the one who trusts in God. It is only God's love which can empty the guilty, troubled heart of its sin and fill it with song (see 32:11). "How great is the love the Father has lavished on us, that we should be called children of God!" (1 John 3:1).

ENDNOTES

[1] Derek Kidner, *Psalms 1–72,* Tyndale Old Testament Commentaries, ed. D.J. Wiseman (Downer's Grove, Illinois: InterVarsity Press, 1973), p. 133. The psalmist's happiness informs our understanding of the Old Testament sacrificial system (see Hebrews 9:9).

[2] Cohen sees the metaphor as botanical, with the psalmist's "sap" withering (A. Cohen, *The Psalms,* Soncino Books of the Bible, ed. A. Cohen [London: Soncino, 1950], p. 93) while Craigie takes it to be biological: the psalmist's "tongue" curled during the summer heat (Peter C. Craigie, *Psalms 1–50,* Word Biblical Commentary, vol. 19, eds. David A. Hubbard and Glenn W. Barker [Waco, Texas: Word Books, 1983], p. 263).

[3] For a New Testament passage echoing this, see Jesus' demonstration of forgiveness in Luke 7:44-50.

32

"THE EARTH IS FULL OF HIS UNFAILING LOVE"[1]

Psalm 33:1-22

This psalm begins where Psalm 32 concluded, with a call to praise (see 33:1-3).[2] It is a joyful song taken up by instruments; **harp** and **lyre** are mentioned, but all were probably invited (33:2). **A new song** (33:3) implies a fresh word of praise; since God's mercies are new every morning, stale praises will never do. The psalmist calls for God to be praised with loud shouts, like those raised by Israel at some of her highest moments.[3] Verses 4 through 19 provide the reasons for praise: God's praiseworthy character (33:4-5), His creative **word** (33:6-9), His sovereign **plans** (33:10-12), and His tremendous power (33:13-19).

The rich description of God's character in 33:4-5 begins with praise for God's word. Because it is always right and true, God can be depended on—**he is faithful in all he does** (33:4). According to verse 5, God will never be anything but faithful, for He **loves righteousness and justice.** A different word for **love** is used at the end of verse 5 *(chesid)* to emphasize God's covenant relationship with Israel. God's compassionate commitment to His people fills the earth, implying overabundance (see 119:64).[4]

Before God filled the earth with His **unfailing love,** He called it into being with His **word** (33:6; see Genesis 1). Because God's word is **right and true** (Ps. 33:4), what that word creates possesses these same qualities and demonstrates God's love. When He piled the waters into **jars** (or heaps or bottles or wineskins) and placed them in vaults to be released only at His command, God demonstrated His control of the waters (33:7). This force that troubled many in the ancient Near East was subject to God's authority (see 32:6).

Because of what God accomplished with His words, all the earth ought to fear Him (see 33:8-9). Verse 8 provides the call to reverence, while verse 9 gives the reasons: **For he spoke, and it came to be; he commanded, and it stood firm** (**he** is emphasized both times in the Hebrew). The psalmist treats creation not as an abstract doctrine to satisfy curiosity about the world's origin but as a reason to praise and obey the Creator.[5]

God's commands and the firmness with which they stood leads to a celebration of God's plan. The psalmist makes a pointed contrast between human plans and purposes which do not stand and the plans and purposes of God which do not fall. For the psalmist, the most praiseworthy element of God's plan is His choice of Israel as God's people. This is more than nationalistic pride, for the call of Israel was part of God's plan to reconcile all the world to himself; it demonstrated His personal, permanent and powerful love for people.[6]

Not only does God love all people, He is sovereign over **all mankind** (33:13-19). From the **heavens** He created (33:6), God **looks down** into the hearts of humankind, which He also created.[7] No human power can succeed against Him; the finest military weapon then available (see 33:16-17) could not even aid one's escape (see 33:17b).

While He watches all, His eye is especially on **those who fear him** (33:18-19). Difficulties may arise, even serious national dangers like famine and the threat of death, but God's protection and provision belong to those who fear Him and not difficulties and dangers.

The psalm ends with a communal affirmation of these truths about God and an implied commitment to praise Him (see 33:20-21). Security is directly related to that in which one has placed one's confidence. Consequently, trusting in God's holy name—that is, His righteous, true, faithful, and loving nature (see 33:4-5)—brings confidence and praise.

ENDNOTES

[1]Psalm 33:5b.

[2]This link, along with similar vocabulary and concepts may explain why these psalms are placed alongside one another. Some even think they were originally one psalm (Peter C. Craigie, *Psalms 1–50*, Word Biblical Commentary, vol. 19, eds. David A. Hubbard and Glenn W. Barker [Waco, Texas: Word Books, 1983], p. 270).

[3]See the use of the word "shout" in 1 Samuel 4:5-6; 2 Samuel 6:15; 2 Chronicles 15:14; Ezra 3:11-13.

⁴Isaiah provides insight into the meaning of **full** when he speaks of the earth being full of the knowledge of the Lord "as the waters cover the sea" (Isa. 9:11).

⁵Craigie, p. 275.

⁶For God's plan, see His call of Abram in Genesis 12:1-3. The psalmist makes this point by placing this statement precisely in the middle of the psalm (Ps. 33:12).

⁷The Hebrew seems to emphasize that God examines each one individually (Craigie, p. 269).

"TASTE AND SEE THAT THE LORD IS GOOD"[1]

Psalm 34:1-22

A ccording to its title, this psalm arose from an episode in David's life when he was running from Saul.[2] Sometime after this event, David arranged these verses in a rough alphabet acrostic.[3] The opening call to praise (see Psalm 34:1-3) announces David's intention to praise God and summons others to join him. To **extol the Lord at all times** could be translated "at every time," suggesting praise is called for even in periods of difficulty. The Hebrew of 34:2 places the emphasis on God's name, stressing David's intent to boast in God and nothing else. David may be observing the Mosaic requirement for the celebration of a fulfilled vow.[4] The testimony given during the communal meal which followed would **exalt** God (34:3) and build confidence in His greatness.

David calls for praise because he sought God and was answered with deliverance (see 34:4). This thought is repeated in similar language in 34:6. In between, in 34:5, David concludes that not only he but all who fix their eyes on God find deliverance rather than disgrace. **Radiant,** translated variously as "shine," "glitter," "beam," or "grow bright," is used in Isaiah 60:5 to describe a mother's delight when she again sees her children whom she had given up for dead.[5]

The deliverance of the poor man is described in powerful terms: An angel of God **encamps,** or is camping (the verb suggests a present, ongoing reality) around those who fear Him (Ps. 34:7). Deliverance results, not from a frontal attack on the enemy lines, but from God's continuing presence throughout the battle.

In 34:8-22, David relates the lesson learned through this experience: **fear the LORD.** The fear of the Lord represents the essence of Israelite religion. It is not a terror of God, but a healthy reverence which provides the foundation for true wisdom (see Proverbs 1:7). It is an attitude of the heart which must manifest itself in behavior (see Psalm 34:12-14).

David invites his hearers to experience the blessing of such reverence (see 34:8-10). **Taste and see** (34:8) not only alludes to the sacrificial meal at which these words are spoken, but employs that meal as an object lesson: As food benefits only the one who eats, God's blessings benefit only the one who trusts. These blessings are summarized in the Old Testament creedal statement, **the LORD is good** (34:8). He not only meets and exceeds all expectations but is himself the source of all that is good.

Those who, out of reverence for God, have taken refuge in Him alone find they need nothing else: They **lack nothing** (34:9-10). Haunting **fears** (34:4) are replaced by the fear of the Lord. Poverty and affliction (34:2, 6) give way to abundant provision (34:9-10). Even if young lions go without, those who seek the Lord will not (34:10). Lions, of all animals, are the least likely to go hungry; young ones are even less likely than old. This is not a promise of affluence but a reminder that God, if pursued as a lioness hunts her prey, will always let himself be caught.

Having celebrated the blessing of reverence for God, David now explains to his pupils how to learn it (34:11-14): Do not speak deceitfully (34:12-13), live a righteous life (34:14a) and pursue peace (34:14b). In order to experience **good days** (34:12), the good things He gives (34:10), and the goodness of God himself (34:8), one must **do good** (34:14).

The concluding section (34:15-22) affirms that Yahweh will deliver the righteous. Like a protective mother, He lovingly watches over them, constantly **attentive to their cry** (34:15). He has also been watching the evildoers, however, and will wipe them off the face of the earth (34:16). Although 34:17 may refer to **the righteous** (as in the NIV), the Hebrew has only "they." This could refer to the wicked who repent, a notion in line with Jewish thought which "exalts the power of true repentance."[6]

God delivers the **brokenhearted** (34:18) but does not promise their hearts will not break. Those who take refuge in God (34:8, 22) may have troubles, even many of them (34:19), but God takes their pain seriously and provides a way of escape (34:19-22).

ENDNOTES

[1]Psalm 34:8a.

[2]According to 1 Samuel 21:10-15, David took refuge with Achish, a Philistine king. Abimelech, the name mentioned in the title of this psalm, may be the title for Philistine rulers as Pharoah is the title for Egyptian monarchs. Psalm 34 contains no clear link to this setting; the connection must have been known from tradition (F. Delitzsch, *Psalms,* Commentary on the Old Testament, vol. V, translated by James Martin [reprint, Grand Rapids, Michigan: Wm. B. Eerdmans Publishing Co., 1978], p. 408).

[3]One letter *(waw)* is missing, while the letter *pe* is used in two places. For more on acrostics, see the discussion on literary elements in Hebrew poetry in the introduction to this commentary.

[4]For more on such songs of thanksgiving, see the discussion on psalm types in the introduction to the commentary.

[5]The New International Version has taken some liberties to translate this as **those who look to him** since the Hebrew only reads "They looked to him," which raises the question, who are "they"? It has been suggested that "they" may be the fears referred to in verse 4, which looked at God and flowed away (an alternate translation for **are radiant**); their faces do not try to find them anymore.

[6]A. Cohen, *The Psalms,* Soncino Books of the Bible, ed. A. Cohen (London: Soncino, 1950), p. 102.

34

DIVINE LEGAL AID

Psalm 35:1-28

Anyone who has had to face slanderous accusations can appreciate Psalm 35. It contains not one call for divine justice, but three, a reminder that such problems are not often quickly resolved and that one's best defense is divine. The promise of praise with which each call concludes turns our thoughts from earth to heaven, from our cause to God's.

The first call (see 35:1-10) summons Yahweh the warrior to fight for David (see 35:1-3). The battle is not primarily literal but legal, for **contend** (35:1) is the language of the law court (see Isaiah 3:13; 57:16; Psalm 103:9). The contest is as fierce as a battle, so God is summoned to take up the weaponry of war (see Psalm 35:2-3). The **shield** is a hand-held piece of armor while the **buckler** is a large shield designed to protect the whole body and is carried by an aide.[1] For offensive weaponry, God's spear is to be drawn out and readied for use. The next phrase could refer to another weapon (**javelin** or battle-axe) or could be a request for God to bar the way of the enemy (see the NEB). The psalmist also asks for a word of reassurance from God, a promise of salvation (see Psalm 35:3).

Having summoned his Defender, David requests what he would like to see happen to his enemies (see 35:4-8).[2] The shift to the passive voice emphasizes that any revenge is to be God's doing, not David's. Like chaff before the wind these "lightweights" will disappear, hurried on by the **angel of the Lord** (35:5, 7). This and Psalm 34:7 are the only references in Psalms to the angel of the Lord.[3] In these verses, David wants nothing more than justice; they have wronged him without cause and he wants them to experience some of their "own medicine." If his soul is preserved from disaster, David will **rejoice in the Lord** (35:9-10), knowing that salvation would be God's doing, not his own.

The second call for help (see 35:11-18) begins with a description of David's enemies (see 35:11-16). Mention of **ruthless witnesses** and harsh interrogation suggests the law court. David had shown his enemies kindness, interceding when his enemies were ill, persisting when his prayer went unanswered. Even though he had afflicted himself for them, they responded by afflicting him. It is as if the Good Samaritan found himself attacked and robbed by the very man he had helped on the road.[4]

Based on this unjust attack, David calls for God's help (see 35:17). He wants God to preserve his **precious life** (the same Hebrew word found in 35:3, 4, 9) from the ravenous lions. When God answers, David will publicly praise, perhaps through a vow fulfillment ceremony.[5]

The final call for God's help (see 35:19-28) also begins with a description of David's enemies, this time highlighting their falseness (see 35:19-21). Their eyes wink maliciously, their mouths are open in a gesture of evil glee (see Isaiah 57:4), while they claim to see what never really happened. They are truly dangerous, for they attack **those who live quietly in the land**, those like David who have given no cause for such treatment. No clearer illustration of such an attack can be found than the life of Jesus, who quotes a portion of Psalm 35:19 in John 15:25.

Unlike the enemy, who has falsely claimed to have seen (see Psalm 35:21), the Heavenly Judge actually *has* seen and heard the evidence; now it is time for Him to speak and act (35:22-25). While the enemies are utterly ashamed (note the similar terms in 35:4), those who rejoice in righteousness will have reason to rejoice continually (35:26-27). David too will join in this continual song of praise for God's righteous judgment (35:28).

Trusting God is sometimes frightening. Disasters arise and He does not always come the first time we call. We must continue to pray, remembering that we serve a just God who gets the glory when the victory comes.

ENDNOTES

[1]Peter C. Craigie, *Psalms 1–50*, Word Biblical Commentary, vol. 19, eds. David A. Hubbard and Glenn W. Barker (Waco, Texas: Word Books, 1983), p. 286.

[2]For more on imprecatory psalms, see the introduction to the commentary.

[3]See *Psalms 1–72* by Derek Kidner, Tyndale Old Testament Commentaries, ed. D.J. Wiseman (Downer's Grove, Illinois: InterVarsity Press, 1973), p. 142. Some have suggested that this is why these psalms were placed alongside one another.

[4]Kidner, p. 143.

[5]For more on songs of thanksgiving, see the discussion on psalm types in the introduction to the commentary.

35

THE LIMITLESS LOVE OF GOD

Psalm 36:1-12

For a psalm whose purpose is to celebrate the love of God, Psalm 36 begins curiously with a picture of the wicked person. But set against this dark background, God shines more brightly—His good deeds against their bad, His faithfulness against their faithlessness. Because God is who He is, the folly of the wicked is even more foolish. This is true not just because God will punish (there is little here of divine judgment), but because His love is so winsome.

This psalm begins with an unusual expression that translates literally as "oracle of transgression" (Ps. 36:1). Since **oracle** is usually used with God's name, Bible commentator Peter Craigie suggests that God's name was originally in the Hebrew text but has dropped out. The New International Version simply separates **oracle** from "transgression" (**sinfulness**). It may be better to take the phrase "oracle of transgression" as a forceful expression describing those who live by wickedness instead of God's self-revelation.[2]

To have **no fear of God** (36:1b) suggests more than a lack of reverence for God. It indicates that the enemy has no fear of God's judgment. Without qualm he proceeds down a path marked by self-flattery (see 36:2), deceitful words, and evil deeds (see 36:3). His godless character is evident in nightly plotting—**on his bed** suggests premeditated malice—and in his commitment to a **sinful course** (36:4). Finally, his conscience has become too dulled even to be able to reject what is wrong (see 36:4).

Abruptly, the theme changes from the sinfulness of the wicked to the love of God. Beginning this section (see 36:5-6) with carefully crafted and worshipful words, the psalmist describes this unsearchable, impregnable, and inexhaustible love. Rendered more literally, these verses read,

> Oh LORD, in the heavens is your love,
> Your faithfulness [is] to the skies.
> Your righteousness [is] like mountains of God
> Your justice like the great deep.
> Man and animal you save, Oh LORD.

Note how the poet reverses the order of the location and the divine attribute in the first two lines ("heavens . . . love . . . faithfulness . . . skies"). Lines 3 and 4 sharply contrast magnificent height and great depth. Line 5 describes the practical consequences of what is praised in line 1: God's limitless love which cares about humanity and even animals. Framing this beautiful poem is the holy name of Yahweh.

In 36:8-9, the metaphor changes from protection to provision with God described as a gracious host. **They feast on the abundance of your house** (36:8a) is striking. With no subject supplied, the reader must go back to 36:7 to find who is being so bountifully fed. Surprisingly, all humanity, **both high and low among men,** feasts at God's table, including the wicked described in 36:1-4.

God's **river of delights** satisfies thirst (36:8). The Hebrew word translated **delights** may have been chosen because it sounds so much like the word for Eden (see Genesis 2:10). Very likely this river originates from the **fountain of life** (Ps. 36:9), for having God means having not only a continual supply of delights but the very source of those delights. This seems to be the sense of 36:9b also, **in your light we see light.** While the light we see could be physical (God has given the sun) or spiritual (that is, the true perception of things, as demonstrated by this psalm), **light** can refer to life itself with all its blessings (see Psalm 4:6; 97:11; Esther 8:16).

David's final prayer echoes the themes of this psalm: the wicked and the love of God. While he knows that God's love provides for all humanity (see Psalm 36:7-9), David prays that God will be especially attentive to the needs of the righteous, **the upright in heart** (36:10). After all, the proud and wicked continue to trouble the psalmist, so he asks, in 36:11-12, that they not be allowed to triumph. In battle, the victorious commander could place his foot on the neck of his prostrate foe (see Joshua 10:24). This is probably how Psalm 36:11a should be understood. David asks for complete protection, not only from **the foot of the proud** but also from his **hand** (36:11). So certain is the psalmist of victory that he speaks of it in 36:12 as an accomplished fact.

To see the love of God does not make us blind to evil. Instead, it fills us with praise for a God who continues to show kindness, even to His enemies. Those who know God's love can pray confidently for safety, even in the midst of danger.

ENDNOTES

[1]See the outline of Psalm 36 in the discussion of parallelism in the introduction to this commentary.

[2]The first view is held by Peter Craigie (*Psalms 1–50* by Peter C. Craigie, Word Biblical Commentary, vol. 19, eds. David A. Hubbard and Glenn W. Barker [Waco, Texas: Word Books, 1983], p. 289; the last by the Revised Standard Version and Derek Kidner (*Psalms 1–72* by Derek Kidner, Tyndale Old Testament Commentaries, ed. D.J. Wiseman (Downer's Grove, Illinois: InterVarsity Press, 1973), p. 145.

36

SAFE IN THE PALM OF HIS HAND

Psalm 37:1-40

A prevailing problem for the godly has been the presence, and often the prosperity, of the wicked. Psalm 37 advises how to respond to such a problem and does so in rough acrostic style.[1] David has structured this advice as a series of commands surrounded and supported by reasons to put one's confidence in God. In spite of how things might appear, God is still in control and is working out His will in the world.

The psalm begins with **Do not fret** (37:1), a command important enough to be repeated twice more (see 37:7, 8). Such advice implies that, in spite of confidence in God (see 36:12), the problem of the wicked continues to trouble the devout Israelite. Take the long view, counsels David, and see that their prosperity is only seasonal (see 37:2).

In place of fretting and anxiety, one is to **trust in the LORD and do good** and **dwell in the land and enjoy safe pasture** (37:3). Trust in God is shown by acknowledging His good gifts (such as the land) and, literally translated, "grazing on His faithfulness" (**enjoy safe pasture;** see withering **grass** in 37:2). To delight oneself in God's good gifts (not a command in the Hebrew), like sheep who safely graze in God's green pastures, is to experience all the good one's heart could desire (see 37:4).

Again the command to **trust** in God is repeated (37:5), this time with the promise of public vindication (37:6). Such a promise implies that vindication, while not always immediate, will come. Waiting should be done **patiently** (37:7-9), not allowing frustration to boil into anger against God. Anxiety doubts God's coming vindication.

The appeal to patient trust (37:1-9) is supported by an extended contrast between the eventual outcome of the wicked and the righteous (37:10-26), making frequent use of antithetic parallelism. In only **a little**

while, the wicked will disappear (37:10). Meanwhile, those who trust in Yahweh and not themselves will inherit the earth (37:9, 22, 29, 34) and live there in **great peace** (37:11).[2]

The wicked may plot, but God only **laughs** at them; He knows their day is coming (37:12-13). Perhaps God is also humored by the knowledge that their attack will bring about their own destruction (37:14-15; see Joshua 8:22). He will place His divine arms beneath the righteous to hold them up but will break the arms of the wicked, rendering them too powerless to wield weapons or secure wealth (see Psalm 37:17).

Upheld by God, the righteous are eternally secure (37:18) and blessed even when all around them withers (37:19). By contrast, the wicked, who may look beautiful now, will wilt like a fragile flower in the summer sun. **They will vanish—vanish like smoke** (37:20); the Hebrew emphasizes the certainty of this judgment.

While the righteous may be poor and the wicked rich, it is the righteous who **give generously** and for this reason, prosper (37:21-22). The hoarding and stealing wicked cannot buy security; only God's smile can produce this (37:23-24). As if to substantiate his claim, David testifies to God's blessing on the righteous (37:25-26). This passage must be kept in its context; sometimes the righteous do suffer (37:24, 33, 39), but God's love never fails.

Having provided ample reason to trust in God, David again issues a series of commands which echo those at the psalm's beginning. **Turn from evil and do good** (37:27-33), David writes, clearly confident of eternal rest because of God's eternal love (37:27-29). Feet that are firmly planted on the path of God's law will not slip but will know protection in spite of real danger (37:30-33).

Wait for the LORD and keep his way (37:34), for He will accomplish what He promised. Everyone knows that wild flowers soon wither (37:20), but David has seen the wicked **flourishing like a green tree in its native soil** (37:35); this is the picture of security (see 1:3). And yet, one day he passed by and "behold, he was not!" Not a trace remained (see 37:36).[3]

Because justice is as certain as God's character (see 37:37-40), the psalmist concludes on a note of confidence: The righteous have a future, but the wicked do not because there is a powerful God who knows and cares. Such advice gives reason to pause in humanity's reckless dash toward financial prosperity and provides hope in a world where vindication is long in coming.

ENDNOTES

[1]Approximately every other verse begins with a succeeding letter of the Hebrew alphabet. For more on acrostics, see the discussion on other literary elements in Hebrew poetry in the introduction to this commentary.

[2]Jesus' blessing on the meek in Matthew 5:5 is drawn from this verse.

[3]Reading this passage with the Dead Sea Scrolls; see *Psalms 1–50* by Peter C. Craigie, Word Biblical Commentary, vol. 19, eds. David A. Hubbard and Glenn W. Barker (Waco, Texas: Word Books, 1983), p. 296.

37

SIN AND ITS EFFECTS

Psalm 38:1-22

S in has disastrous consequences for the body, relationships, and souls. David describes these effects in Psalm 38 and provides a model for us to deal with sin's wounds. This psalm does not request forgiveness but pleads that the consequences of sin would be lessened.[1] The sins that prompted Psalm 38 were already forgiven, but their effects continued to be painfully experienced. This may explain the title: **A petition.** David is appealing to God for divine help to deal with his suffering.

Verses 2 through 10 concern the physical effects of sin. God shot piercing **arrows** and lowered His **hand** of judgment in wrath (38:2-3) because of sin. In verse 3, **sin** is singular and may suggest unintentional failure to satisfy God's demands. **Guilt** (38:4) should probably be translated "iniquity" (as it is in 38:18). Temptation reveals sin's attractions; its consequences reveal its foolishness (see 38:5). Ancient rabbis said, "A man does not commit a transgression until a spirit of madness has entered into him."[2]

In the Hebrew, **there is no health in my body** frames verses 3 through 7. Sin leaves one too miserable to sit but too exhausted to move (see 38:4). It creates festering **wounds** (38:5). The root word from which we get **loathsome** (38:5) is used elsewhere to describe rotting fish and human corpses (see Exodus 7:18, 21; 8:14; Amos 4:10). Sin humiliates and saddens (see Psalm 38:6); it fills one (one's **back** [38:7]) with burning pain. Out of his anguished, broken heart David groans to God who, he believes, is watching all that transpires (38:8-9). According to verse 10, death is near, for his **heart pounds,** his strength fails and the light has already faded from his eyes (see 13:3).

Sin also kills relationships, as 38:11-20 describes. David is avoided by his **friends and companions** as if he had leprosy (38:11). His enemies take the opportunity to trap, harm, deceive, and ruin him (38:12). David is left physically incapacitated and defenseless (vv. 13-14), left with nothing to do but wait on God (vv. 15-16). David is convinced that God will answer in spite of His earlier silence, for **you will answer** (38:15b) is emphatic in the Hebrew.

While he waits, however, the situation deteriorates. His enemies are about to topple him and his pain continues (see 38:17). The phrase translated as **I confess my iniquity** (38:18) is better rendered "I will declare my iniquity." David will willingly acknowledge that he suffers the effects of his own sins, but he is not willing to be persecuted by unrighteous people (38:19-20). Such words are inappropriate for the repentant sinner but fit well in the mouth of one who, having been forgiven, knows that no further judgment is deserved from human enemies. The final call for mercy (38:21-22) brings the irony of this psalm into bold relief. Even in the face of God's silence, David remains confident that God will help him (38:22).

Although not all suffering is due to sin, sin has its consequences, including physical suffering and alienation. God remains willing to listen to our cries for mercy, even when we are suffering from our own foolish choices.

ENDNOTES

[1]David learned, if nowhere else, at the death of Bathsheba's first child that even forgiven sins have consequences (see 2 Samuel 11-12).

[2]As cited by A. Cohen, *The Psalms,* Soncino Books of the Bible, ed. A. Cohen (London: Soncino, 1950), p. 118.

38

"MY HOPE IS IN YOU"[1]

Psalm 39:1-13

Questions about the meaning of life are as old as humankind. Psalm 39 not only raises these questions, but provides a model for facing them. Knowing the wicked are watching, David did not wish to call God's righteousness into question by challenging the fairness of life. He determines to keep silent, watching both his **ways** and his **tongue** (39:1), even muzzling his mouth.

His need for meaning, however, overpowered his need for silence. The longer he was silent, **not even saying anything good** (39:2), the more he felt the need to speak. His **heart grew hot,** a description of intense passion. The same phrase is used in Deuteronomy 19:6 to describe the desire for revenge that burns within one whose family member has been murdered.[2] When he could hold it no longer, he spoke with his tongue, the organ he earlier intended to restrain.

The outburst in 39:4-6 reflects not only his frustration with life, but a hint as to what made him question the meaning of life in the first place. References in verses 4 and 5 to the brevity of life suggest that David is suffering, an idea supported by mention of his **anguish** (39:2) and **scourge** (39:10). David may also have been frustrated by the **wealth** of the wicked (39:6, 11). Compounding this was the transience of life (see 39:4-5, 11-12); his allotted time was nothing more than a **handbreadth** (v. 5), a small measurement equal to only the width of four fingers.[3]

Each man's life is but a breath (39:5c), even under ideal conditions (the Hebrew includes the phrase "when standing firm"). His fervent assertion (see 39:6) that life is short and meaningless brings him to a crossroads; if life is meaningless, then God does not care about humanity. By stating the matter so abruptly, David is startled back to reality and to hope in a God who cares.

Verse 7 marks the turning point in the psalm. Placed at the psalm's midpoint and beginning with the grammatically striking phrase **But now,** David's dilemma begins to be resolved. He will not trust in health, vindication, or longevity, but in Yahweh.

It is important to note that the resolution of this dilemma (see 39:7-13) does not reflect a change in David's circumstances, only a changed perspective on those circumstances. He continues to suffer, but now he understands more clearly its cause (see 39:8-11a). Perhaps David is saying in verse 9, "I was silent (for I thought I had reason to complain) but I will not open my mouth, for you have done this (and had every reason to do so)."

Having recognized God's right to punish him, David asks God to stop: **Remove your scourge from me** (39:10). This request indicates David's confidence in divine compassion. When he says **I am overcome by the blow of your hand** (39:10), he makes the **I** emphatic, as if to remind God that He is hurting one of His own.

In 39:11b, David returns to the theme of the prosperity of the wicked. Earlier he raised the question, "Who will get the money of the rich when they are gone?" (see 39:6). In verse 11, he answers that question by saying that God will get the money: **You consume their wealth like a moth.** While the wicked might continue to prosper, they cannot escape God's judgment. Here again meaning is restored to life, not by altering the circumstances, but by seeing them more clearly.

David's cry of frustration at the beginning of this psalm was prompted by the brevity of life (see 39:5). In verse 12, he accepts this fact but reminds God of His instructions to Israel to protect the rights of aliens. This **alien** prays for help and weeps, considered the highest degree of prayer by the rabbis.[4]

The last verse contains a curious request, that Yahweh would **look away from** David so he could rejoice in what little remains of his sojourn. Usually joy is the result of God turning His face toward someone, rather than away. These words are best understood as a request, like that in verse 10, for an end to God's discipline so that he can **rejoice again** (39:13).

While we cannot escape questions about the meaning of life, we can learn to face them. God's love rules out a meaningless universe. Our circumstances may not change, but our perception of those circumstances will when we put our hope in a loving God.

ENDNOTES

[1]Psalm 39:7b.

[2]Peter C. Craigie, *Psalms 1–50,* Word Biblical Commentary, vol. 19, eds. David A. Hubbard and Glenn W. Barker (Waco, Texas: Word Books, 1983), p. 309.

[3]Ibid.

[4]"From the day the Temple was destroyed, the gates of prayer were locked; but although the gates of prayer were locked, the gates of tears remained unlocked" (as cited by A. Cohen, *The Psalms,* Soncino Books of the Bible, ed. A. Cohen [London: Soncino, 1950], p. 122).

39

"O MY GOD, DO NOT DELAY"[1]

Psalm 40:1-17

While Psalm 40 begins as a testimony of divine rescue (see verses 1-10), it concludes with a cry for God's prompt action on David's behalf (verses 11-17). David intends, using this strategy, to build a case for why God should come to his aid. When in trouble before, he cried out to God and **waited patiently** (40:1). The Hebrew indicates this was fervent waiting (see the NEB, "I waited, waited for the Lord.") He was rewarded when God stopped, bent down and attentively listened to his cries for help (see 40:1).

Trapped in a **slimy pit** of **mud and mire** (40:2), escape was impossible, for no solid footing could be found. The mud clung to his feet and weighed him down still more. Each attempt up the slippery walls only worsened matters; death appeared imminent. But God, hearing David's cry, reached into the pit, lifted David out, and set his **feet on a rock,** on a **firm place to stand** (40:2).

With this rescue came a **new song** to sing, praising God for deliverance (40:3). In response to his song of praise, **many will see and fear and put their trust in the LORD** (40:3). Seeing the goodness of God should lead to an attitude of reverence for God and to trust in God, the path of true blessedness (40:4-5). Those who **look to the proud**— that is, trust in them—find these "fabricators of falsehood" wholly unreliable and deceitful. Yahweh, by contrast, has already done great things and has many more wonders in store (40:5).

With such a faithful God to trust, willing obedience is the only reasonable choice (40:6-10). When David speaks of God not wanting or requiring **sacrifice and offering** (40:6), he is not speaking absolutely but comparatively. God certainly wanted them, for He commanded His people how and when they should be offered. God required animal sacrifices as a token of willing submission to Him. It is submission that He most desires and what the psalmist offers in verses 6 through 8.

My ears you have pierced (40:6) puzzles interpreters. The verb translated **pierced** is more commonly used to describe the digging of a well, grave, or pit. By taking the less common but more literal use of the verb, the New International Version calls to mind the ritual whereby a slave could make himself the lifelong property of his master (see Exodus 21:5-6). Different words are used for pierce, however, and Psalm 40:6 speaks of "ears" rather than "ear" being pierced. If "dug" is being used metaphorically to refer to the unblocking of the ears,[2] David could be saying that God enabled him to hear His voice and obey. Either reading prepares for the submission described in Psalm 40:7a: **Here I am, I have come**. He obeys **the scroll**— probably the Law of Moses—with delight; it is not merely in his hands or on his mind but is **within my heart** (40:8).

David claims that wholehearted submission to God's law is superior to sacrifice. The writer of Hebrews (10:5-7) uses these verses to show that sacrifices are not only surpassed, they are set aside by Christ's willing submission to the Cross. The Law spoke about the Messiah, as did the Prophets and the Writings (see Luke 24:27).

David's willing obedience is shown in his faithful expression of God's character among his fellow worshipers (see Psalm 40:9-10). That God is well aware of this act of piety, David is sure; the **you** in **as you know, O LORD** is emphatic (40:9). God is extolled as righteous, faithful, the savior, steadfast in His love *(chesed)*, and truthful. It is because of these qualities that David can pray for God's **mercy** (40:11-17). When David prays, **Do not withhold your mercy from me** (40:11), he uses the same verb as in verse 9 to refer to his testimony. As he did not refrain from testifying for God, he does not want God to refrain from helping him. Just as there were too many of God's wonders to tell (see 40:5), now there are too many troubles to count (**without number** [40:12]).

David's prayer becomes more specific in verses 13 through 16, beginning with a cry for rescue (40:13). The rest of the prayer is for God's judgment on the wicked (40:14-15) and vindication for the righteous (40:16). In the end, David returns to a call for prompt action (40:17), highlighting the desperateness of the situation. David suggests, by his use of **think of me** (40:17), that now would be a good time for God to carry out what He has **planned** (40:5; the Hebrew words for **think of me** and **planned** are related).

The psalm ends as it began, with David waiting. God came through in the first instance, and David appears confident that He will this time, too. Waiting should be done in patient trust and humble submission, desiring, even more than our own vindication, that **the LORD be exalted!** (40:16).

ENDNOTES

[1]Psalm 40:17d.
[2]Examples of such use in reference to the ears are not frequent.

40

PRAYER FROM A SICKBED

Psalm 41:1-13

A time of illness, perhaps of a prolonged and serious nature, has left David feeling vulnerable. In addition to having to remain in the defenseless posture of lying on his bed, there is the question, How much longer must he suffer? And will he ever recover (even more serious if *King* David is the author)? Is this illness an evidence of God's displeasure? Given David's vulnerability, the confidence (see 41:1-3, 10-12) with which he frames his request (see 41:4-9) is even more profound.

He begins by reminding all who are listening (including God) that one **who has regard for the weak** is blessed (41:1). To **have regard for** goes beyond doing a kind act. It is carefully considering how best to be kind to those in need. This is rewarded with deliverance, protection, and preservation in such effusive quantities that everyone pronounces this person blessed (see 41:1b-2). The one who has shown such kind regard will find that, in times of illness, God himself attends to **his sickbed** (41:3).[1]

From this confident but vulnerable posture, David makes his appeal to God. **I said** (41:4) does not adequately bring out the emphasis in the Hebrew; "As for me, I say . . ." comes closer to capturing the psalmist's determination to be heard.[2] Recognizing that he is not without fault, he appeals for forgiveness (41:4) and receives it (41:12). When he asks for healing, he reasons not only that his past kindnesses would be remembered (41:3) but also that a God who blesses the kind will himself be kind.

According to verses 5 through 9, David's **enemies** are not kind at all. Like vultures, they circle his sickbed, watching, waiting and hoping for his death. Under the guise of friendship they deceive, slander and betray.

They imagine him possessed by a **vile disease** (41:8), more literally "an evil thing" or "a thing of Belial." They want others to know this man is being punished for his sins. The cruelest blow came from a **close friend** whom he trusted and with whom he had shared fellowship (41:9). While the precise meaning of **lifted up his heel against me** is unclear, its general sense of "cruel advantage" is obvious.[3]

If David is the author of this psalm, we have no difficulty locating incidents in his life to correspond to this psalm. His own son, Absalom, as well as his trusted counselor, Ahithophel conspired against him (see 2 Samuel 15–17). According to Jesus, Psalm 41:9 perfectly describes His betrayal by Judas (see John 13:18).

But you, O LORD, signals David's conviction that God is not like these false friends; he can be counted on to show mercy (Ps. 41:10-12). While David's motive in 41:10b appears vindictive—**raise me up, that I may repay them**—as king he has a moral obligation to punish treason. Some translate 41:10b as "I will requite them good for evil," citing Psalm 35:13 as an example of David's true heart.[4] David concludes this psalm confident that God will reward him in the end.

Although the doxology of 41:13 was added later as a liturgical response to the reading of Book 1, its call for eternal praise to Yahweh and its double "so be it" make it an appropriate **Amen** to this prayer from a sickbed.

ENDNOTES

[1]Verse 3b is literally "all his lying down you have turned in his sickness." **Restore him from his bed of illness** is accurate but ignores the "you" which makes the "turning" more personal.

[2]F. Delitzsch, *Psalms,* Commentary on the Old Testament, vol. V, translated by James Martin (reprint, Grand Rapids, Michigan: Wm. B. Eerdmans Publishing Co., 1978), p. 44.

[3]Suggestions include "to trip" (A. Cohen, *The Psalms,* Soncino Books of the Bible, ed. A. Cohen [London: Soncino, 1950], p. 129), "to kick" (Delitzsch, p. 48), "to be a heel" (Peter C. Craigie, *Psalms 1–50,* Word Biblical Commentary, vol. 19, eds. David A. Hubbard and Glenn W. Barker [Waco, Texas: Word Books, 1983], p. 321) or "cruel advantage" (Francis Brown, *The New Brown-Driver-Briggs-Gesenius Hebrew and English Lexicon* (Peabody, Massachusetts: Hendrickson Publishers, 1979), p. 784).

[4]Cohen cites early and medieval Jewish scholarship for this view.

Part Two

BOOK 2

Psalms 42:1–72:20

The second book of the Psalter is slightly shorter than Book 1 and contains a considerably smaller percentage of psalms attributed to David (less than sixty percent). A sizable minority of Psalms are attributed to authors other than David. One psalm is ascribed to Asaph (Psalm 50), seven are ascribed to the Sons of Korah (Psalms 42, 44–49), and one to Solomon (Psalm 72). Four are not attributed to any author (Psalms 43, 66–67, 71) and one has no title at all.

When God's name is used in Book 2, more than seventy percent of the time it is the name Elohim. Book 2 ends with a doxology in Psalm 72:18-19 and with the statement, **This concludes the prayers of David son of Jesse.** Surprisingly, it is attached to a psalm attributed to Solomon and is followed in subsequent books by more psalms attributed to David.

41

"PUT YOUR HOPE IN GOD"[1]

Psalms 42:1–43:5

All indications are that Psalms 42 and 43 were originally composed as a single poem. They share a common theme— vindication—and a common refrain (see 42:5, 11; 43:5). If separate, Psalm 43 would be the only psalm in Book 2 (Psalms 42–72) without a title.[2] Taken together, there are three stanzas (42:1-5; 6-11; 43:1-5), each composed of a prayer to God and a word of self-encouragement. The psalmist's unfulfilled longing to worship in God's house suggests he was a Temple singer prevented for some unknown reason from returning to Jerusalem. Oppressed by those around him who saw his exile as evidence that Yahweh was powerless, this son of Korah prayed to return.

His prayer begins with a powerful word picture which compares his desire to be in God's house to a deer audibly panting for **streams of water** (42:1). **Streams** is the translation of a Hebrew word used for channels which sometimes flow with water, but which are only ravines in the arid season (see Job 6:15; Joel 1:20). The **deer,** who has come to this wadi for a drink, has found only dust.

Nor has the psalmist found that for which his soul thirsts: **the living God** (Ps. 42:2). **Living,** when referring to God, describes His ongoing activity. When applied to water, **living** means flowing, that for which the deer pants. All day long, the psalmist must bear the taunts of his oppressors who see the psalmist's exile as proof that God is absent (see 42:3). Their taunts only heighten his tearful longing for God, but those salty tears do not bring satisfaction, only a greater thirst for God.

The psalmist's thoughts turn to better days when he led the crowd of pilgrims, shouting and giving thanks, into the Temple (see 42:4).

Those were days of fellowship and joy; now he knows only taunts and tears. Then he shared the feasts associated with Temple worship; now his diet is only tears.

With what confidence remained, he counsels himself (see 42:5). Although he is **downcast** and disturbed because he cannot find God, he instructs his soul to **hope in God,** certain that one day he will again stand in the Temple and worship his Savior and God.

The second stanza (42:6-11) begins by prescribing a cure for his soul's discouragement. He will remember God from **the land of the Jordan, the heights of Hermon—from Mount Mizar** (42:6). **Mount Mizar** may be a literal mountain in the Hermon range which has not been identified. Perhaps **Mizar** (*mizar* in Hebrew) should be translated literally as "small hill" and be taken as a reference to the hill in Jerusalem where the Temple is located. Or the "small hill" could be an ironic reference to Mount Hermon, greater than Zion in elevation but, in spiritual significance, much smaller (see Psalm 68:15-16; 133:3). Such recollections overwhelm the psalmist like the waters of the Jordan which tumble among rocks and over waterfalls from their source near Mount Hermon (see 42:7). It is ironic that in a land of deeps, waterfalls, waves and breakers, such spiritual dryness could predominate.

Even though he continues to long for the Temple and mourn his absence from it, the psalmist has come to trust in Yahweh's **love** (*chesed;* 42:8). In light of his longing for the living God in 42:2, perhaps this expression, **God of my life,** almost identical in the Hebrew, should here be translated "living God." Only because of his confidence in God's love (see 42:8) can he ask the questions found in 42:9-10. The refrain counseling him to **put your hope in God** (42:11) is all the more powerful, coming as it does immediately after the question, **Where is your God?** (42:10b).

The final stanza (Psalm 43) begins on a more aggressive note, **Vindicate me,** appealing to God for vindication against an ungodly nation (43:1), probably his captors. In 43:2, we return to the questioning mood (and wording) of 42:9, but only briefly. His call for **your light and your truth** (43:3) signals the psalmist's renewed conviction that all is not as it appears. God has not forgotten or rejected him; this is clear from God's light and truth, which will accompany and guide him back to the place for which his heart longs: God's **holy mountain** (43:3). There he would again find joy (43:4; see 42:4) in the presence of his God. The fourfold repetition of God's name in 43:4 leads to the refrain, this time spoken in solid confidence.

The experiences of this anonymous son of Korah demonstrate that the life of a believer is not free of trouble. Troubles do not vanish with a prayer, even for one so passionate about being in God's presence. The one who perseveres through pain, abandonment, ridicule, and disappointment—remembering to hope even when the reasons seem few—will not be disappointed by God.

ENDNOTES

[1]See Psalm 42:5; 43:5.
[2]Psalm 71 also lacks a title but is thought to be one with Psalm 70.

42

THE PRAYER OF A NATION IN DISTRESS

Psalm 44:1-26

While psalms like 42 and 43 sound like the meditation of a righteous individual, others seem to have arisen during a national calamity. Psalm 44, an example of the latter, was written during a military crisis when God was silent and Israel's future seemed uncertain. Out of this difficulty comes a call for help (44:23-26) built on the basis of God's past help (44:1-3), on Israel's trust in God (44:4-8), on the seriousness of Israel's present difficulties (44:9-16), and on the basis of their innocence (44:17-22).

In verses 1 through 4, the psalmist reminds God that the land became theirs in the first place only by His help. "You, your hand drove the nations out" would be a more literal rendering of verse 2. This example of God's past help is chosen because Israel appears to be losing the very land it was given (see 44:11-12). These verses provide a good commentary on the book of Joshua where the point is made repeatedly that God brought the victory, not Israel's army (44:3; see Joshua 5:14; 6:2ff; 7:12; 10:11, 14). Canaan was given to them out of the kindness of God's heart (**for you loved them** [Ps. 44:3]).

Having reminded God of His help in the past, verses 4 through 8 demonstrate that Israel, because of its trust in God, still deserves that help. This trust is demonstrated by an assertion of loyalty in verse 4: **You are my king.**[1] It is in divine, not human, power that victory will be found (see 44:5-7). To **push back** one's enemies (44:5) translates a Hebrew expression used elsewhere to describe the goring of an ox (see

Deuteronomy 33:17) or the butting of a sheep (see Ezekiel 34:21). By extension, this verb came to be used, as here, for military victory. Israel will trust, but not in the bow; it will be victorious, but not due to the sword. Its boast will not be in itself but always and only in God.

In Psalm 44:9-16, the psalmist describes another reason for God to intervene—Israel's desperate circumstances. Using terms strongly reminiscent of Deuteronomy 28 and emphasizing divine judgment (note the frequent use of **you**), Israel is portrayed as rejected and disgraced because of military defeat. Ironically, Psalm 44:10 uses the same terms for **the enemy** as were found in 44:7. In 44:7, it was the foes who were defeated and ashamed; in 44:10, Israel is defeated, forced to retreat, and plundered at will by its enemies.

Like sheep without a shepherd, the nation has been attacked and **devoured** by a marauder (44:11a). It is unclear what event is referred to by **scattered us among the nations** (44:11b). It may be the Assyrian attack on Judah in 701 B.C. when a number of cities were defeated and, according to Assyrian records, over 200,000 were carried off as prisoners.[2] It may refer to the Babylonian deportations in 605, 597, and 586 B.C., or to some point during Israel's subsequent history. It is possible the exile was relatively minor, such as those described in Amos 1:6, 9. Israel was sold, but not for a profit, like a merchant unloading unwanted goods below cost. Because of such treatment, Israel was humiliated. It had become a **byword** (44:14), the "theme of derisive songs."[3] Israel was **covered with shame** (44:15).

The final appeal for divine intervention is based on Israel's innocence (see 44:17-22). Although they had **not forgotten you** (God), nor broken His **covenant,** or even **strayed from your path** (44:17-18), they had been **crushed** into desolation (**made . . . a haunt for jackals**) and **covered** with the **darkness** of death (44:19; see the same word in 23:4). The God who **knows the secrets of the heart** (44:21) must know what Israel is unfairly experiencing, yet He refuses to act. Even more baffling, they suffer for His sake, and *still* He leaves them like a flock without a shepherd (see 44:22; also 44:11).[4] This protest of innocence is not a claim of absolute perfection, only that they have done nothing to deserve such severe punishment.

Having built his case for God's intervention, the psalmist finally makes his request in verses 23 through 26. Since God's absence suggests slumber, the psalmist commands Him to **Awake, O Lord!** (44:23). Time is running out according to 44:25, for they are dying. The final Hebrew word in this psalm translates **your unfailing love**

(44:26). The inexplicability of Israel's difficulties could not move the psalmist from his conviction of the love of God; it is on this love that he rests his case and his future.

ENDNOTES

[1]The difference between

You are my King and my God,
who decrees victories for Jacob

and the alternative reading,

You are my King, O God;
Command victories for Jacob (see the NIV footnote),

depends on one Hebrew letter. Either reading is equally possible, and both fit the context well.

[2]*Ancient Near Eastern Texts Relating to the Old Testament,* 3rd ed. with supplement, ed. James B. Pritchard (Princeton: Princeton University Press, 1969), p. 288.

[3]A. Cohen, *The Psalms,* Soncino Books of the Bible, ed. A. Cohen (London: Soncino, 1950), p. 137.

[4]Paul (see Romans 8:36) found this passage a close parallel to the sufferings experienced by Christians.

43

SONG FOR A ROYAL WEDDING

Psalm 45:1-17

N early all scholars agree that this psalm was originally written for the wedding of an Israelite king. After a brief introduction (45:1-2), the poet sings the praises of the king (45:3-9) and the new queen (45:10-15), and concludes with a final word to the king (45:16-17).

The poet, after acknowledging his delightful task (45:1), describes his subject as **the most excellent of men** (45:2). He had physical beauty, an important quality for a king (see the descriptions of Saul and David in 1 Samuel 9:2; 16:12). Beauty extended to his character, as seen in the description, **your lips have been anointed with grace** (Ps. 45:2). "Gracious speech" was important for the king. In praising his monarch, the psalmist praises God as the source of his excellence (see 45:2).

Although the king possesses tremendous military prowess (45:3-5), his goal is not personal gain but the triumph of what is true, meek and right (45:4). There is some question as to how the first part of verse 6 should be translated. **Your throne, O God, will last forever and ever** clearly renders the Hebrew but does not fit the context which addresses the king, not God. Some take the word translated **God** *(Elohim)* as an adjective which modifies **throne** ("Your divine throne is everlasting" [Tanakh/NJPS]; see 1 Chronicles 29:23). *Elohim* is sometimes used of humans (Exodus 21:6; 22:8; Psalm 82:1; 138:1), and the king is elsewhere addressed as the "son" of God (Psalm 2:7; 2 Samuel 7:14). For these reasons and because it makes more sense in this context, the psalmist may be speaking of the king's throne. To avoid confusion, he quickly draws a distinction between the earthly Elohim and the divine Elohim by speaking to the king of **your God** in Psalm 45:7. The writer of Hebrews, following the Septuagint,[1] believes these verses refer to Christ (see Hebrews 1:8-9), which in their fullest sense, they most surely do.

The description of the king in his wedding array is luxuriant (see Psalm 45:7-9). At his enthronement, the king was set apart by being anointed with **oil** (45:7); therefore, "Anointed One" (from which "Messiah" derives) originally designated the king. Here the **anointing** symbolizes the king's joy. The fragrance of the **myrrh and aloes and cassia** is so strong his clothes seem to be woven of spices.[2] The beauty of the palace **adorned with ivory** awes the eyes, while the **music** of stringed instruments delights the ear (45:8). All this luxury is meant to reward the king for his love of **righteousness** (45:7).

More beautiful than anyone in the king's court is the bride who stands at the king's right hand (see 45:10-15), splendidly adorned in the finest **gold of Ophir** (45:9).[3] He exhorts the foreign-born queen to **forget your people** and her childhood home (45:10-11). This difficult task would be made easier by the blessings awaiting her in her new home.

She will know the love of the king to whom she must now transfer her loyalties (45:11), and the honor and gifts of many (45:12). **Daughter of Tyre** may refer to wedding guests from Israel's wealthy northern neighbor (as suggested by the New International Version), the gift of a Tyrian robe, or the bride herself ("O Tyrian lass" [Tanakh/NJPS]). Her appearance will be glorious in a **gown . . . interwoven with gold** (45:13) and **embroidered garments** (45:14).

The psalm concludes with the promise, directed to the king (clear in the Hebrew from the masculine singular pronouns), of a permanent place among the people of God (see 45:16-17). Permanence will come through male descendants who will rule in his place and continue his dynasty. It will also come through the song of the poet who will perpetuate the king's memory **through all generations** (45:17; note how verse 17 echoes verse 2).

As a wedding song, this psalm provides a beautiful picture of God's delight in human love and joy. When seen in its clearest light as a description of the majesty of Christ, one finds ample reason to praise Him **for ever and ever** (45:17).

ENDNOTES

[1]The Greek translation of the Hebrew Bible prepared between 200 and 300 B.C.

[2]F. Delitzsch, *Psalms,* Commentary on the Old Testament, vol. V, translated by James Martin (reprint, Grand Rapids, Michigan: Wm. B. Eerdmans Publishing Co., 1978), p. 85.

[3]Gold from Ophir, a city possibly located in Saudi Arabia between Mecca and Medina, is considered to be of the finest quality (see 1 Kings 9:28). (Peter C. Craigie, *Psalms 1–50,* Word Biblical Commentary, vol. 19, eds. David A. Hubbard and Glenn W. Barker [Waco, Texas: Word Books, 1983], p. 340.)

44

A MIGHTY FORTRESS IS OUR GOD

Psalm 46:1-11

This psalm, which inspired Martin Luther's well-known hymn "A Mighty Fortress Is Our God," was apparently composed in a time of crisis. Perhaps it was written after Jerusalem's rescue from the Moabite coalition in the days of Jehoshaphat (see 2 Chronicles 20) or after Jerusalem's escape from the Assyrian siege in 701 B.C. (see 2 Chronicles 32). By describing the security of Zion, Psalm 46 would have inspired confidence in Zion's God. He had chosen this city as His capital, symbolizing His election of Israel. Even in the post-exilic and New Testament periods, God's restored favor on His people is described in terms of a reestablished Jerusalem (see Isaiah 60-66; Revelation 21-22). By avoiding explicit reference to Jerusalem, however, this becomes a song of confidence for any place where God elects to dwell.

The psalm is composed of three stanzas (see Psalm 46:1-3; 4-7; 8-11); the second and third conclude with a refrain (see Psalm 46:7, 11). It begins with a strong affirmation of trust in God based on His faithfulness. **God is our refuge and strength** (46:1), our security when attacked, and our source of power to attack. **An ever-present help in trouble** implies both a willingness to be called upon and a past history of invaluable aid (see 2 Chronicles 15:4). Small wonder, then, is the people's response: **Therefore we will not fear** (Ps. 46:2). They will not fear even while the very pictures of permanence—**earth** and **mountains**—are collapsing around them (literally, "we will not fear while the earth is giving way and while the mountains are falling").

The poet refers to more than just a cataclysmic end, however. To the Hebrews, the consumption of the earth by the sea suggested a return to the chaos that existed before creation. Even then, **we will not fear.**

After such a claim, verse 3 in the New International Version seems anticlimactic. Bible commentator F. Delitzsch's translation avoids this anticlimax:

> Let the waters thereof roar, let them foam;
> Let mountains shake at the swelling thereof.[1]

"Go ahead and roar," the poet says to the impending chaos, "for we are safe in God's city."

In contrast to the terror such chaotic seas might produce, those in God's city are gladdened by **a river** (46:4a). Jerusalem had no river running through it, but it had something better, a faithful God living in His holy house (46:4b). With God in residence, there is no fear of chaos. **Not fall** (46:5) is the same word used to refer to the action of the mountains in 46:2b. **At break of day** could symbolize a fresh start, a new beginning, or a release from deep darkness (see 23:4; 44:19). Dawn was often the time when armies would attack; the phrase may promise God's protection at the height of the crisis. There may be an historical allusion to the Exodus, for dawn was the time God released the waters of the Red Sea onto the Egyptian army (see Exodus 14:27). Dawn was also the time when Jerusalem discovered 185,000 dead Assyrian soldiers on their doorstep (see Isaiah 37:36).

Nations are in uproar (Ps. 46:6; the same word is used for the roaring sea in 46:3a) and **kingdoms fall** (the same word used for the falling mountains in 46:2b); not only in nature but in international chaos too, God is in charge. He need only **lift his voice** (46:6)—an idiom that elsewhere means thunder (see Exodus 9:23)—and **the earth melts** as if struck by lightning. The same force—God's voice—which created the world can destroy it; it cannot be destroyed (see Psalm 46:2) until God says so.

The LORD Almighty is with us the refrain begins (46:7), as the people affirm the security of God's presence. The mention of Yahweh here is for emphasis since it is used so infrequently in Book 2 of the Psalter. **LORD Almighty** refers to God's role as commander in chief of the armies of heaven who stand prepared to defend Jerusalem. **God of Jacob** anchors this might to a loving and ancient relationship, a relationship marked by God's loyalty (see Genesis 35:3). This mighty, loving God is a **fortress** (or high tower), impregnable and secure.

Come and see the works of the LORD for yourself, the psalmist invites (Ps. 46:8); perhaps better is "Come consider the wonders of Yahweh" (NJB). Ironically, what He destroys are the weapons of destruction; the end result is peace (see 46:8-9). Not only weapons but even "wagons" will be burned (a better translation than **shield** or "chariots" as suggested by the NIV footnote) for with peace, there is no more need for the military supplies they carry.

God himself now speaks: **Be still and know that I am God** (46:10). These may be words of comfort to His people; more likely He is commanding the nations to "desist" and "acknowledge" that He is God.[2] His lordship over the earth has been demonstrated in this psalm (see 46:2, 6); here He proclaims it himself. To this, His people enthusiastically respond,

> **The LORD Almighty is with us,**
> **the God of Jacob is our fortress** (46:11).

That exaltation which God demands is already established among them, and they are reaping the joy His presence brings. God's people can still join in this refrain, however chaotic life may be.

ENDNOTES

[1] See *Psalms* by F. Delitzsch, Commentary on the Old Testament, vol. V. translated by James Martin (reprint, Grand Rapids, Michigan: Wm. B. Eerdmans Publishing Co., 1978).

[2] See *The Psalms* by A. Cohen, Soncino Books of the Bible, ed. A. Cohen (London: Soncino, 1950), p. 146.

45

KING OF ALL THE EARTH

Psalm 47:1-9

While in Psalm 46:10 God asserted that He would be "exalted among the nations . . . and in the earth," Psalm 47 explores what this exaltation implies. In so doing, it sounds an important theme in the Psalter: the universal reign of God. Some have seen this and other psalms as part of an annual ceremony in Israel during which God's kingship was reaffirmed. While we know of a festival like this in Babylon, evidence for such an Israelite celebration is sketchy. Others believe this psalm arose from an event in Israel's history, perhaps when David transported the ark to Jerusalem (see 2 Samuel 6) or when Jehoshaphat and his army returned from victorious battle (see 2 Chronicles 20).[1]

Psalm 47 opens with a call to exuberantly praise God's sovereignty (see 47:1). While this call is issued to all nations, the reasons to praise God concern the victories He has worked for Israel (47:2-4). The One who has revealed himself as **awesome** and **Most High** is Yahweh, their covenant God (Ps. 47:2).[2] To have other nations **under** their **feet** (47:3) symbolizes military victory (see Joshua 10:24). God gave Israel the land because of His love for that nation.[3] He may be King **over all the earth** (Ps. 47:2), but God is especially generous to Israel.

Between the two stanzas that make up this psalm is a verse which describes God taking His throne (47:5). Once again the name Yahweh is used to refer to this One who ascends **amid shouts of joy** and **the sounding of trumpets** (47:5).

A call to praise (47:6) also begins the second stanza (47:6-9). Without specifying who is to praise (47:6), the command to **sing praises** appears four times. As in stanza 1, the reasons for this praise follow in the next three verses (47:7-9). While in verses 2 through 4 God was praised for His victories to Israel, now the command is to "sing a maskil of praise" for His kingship over the whole earth (47:7; see the NIV footnote). The nature of a maskil is mysterious, which prompts some to leave it untranslated, others to treat it as a musical term such as a **psalm** or "songs" and still others to regard it as a qualitative term or "with understanding."[4]

The nations, which are told to praise God joyously in 47:1, are told why: **God reigns over the nations** (47:8). This thought continues in 47:9 with **the nobles of the nations assemble** before him. The Hebrew of 47:9 reads, literally, "The nobles of the people have assembled, the people of the God of Abraham." The Septuagint translated "with" between the phrases, suggesting that the nobles and Israel gathered together before God.[5] The New International Version supplies **as,** which could mean that the nobles assemble *like* Israel does. It could also imply that the nobles and Israel have become one—that is, the nations have now become God's people. While the **great king over all the earth** was especially kind to Israel (47:2, 3-4), His ultimate objective was to make Jews and all other nations into one people under His lordship. This view, developed in New Testament passages such as Galatians 3:7-9 and Ephesians 2:11-22, is supported by **for the kings of the earth belong to God** (Ps. 47:9). It also explains the link with **Abraham** (47:9) who was promised that all nations would be blessed through him (see Genesis 12:3).

This God is **greatly exalted,** not only because of His military strength or kindness to Israel but also because of His wonderful plan to bring about reconciliation with Him and with one another. It took another exaltation, the lifting up of Christ on the cross, to accomplish this plan, "to the glory of God the Father" (Philippians 2:11).

ENDNOTES

[1] Derek Kidner cites the similarity between Psalm 47:5 and 2 Samuel 6:15 (*Psalms 1–72* by Derek Kidner, Tyndale Old Testament Commentaries, ed. D.J. Wiseman [Downer's Grove, Illinois: InterVarsity Press, 1973], p. 177); F. Delitzsch supports the reference to Jehoshaphat (*Psalms* by F. Delitzsch, Commentary on the Old Testament, vol. V, translated by James Martin [reprint, Grand Rapids, Michigan: Wm. B. Eerdmans Publishing Co., 1978], p. 97).

[2] The use of "Yahweh" is striking in Book 2 of the Psalter, which usually refers to God using the name "Elohim."

[3] Some see **pride of Jacob** (v. 4) as referring to the Temple (see *The Psalms* by A. Cohen, Soncino Books of the Bible, ed. A. Cohen [London: Soncino,

1950], p. 147); a case could also be made for Jerusalem (see Psalm 87:2).

⁴See *Psalms 1–50* by Peter C. Craigie, Word Biblical Commentary, vol. 19, eds. David A. Hubbard and Glenn W. Barker (Waco, Texas: Word Books, 1983), p. 347; see NIV (**psalm;** see also RSV), TEV ("songs"); see NEB ("with skill"), Cohen (p. 147), NJB ("with understanding"). There may be an echo of this phrase in 1 Corinthians 14:15, where Paul speaks of singing "with my mind."

⁵Craigie, p. 350.

46

CITY OF OUR GOD

Psalm 48:1-14

For the Israelites, the city of Jerusalem was more than a national or religious center. It was a tangible demonstration of God's selection of Israel as His chosen people. For this reason, many psalms sing the praises of Zion, perhaps to such an extent that these became almost a trademark of Israel's worship (see Psalm 137:3). Psalm 48 appears to have been written after the deliverance of Jerusalem from some threat, although the particular circumstances are beyond recovery.[1]

While Jerusalem was highly honored among the Israelites, 48:1 makes clear who is to be worshiped: **Great is the LORD.** In verse 2, Jerusalem is described as a source of **joy** to the world. This joy may be known by the nations when, in fulfillment of the promise to Abraham, they are blessed through the Jewish nation (see Genesis 12:3). **Zaphon** could be translated as "north," but the New International Version is probably correct to treat it as a place name. Mount Zaphon was regarded by Israel's neighbors as a residence for their gods. By comparing Zion to Zaphon, the psalmist sets the record straight: The one true God has only one address, Jerusalem, **the city of the Great King** (Ps. 48:2). Verse 3 extends the thought of God's presence there by locating Him in the **citadels,** where He mans the fortifications against attack. With God as defender, what can the enemy do but flee in terror (see 48:4-8)?

Each stage of the battle—the attack, the confrontation, and the retreat—is presented in the strongest terms. Not one army, but a coalition advances.[2] One look at Jerusalem and these kings flee, terrified. The destruction of the **ships of Tarshish** (48:7) is symbolic since Jerusalem, located miles inland, would not be a target for attacking navies. Further, the destruction of such ships appears to be a fitting metaphor for the sudden demolition of weapons of great strength and size.[3] This battle, having been witnessed by the residents of Jerusalem, now confirms what they had previously heard about Zion's stability (see 48:8).

More confident than ever, the congregation now addresses itself to God (see 48:9-11). Victory has brought them not self-confidence but a clearer sense of God's steadfast, **unfailing love** (*chesed;* 48:9). This love brings more than military victory; it brings enough justice and righteousness for the whole world (see 48:10-11). **Zion,** earlier presented as a source of joy (48:2) now rejoices along with its **villages** (48:11).

The psalm concludes with a walking tour of Jerusalem. The congregation is instructed to **count her towers** (48:12) in order to **tell of them to the next generation** (48:13). There is a play on words in the Hebrew, approximated by **count** and "recount" in English. If, as some suggest, the congregation is composed of pilgrims who have come to Jerusalem to worship, they are instructed to take the sights and security of Jerusalem back to their children, those too young to make the journey.

We conclude where we began, not with the worship of a city, but of the God who has taken up residence within her. **For this God is our God** (48:14) could perhaps be better rendered "Such is God" or "For this is God."[4] One might see the **towers, ramparts** and **citadels** of Jerusalem, but until one sees **God . . . in her citadels** (48:3), the picture is incomplete.

It is God, not Jerusalem, who will remain **for ever and ever.** This God will **guide even to the end** (48:14). **Guide** is used elsewhere in the Old Testament to describe the actions of a shepherd who leads the flock to rich pastures (see Psalm 78:52; Isaiah 49:10; 63:14). The security of God's people was not to be found in a location but in the company of their Shepherd. This Shepherd will never abandon His sheep; He will remain with them **even to the end,** or more literally "until death" (Ps. 48:14), the "strongest expression one can use for constancy."[5]

The security and guidance with which this psalm concludes are in great demand now as then. They cannot be found in a place, even a good and holy place, but can be found only in fellowship with God. Such a shepherd, if followed, will be with us always, even "to the very end of the age" (Matthew 28:20).

ENDNOTES

[1]Derek Kidner, *Psalms 1–72,* Tyndale Old Testament Commentaries, ed. D.J. Wiseman (Downer's Grove, Illinois: InterVarsity Press, 1973), p. 179; Robert Alter, "The Psalms: Beauty Heightened Through Poetic Structure," *Bible Review,* vol. 2 (1986), pp. 29–41.

[2]There is a play on words between the assembling of kings *(no'adu)* in verse 4 and God who has become known *(nod'a)* in verse 3.

[3]See *The Psalms* by A. Cohen, Soncino Books of the Bible, ed. A. Cohen (London: Soncino, 1950), p. 150; Kidner, p. 179. Tarshish and the east wind are legendary, the first as a symbol of the open sea (Peter C. Craigie, *Psalms 1–50,* Word Biblical Commentary, vol. 19, eds. David A. Hubbard and Glenn W. Barker [Waco, Texas: Word Books, 1983], p. 354), the second to describe a powerfully destructive force (see Exodus 14:21; Ezekiel 27:26).

[4]See NEB; Craigie, p. 347.

[5]Kidner, p. 181, note 1.

47

A RIDDLE EXPLAINED

Psalm 49:1-20

"Why do the wicked get all the breaks?" is not a new question. This is the riddle that Psalm 49 explains. Implicit in its explanation is a call to be rich in wisdom.

The introduction (49:1-4) begins with a summons to **listen** to the poet's words (49:1-2). Because of the universal importance and applicability of his message, he addresses **all who live in this world** (49:1). He wants to be heard by all levels of society, both **low and high, rich and poor alike. Low and high** represents one way of understanding the phrase which translates literally "both sons of Adam, and sons of man" (49:2); another possibility would be "all mankind, every living man" (NEB). The poor are invited to learn that money is not all it is advertised to be, the rich to learn not to place their trust in wealth.

In verses 3 and 4, the poet announces his intention to **speak words of wisdom** (49:3)—that is, words which provide divine insight into human existence. The **proverb** *(mashal)* to which he will pay attention (49:4) can refer to a comparison (see Ezekiel 17:2) or to a message from God in poetic style, which is probably the meaning here. **Riddle** describes a puzzling problem which he will **expound** with his **harp** (Ps. 49:4). The music of the harp may serve not as the musical accompaniment to the message but as the vehicle whereby God would communicate the solution of this puzzle (see 2 Kings 3:15). This would fit the literal meaning of **expound,** which is "open" or "draw out." The solution to the puzzle of the prosperous wicked comes from God rather than the poet.

The first stanza (Ps. 49:5-12) emphasizes that wealth cannot protect a person from death. For this reason, one need not fear when **evil days come** (49:5-6). The **wicked deceivers**—those who have put their trust in their

157

riches—will ultimately discover, to their dismay, that wealth is much weaker than righteousness. It cannot buy off God (49:7-9) or keep anyone alive. The Hebrew could hardly state the point more strongly in verse 7a: There is no way a person can **redeem the life of another.** After a parenthetical comment (see 49:8), this thought resumes. It is not money that is condemned, but putting one's trust in wealth rather than in God. Although such a truth is self-evident, it should be noticed that while **wise men die, the foolish and the senseless alike perish** (49:10). The Hebrew suggests that while the former cease to live, the latter fail to leave any trace of ever having lived.

There is some question whether verse 11 refers to the eternal destiny of the wealthy wicked (see the NIV) or to their inward thoughts (see NIV footnote). Either way the point is made clearly in the following verse: **But man, despite his riches, does not endure** (49:12). Ironically, the verb translated **endure** can be rendered "spend the night." The wicked rich imagine themselves living forever, but their tenure on this earth is not even an overnight stay.

The second stanza (49:13-20) begins with the warning that all who **trust in themselves** (the same as trusting in wealth in verse 6) are doomed to die like animals (49:12). More specifically, they are like sheep led to slaughter with death as their shepherd (see 49:14).[1] The righteous, on the other hand, will rule over them **in the morning.** While the morning could refer to better days, here it probably refers to the resurrection.[2] This fits not only the reversal of oppressor and oppressed, but also verse 15. Instead of decomposing in **the grave** (Sheol; 49:14), God takes the righteous to himself. Money cannot **redeem** a person, but God can (the same verb is used in verses 7 and 15).

Having learned his lesson, the psalmist counsels others (49:16-20): Now that you know the true worth of wealth, **do not be overawed** by it, for money and the blessings it buys are only temporary (49:17). The refrain, sounded first in verse 12, is repeated again in verse 20, slightly modified to emphasize the point of the second stanza. The modifications help unify the psalm since the **understanding** offered in verses 3-4 is what is needed in verse 20 (the two words are closely related).

Such understanding continues to be needed today. Wealth remains a powerful magnet which can draw us away from God's value system. **Do not be overawed when a man grows rich** (49:16) is still good advice. To follow the counsel on the United States' coins—"In God we trust"—is to place our hope in the only One capable of redeeming our lives from the grave (see 49:15).

ENDNOTES

[1]This reading, following the New English Bible and the Tanakh (NJPS) seems more likely, although the New International Version reading is possible.

[2]See *The Psalms* by A. Cohen, Soncino Books of the Bible, ed. A. Cohen (London: Soncino, 1950), p. 154.

48

HONOR HIM WITH SACRIFICES FROM THE HEART

Psalm 50:1-23

Psalm 50 borrows much of its imagery from the courtroom, with God as plaintiff and judge and Israel as defendant. Preparation for the proceedings and the arrival of the Judge (50:1-6) are followed by an address to the righteous Israelites (50:7-15) and to the wicked (50:16-23).

With great dignity, God is addressed in a threefold way: **The Mighty One, God, the LORD** (50:1) to express the solemnity of what follows. Verse 1b speaks of God's sovereignty over the whole earth, while verse 2 describes His shining forth from Jerusalem. By pairing these descriptions, one is reminded that God has universal dominion but chose to take up residence in Jerusalem.

God's arrival is described in terms reminiscent of Mount Sinai (see Exodus 19) as He comes and speaks with surrounding fire (see Psalm 50:3). When the covenant was renewed in the wilderness, heaven and earth were called as witnesses (see Deuteronomy 32:1). So, too, in Psalm 50:4 these witnesses are subpoenaed to testify to the actions of these people.

The defendants are summoned (50:5), and the **heavens** call the court to order by proclaiming God's **righteousness,** not unlike when the modern bailiff calls the court to order and announces that the "honorable judge" is presiding. With the heavenly court now in session, the Judge speaks first to the righteous (50:7-15). He does not fault them but corrects their misunderstanding about the purpose for sacrifices (50:8-13) and counsels them about what really matters (50:14-15).

God makes it clear that He does not need their sacrifices (50:9). He does not hunger (50:13), but if He did, He has plenty of animals to eat (50:9-12). What He really wants is **thank offerings** and the fulfillment of **vows** (50:14), not because these were the only good sacrifices, but because they were voluntary and thus sprang from the willing heart of the giver. God wanted His people to exercise their covenant privileges: calling upon Him when they were in trouble, experiencing His deliverance, and elevating Him as their God (see 50:15).

In 50:16-23, the Judge challenges the wicked: How dare you identify yourself as my covenant people? (50:16). This group merely mouths the terms of the covenant. The **words** they cast behind them may be the Ten Commandments, referred to in Exodus 20:1 as the "words" God spoke to Israel. Such a connection seems likely since the vices described in Psalm 50:18-20 violate the eighth, seventh, and ninth commandments.[1]

They do not simply steal and commit adultery, but they habitually do so with joy. They bear false witness (see 50:19-20). While the New International Version's **You use your mouth for evil** is possible, a better rendering of verse 19 may be "You release your mouth to speak evil and harness your tongue to deceit," opposite actions with the same result.[2] Worst of all, they say such things not against a neighbor but against their closest family member (see 50:20).

The Judge warns that punishment, although delayed, will come: **But I will rebuke you** (50:21). Surprisingly, His only explicit counsel to the wicked is to sacrifice **thank offerings** (50:22-23), but, as we have seen, there is a great deal implied here. To give such offerings from a willing heart means they neither **forget God** (50:22) nor sin against His words. **Thank offerings** honor God and make it possible to experience His salvation (see 50:15).

If their hearts do not change, however, **I will tear you to pieces** (50:22; perhaps with one of His wild beasts—see 50:10). "Tearing" echoes verse 5b: **made a covenant with me by sacrifice**—literally, "those cutting my covenant by sacrifice." This idiom suggests the cutting of animals which sealed and celebrated Israel's agreement with God (see Genesis 15:10). The psalmist counsels either "cut a deal" with God or else be torn apart by Him. The courtroom scene closes, not with the condemnation of the wicked, but with the promise of salvation. Ours is a Judge who must condemn sin, for He hates the sight of it. But He is also a Judge who has paid the price on the cross to remove that sin.

ENDNOTES

[1]Peter C. Craigie, *Psalms 1–50,* Word Biblical Commentary, vol. 19, eds. David A. Hubbard and Glenn W. Barker (Waco, Texas: Word Books, 1983), p. 366.

[2]See *The New Brown-Driver-Briggs-Gesenius Hebrew and English Lexicon* by Francis Brown (Peabody, Massachusetts: Hendrickson Publishers, 1979), p. 1018; *Psalms* by F. Delitzsch, Commentary on the Old Testament, vol. V, translated by James Martin (reprint, Grand Rapids, Michigan: Wm. B. Eerdmans Publishing Co., 1978), p. 121.

49

FROM A CRUSHED TO A PURE HEART

Psalm 51:1-19

This psalm arises from a heart crushed by the recognition of its own sinfulness. Traditionally understood as David's prayer after his sins of adultery and murder were confronted by Nathan, it expands the painful scene described in 2 Samuel 12. Israel and the church later employed the psalm to express penitence.

Psalm 51:1-9 expresses David's desire for forgiveness. Because of the nature of his sins, he recognizes that he has no basis to even address God, much less ask His forgiveness. Therefore, verse 1 begins with a cry for **mercy,** followed by appeals to God's covenant love and **great compassion;** only then comes the appeal for forgiveness. **Transgressions** suggests rebellion and willful disobedience (see 2 Kings 3:7), **iniquity** may imply waywardness, while **sin** carries the idea of failure due to wrong choices.

David asks God to **blot out** his transgressions, that is, erase them if written, break them if carved onto tablets, or wipe them clean as one would wipe a dirty dish. He desires to be laundered again and again until the stain is completely removed and he is pronounced clean. More than the slightly different meanings these words may suggest for sin and forgiveness, their repetition indicates the urgency of David's appeal: Use whatever means are necessary, but let no sin remain.

The reason for his desperate desire for purity appears in Psalm 51:3-6. He now understands the full horror of his sin (see 51:3). **I know my transgressions**, he admits (**I** is emphatic in Hebrew). Twice in verse 3 he uses the personal pronoun to describe his sin (five times in verses 1 through 3). Continually, his sin looms before him.

David realizes his sins were against God and God only (see 51:4). This is striking in light of his murderous and oppressive actions to Uriah

165

and Bathsheba, but reminds us that all sin is ultimately against God. For this reason, God is justified in bringing down the full force of divine judgment on David (see 51:4d).

David's desire for forgiveness is driven by the newly sharpened awareness that his sins were symptomatic of a deeper problem, one present even before birth (see 51:5). Both verses 5 and 6 begin with the same word (translated **surely**) and speak of what goes on in a hidden, inner place. Verse 5 explains the nature of humanity which is so unlike what God desires (see verse 6).

Given such reasons, David again asks for cleansing. **Hyssop** (51:7a), a small bushy plant, is probably Syrian marjoram. It was used at the first Passover (see Exodus 12:22)[1] and in several rituals for ceremonial cleansing. David requests a washing to make him **whiter than snow** (Ps. 51:7b), something rare in Palestine but proverbial for whiteness. He seeks in forgiveness a healing and joy which would make broken bones dance with delight (51:8). Finally, David asks God to erase the sin from His sight (51:9).

David is not content to be merely forgiven. Because he now recognizes the danger lurking within (51:5), he wants a new heart (51:10-17). **Create** employs the same verb used to describe the creation of the world, suggesting newness. This new heart would bring him the fellowship with God for which he longs. Having seen what occurred when the Spirit departed from King Saul (see 1 Samuel 16:14), David asks that the **Holy Spirit** not be taken from him (Ps. 51:11). The Holy Spirit would bring unending joy if there was a corresponding **willing spirit** within the psalmist, a spirit which delights in God's will and freely obeys.

David's request for renewal continues with a promise to testify to God's deliverance (51:13-17). He will use his restoration (51:12) to help restore others (51:13; approximating the word play in Hebrew). If preserved from the consequences of bloodshed, David will sing the praises of God's righteousness with lips released from a guilt-induced silence (51:14-15).

God's lack of delight in sacrifice (51:16-17) does not reject that system, but is a reminder that there were no sacrifices to atone for willful sins like murder and adultery. **The sacrifices of God** (that is, those with which God is always delighted) are a **broken spirit** and **a broken and contrite heart** (51:17). An animal with a broken leg is unfit for sacrifices, but a heart that is crushed and contrite is precisely what God desires.

Some suggest that verses 18 and 19 were added in the post-exilic period to balance the perspective on suffering in verse 16. It could well be original since it would be only natural for the king to fear that his sin might have negative consequences for his people.

David's prayer reveals something of God's heart concerning penitence. God is moved to forgive, not by the successful completion of religious requirements but at the sight of a crushed spirit. Such brokenness will be content with nothing less than a new heart and a spirit aligned with the will of God.

ENDNOTE

[1]Passover is the time when the Jews remember their deliverance from Egypt. The word *Passover* refers to the "passing over" of the angel of death (in the tenth plague upon Egypt), who did not destroy any inhabitants of the Israelite homes under the sign of the blood (see Exodus 12).

50

A WARNING TO DECEIVERS

Psalm 52:1-9

Using the historical incident of Doeg's betrayal of Ahimelech (see 1 Samuel 22:9-10), Psalm 52 presents a warning to all who seek to triumph over others by deceitful speech. Its place alongside Psalm 51 balances our perception of David. While in Psalm 51 he feared that his sins would exclude him from God's presence (51:11), in Psalm 52 David describes himself as firmly planted in God's presence because of his righteousness (52:8).

The question (52:1) which begins the description of the wicked person (52:1-7) is rhetorical. This person commits deeds that are not praiseworthy but evil and, therefore, has no right to boast. In fact, even the words **mighty man** are sarcastic. If this indeed refers to Doeg, his only "heroic deed" was to betray innocent blood. There is some question about how to translate the rest of verse 1, which literally reads "the steadfast love of God all the day." Because this appears too abrupt a change from the first line, the New International Version and others have altered the text. Such a change is not necessary, since the more literal reading, while abrupt, makes good sense:

> Why do you boast of your evil, brave fellow?
> God's faithfulness never ceases (Tanakh/NJPS).

The description of this evildoer focuses on his mouth. As the family of Ahimelech discovered, his **tongue** had disastrous consequences (52:2). The problem is traced back to a preference for evil over good, then traced ahead to describe a passion for false and harmful words. The New Jerusalem Bible captures the sting of verse 4:

>You revel in destructive talk,
>treacherous tongue.

Because he brought ruin on others, God will ruin him (see 52:5). It cannot be adequately translated, but the poet has chosen words with harsh sounds and heaped them together to express this destruction. The security and favor he sought to gain by his words will vanish as he is snatched up (the word **snatch** is used to describe how quickly one picks up coals from a fire[1]), torn from his tent, and uprooted from among the living. Such a punishment is even more ironic since Doeg's actions helped to perpetuate David's homelessness, the result of his fleeing from the jealous Saul.

The righteous, upon witnessing the scene, will **see and fear,** then **laugh** (52:6). They do not gloat, since this is condemned in the Old Testament (see Proverbs 24:17-18), but they laugh at the triumph of the righteous as one further proof of God's righteousness.

In contrast to the wicked person stands the righteous, represented by the psalmist (see 52:8-9). While the wicked will be uprooted, the righteous is firmly planted **like an olive tree flourishing in the house of God** (52:8). The **olive tree,** known for its longevity, was important to the Palestinian economy because of its multipurpose olive oil. This tree (see 1:3) is verdant and fruitful. The righteous are **flourishing in the house of God**, like the trees which may have been growing in the courts of the Temple in Jerusalem.[2]

Unlike the wicked person who **trusted in his great wealth** (52:7), the righteous person trusts in **God's unfailing love** (52:8). The contrast between the wicked and the righteous continues in verse 9. The former glorifies himself (see 52:1), while the latter glorifies God. Verse 9 closes with a promise to trust in God's name in the presence of others:

>I shall praise you for ever
>for what you have done,
>and shall trust in your name, so full of goodness,
>in the presence of your faithful (NJB).

While the wicked take matters into their own hands, the faithful wait on God. Others are harmed by the words of the wicked, but the faithfulness of the righteous edifies God's people.

ENDNOTES

[1]Marvin E. Tate, *Psalms 51–100,* Word Biblical Commentary, vol. 20, eds. David A. Hubbard and Glenn W. Barker (Waco, Texas: Word Books, 1990), p. 37.

[2]Othmar Keel, *The Symbolism of the Biblical World: Ancient Near Eastern Iconography and the Book of Psalms,* translated by Timothy J. Hallett (New York: Seabury Press, 1978), pp. 125, 135–136, 354; see Isaiah 60:13.

51

YOU CAN'T IGNORE GOD

Psalm 53:1-6

Most scholars agree that Psalm 53 is a later modification of Psalm 14. The nature of those modifications and why they were necessary will occupy our attention. While the title of Psalm 14 contained only "For the director of music. Of David," this psalm implies new liturgical instructions and thus a different function in Israel's worship by adding **According to Mahalath. A Maskil.**

Although the opening verses are very similar in the two psalms, the changes made are meant to strengthen the message of Psalm 53. Verse 1 uses a stronger word than 14:1 for the **vile** ways of the foolish.[1] In 53:3, **everyone has turned away** replaces "all have turned aside." Differences in the Hebrew, while minor, put greater emphasis on the backsliding which has taken place.[2]

Several times, Psalm 53 (see verses 2, 4, 6) has changed the names used for God. While both psalms use God's name seven times, Psalm 14 employs Elohim three times and Yahweh four. Psalm 53 uses only Elohim. This is not a complete surprise since Elohim occurs much more frequently than Yahweh in Book 2 of the Psalter.

The two psalms differ considerably in 53:4-5. The tone of Psalm 53 is more triumphant. In 14:6 the wicked were addressed, while in 53:5 they have vanished and the psalmist speaks to the righteous. Adding the phrase, **when there was nothing to dread** (53:5), suggests that the enemy has been overpowered by fear and destroyed itself, an idea found elsewhere in the Old Testament (see Joshua 10:10; Judges 7:19-22; 1 Samuel 14:20; 2 Kings 7:3-7). This God (whom the fool denies) has defeated the enemies of Israel, utterly despising them. **God scattered the bones** (v. 5) of their enemies, which, in that culture, brought great shame.[3]

More than likely, a military victory caused a later poet to revise Psalm 14 along more triumphant lines. Among the possible victories are the defeat of the Assyrians who besieged Jerusalem in 701 B.C. (see 2 Kings 18-19), the defeat of the Moabite coalition in the days of Jehoshaphat (see 2 Chronicles 20), or the defeat of the Arameans who had besieged Samaria around 850 B.C. (see 2 Kings 6–7). The prayer for restoration in 53:6 indicates that Israel's triumph is not final. By making salvation plural (not brought out in NIV), the prospects of final victory have increased.[4]

The revision of this psalm raises important questions about how and why such changes occurred. These questions should not, however, prevent us from being encouraged by the psalmist. We serve a God who **restores the fortunes of His people.** Therefore, **let Jacob rejoice and Israel be glad!** (53:6).

ENDNOTES

[1]**They are corrupt and their ways are vile** (Ps. 53:1b) does not reflect the changed Hebrew text. It might be better translated, "They are corrupt and have done abominable deeds."

[2]F. Delitzsch, *Psalms,* Commentary on the Old Testament, vol. V, translated by James Martin (reprint, Grand Rapids, Michigan: Wm. B. Eerdmans Publishing Co., 1978), p. 149; A. Cohen, *The Psalms,* Soncino Books of the Bible, ed. A. Cohen (London: Soncino, 1950), p. 168.

[3]Cohen, p. 169.

[4]The plural signifies "entire, full, and final salvation" (Delitzsch, p. 151); see Cohen, p. 169.

52

SAVED BY HIS NAME

Psalm 54:1-7

This brief prayer of deliverance is thought to have originated during David's days as a fugitive. Hiding from King Saul in the wilderness south of Hebron, fellow Judahites from the clan of Ziph betrayed his whereabouts to the King and put David in a very precarious position (see 1 Samuel 23).

While many passages in the Psalms invoke God's name as the reason for deliverance (see Psalm 31:3), in 54:1 it is God's name which will bring about that deliverance. What this entails becomes clearer in light of the parallel line, **Vindicate me by your might** (54:1b). **Vindicate** can have either legal or military overtones, but the latter is probably preferred since it will occur by God's **might** (see Psalm 110:6).

The psalmist cries for help because he has been attacked by ferocious enemies (see Psalm 54:3) as evident from the terms used to describe them. **Strangers**[1] translates a Hebrew word which usually refers to foreign enemies. To apply such a term to the Ziphites is strange since they belong to David's own tribe. He may be using the term ironically: "My own tribesmen have betrayed me, just as foreigners might do." **Ruthless men** (54:3) conveys the ferocity and terror-striking quality that lies behind this Hebrew word (see Isaiah 25:3-5). Worst of all, these men have no **regard for God** (Ps. 54:3; literally, "they have not put God before them"). They became ruthless because they failed to consider how God would judge their violence.[2] Perhaps by failing to follow His law, they became like foreigners to God (see 54:3).[3]

The tone of the psalm changes in verse 4 to one of hope and confidence, emphasized by the Hebrew word translated **surely.** Unlike the enemies who disregarded God (see 54:3), the psalmist asserts that he has not. Verse 4 repeats the Hebrew word for "soul" (**life** [54:3], **me** [54:4]); it is this that the enemies seek to destroy but that God sustains.[4]

Yahweh's sustenance implies His support for David. **Sustains** is used to describe the lifting up of another (see 145:14), a steadying influence (37:24), and the help given by an ally (Ezekiel 30:6; Isaiah 63:5). What a comfort this knowledge must have been to David while he was being hunted by his king and betrayed by his tribesmen! What a comfort to us to know that God remains an ally who can support us through our times of difficulty!

Psalm 54:5 clearly addresses the problem of those who are unsettling David; how it does this is not so clear. The psalmist may be requesting God's judgment on his enemies (see the NIV) or David may simply be making a statement: God "will requite the evil to mine enemies."[5] **Those who slander me** describes enemies whose weapons are their lips, whose strategy is deception, and whose objective is the destruction of the righteous (see 5:8; 27:11; 56:2; 59:10). They seek to annihilate by their lies; God will destroy them by His truth (**faithfulness** [54:5 NIV]). The empty tomb is the greatest example of how the dark night of deception was pierced with the bright light of God's irrepressible truth.

The psalm closes with a promise of **praise** to the good name of God who will bring victory (54:6-7; see 54:1). The victory may still be in the future and visible to the psalmist only by faith. The final line of this psalm finds David witnessing the defeat of his enemies in divine judgment. God's name has brought salvation.

There are times when we feel like David in Psalm 54. Pursued by those to whom we have done nothing and rejected by our own people, we may be tempted to think that God has forsaken us. Maintain a faith like David's at such a time, and God's name will eventually bring salvation to you as well (see 54:1).

ENDNOTES

[1]The Hebrew contains a play on words between the words for **strangers** *(zarim)* and **ruthless men** *(arizim)*.

[2]A. Cohen, *The Psalms,* Soncino Books of the Bible, ed. A. Cohen (London: Soncino, 1950), p. 170.

[3]Marvin E. Tate, *Psalms 51–100,* Word Biblical Commentary, vol. 20, eds. David A. Hubbard and Glenn W. Barker (Waco, Texas: Word Books, 1990), p. 48.

[4]The word play with strangers and ruthless men (see 54:3) is continued in 54:4 by adding **help** *(azer).*

[5]F. Delitzsch, *Psalms,* Commentary on the Old Testament, vol. V, translated by James Martin (reprint, Grand Rapids, Michigan: Wm. B. Eerdmans Publishing Co., 1978), p. 151.

53

PRAYER OF ONE BETRAYED

Psalm 55:1-23

No slander is more painful than that spoken by a friend. While Psalm 55 is traditionally associated with David's betrayal by Ahithophel during the rebellion of Absalom,[1] it expresses the emotions of anyone who has felt the "knife in his back."

Three times the psalmist goes to God for help. The first prayer (see Psalm 55:1-8) calls for God to deliver him from distress. Verses 1 and 2 are reminiscent of Deuteronomy 22:1-4, when God told the Israelites to be good neighbors; David wants God to be a good neighbor. With each request comes a reason; this time it is the psalmist's personal anguish (see Psalm 55:2b-8). While these verses are not easy to translate, their overall meaning is clear: Enemy oppression has brought the psalmist to the point of death. He longs to escape on **the wings of a dove** and rest securely in solitude (55:6-7).

God's help is requested a second time (see 55:9-14) for direct confrontation with the enemies. Again the language is reminiscent of an earlier passage, specifically the account of the Tower of Babel (see Genesis 11), for God is asked to **confuse** the speech of **the wicked.** Just as Babel had become a place without regard for God, so had the city of the psalmist. He describes this place with seven ominous words. Imagine a city where **violence and strife** keep watch (Ps. 55:9), and where **malice, abuse** (55:10), and **destructive forces** (55:11) thrive. **Threats and lies** are permanent residents of its **streets** (55:11), or perhaps better, its public square, the large open space in a city where people would mingle, conduct business and settle disputes.[2]

As if to illustrate the deception which characterizes this city, David addresses a former friend at whose hand he had suffered (see 55:12-14).

This enemy disregarded their **sweet fellowship** (55:14), perhaps used shared confidences slanderously, and betrayed his covenant with God. There is no wound more painful than that inflicted by a former friend.

Another prayer is offered; this time it is for one thing only: Kill my enemies (see 55:15).[3] He wants them to **go down alive to the grave** just as when the ground opened and swallowed Korah and his followers (see Numbers 16). The psalmist wants his enemy to die suddenly while in good health so that all can see God's vindication of the righteous. Again we are given a reason; this time the reason is as abrupt as the request. The enemies deserve to die because they are evil to the core.

In Psalm 55:16-19a, the tone changes to confidence. Perhaps having seen his enemies at their wicked worst (see 55:15), the psalmist recognizes his only hope is God and resolves to trust in Him.[4] God will answer his calls for He is the universal King (see 55:17-19a).

Surprisingly the song of confidence is interrupted midverse, and we return to the enemy. Such a turn may reflect the resilience of memories and how victory is rarely delivered all at once. What was implied in verses 10 through 14 is stated clearly here: The enemy has an unflinching disregard for God as demonstrated by his deceptive and destructive words. Such wickedness is doubly striking since it follows the picture of God in verses 16 through 19a.

Verse 22 interrupts this rumination with a summons to trust. Peter may have had this verse in mind when he summoned his readers to "cast all your anxiety on him because he cares for you" (1 Peter 5:7). Psalm 55:23 returns to prayer, this time offered in the assurance that what had earlier been sought would be granted. Those who **never change their ways** (55:19b) will be brought down to **the pit of corruption** (55:23) where change is the order of the day. The psalm concludes with David's emphatic assertion: *I trust in you* (my emphasis). Here is that point to which all must come to find peace, regardless of how we have been mistreated and by whom.

ENDNOTES

[1] A. Cohen, *The Psalms,* Soncino Books of the Bible, ed. A. Cohen (London: Soncino, 1950), p. 172. For arguments to the contrary, see *Psalms 51–100* by Marvin E. Tate, Word Biblical Commentary, vol. 20, eds. David A. Hubbard and Glenn W. Barker (Waco, Texas: Word Books, 1990), p. 55.

[2] Tate, p. 57.

[3] For more on imprecatory psalms, see the introduction to this commentary.

[4] See 55:16, with **I** receiving extra emphasis and the unusual use of Yahweh in this section of the Psalter.

54

"IN GOD I TRUST"[1]

Psalm 56:1-13

While Psalm 56 has traditionally been understood to have arisen during David's days as a fugitive, it later came to reflect the suffering of the Jewish nation after the Babylonian exile. The psalm begins with a passionate plea, for the enemies are "hot on his heels": **Men hotly pursue me** (56:1). Their hounding is not merely physical but verbal, for they slander him (see 56:2). If this psalm reflects David's experience, such slander may refer to those who accused David of disloyalty to Saul and thus perpetuated Saul's pursuit of David.

The New International Version may be correct in translating the last phrase in verse 2 as a reference to the enemies' **pride.** The phrase may instead be taken as a request for God to appear on high or raise up the psalmist (see the NEB, NJB) or rather as a title for God—"O Most High"—leading naturally into the refrain in verse 3.

The refrain (56:3-4) is a beautiful affirmation of trust. Fears may come (56:1-2, 3a) but trust in God enables one to be fearless (56:4). More specifically, it is God's **word** that is trustworthy and a cause for celebration (56:4). God's **word** may refer to a general promise of deliverance or to a specific promise God made to David, such as the promise that he would one day become king of Israel (see 1 Samuel 16; also, a word which must have brought David consolation when running for his life). God's trustworthy Word stands in striking contrast to the slanderous, human words of the enemy (see Psalm 56:2, 5).

The description of the enemy's slanderous attacks is expanded in 56:5-6. For the third time, the phrase **all day long** appears. It is this continual, unrelenting pressure which makes God's intervention essential (56:7-9). He asks God to **bring down the nations** (56:7). David may have been requesting God's judgment on the Philistines or on the world in general.[2]

David's next request was for God to take special note of his suffering (56:8). The Jews understood **tears** to be especially influential before

179

God. A passage in the Talmud reads, "Yet though the gates of prayer are locked, the gates of tears are not."³ David asked that his tears be preserved in a bottle (better than the NIV's **scroll**), referring to a container made of animal skin and used to hold water, milk, or wine. He wanted God to carefully preserve these symbols of suffering as one would care for any precious liquid in that arid climate. Such intervention would assure David that God was on his side. **When I call for help** is literally "in the day when I call" which answers the threefold repetition of **all day long** noted earlier.

Although in slightly different words, again the refrain is sounded (see 56:10-11) to affirm David's trust in God. Note that the divine name "Yahweh" is used, an uncommon occurrence in Book 2. This is probably to emphasize God's loving concern for David. The psalm concludes with a promise to praise God for deliverance (see 56:12-13). The fulfillment of vows and thank offerings will be David's happy duty on that day when God plants his feet on level ground where he can walk without stumbling. God's Word is the basis for David's hope. Future deliverance is spoken of in the past tense as if it had already arrived. It was this kind of confidence in God's Word that enabled the writer to the Hebrews to boldly assert in the face of persecution,

> The Lord is my helper; I will not be afraid.
> What can man do to me? (Hebrews 13:6, based on Psalm 118:6).

ENDNOTES

¹See Psalm 56:4.

²Because some scholars question whether **nations** fits the historical background of the psalm, they translate the word as "people" and take it to refer to David's enemies in general (Marvin E. Tate, *Psalms 51–100,* Word Biblical Commentary, vol. 20, eds. David A. Hubbard and Glenn W. Barker [Waco, Texas: Word Books, 1990], p. 65).

³As cited by A. Cohen, *The Psalms,* Soncino Books of the Bible, ed. A. Cohen (London: Soncino, 1950), p. 178. The Talmud was a collection of early Jewish commentaries on the Hebrew Bible.

55

"I WILL AWAKEN THE DAWN"[1]

Psalm 57:1-11

Psalm 57 shares much in common with Psalm 56. Both are attributed to David's days as a fugitive (Psalm 57 can be traced to 1 Samuel 22 or 24), and both begin with the same cry for mercy. Unlike Psalm 56, this psalm ends with victory having come. David's prayer for mercy in 57:1-4 is followed by a refrain (57:5). The second stanza (57:6-10) makes no further request of God but celebrates the defeat of the enemies and the greatness of God. The refrain (57:11) brings the psalm to a triumphant end.

After the initial cry for **mercy** (57:1a), David asserts his confidence in God. Security came not from the cave in which he had taken refuge nor in the rugged mountains which were his hiding place, but in God (see 57:1b). Under His wings David would hide until it was safe to emerge. The expression, **until the disaster has passed** indicates that David viewed his troubles like a storm, fierce and dangerous, but only temporary.

David was sure of finding refuge in **God Most High** (57:2a) because he knew God had a **purpose** to fulfill in David's life (57:2b). Even if we remove the words bracketed by the New International Version and translate this phrase more literally, the meaning is clear: God will accomplish whatever He desires. Furthermore, the Hebrew suggests that God performed this even as David spoke, in spite of what the circumstances suggest. God's plan is best, for it proceeds from **his love and his faithfulness** (57:3). Such reassurance was necessary since those **who hotly pursue[d]** David had the ferocity of **lions** and **ravenous beasts** (57:4). Their words were singled out as being particularly dangerous, perhaps referring to the slander which fed Saul's jealousy and kept David a fugitive.

Following this impassioned cry for help is a refrain full of praise and confidence in God (see 57:5). A more literal translation conveys the artistry and balance of the refrain:

> Be exalted above the heavens
> O God,
> Above all the earth [is] your glory.

In 57:6-10, the tone changes to victory. The enemies are again described, but their defeat is quick and even comical (57:6). The one who had cried out for help now has a steadfast heart (57:7) and is ready to praise God. **Awake my soul!** (57:8) is, literally, "awake my glory," referring to the God-given capacity to praise.[2] To **awaken the dawn** (57:8) may refer to the loudness of the song or to what that song accomplishes, namely relief from the terrors of the night. Such praise will be sounded **among the nations** (57:9; see 56:7)—that is, beyond the boundaries of Israel. This phrase finds its fullest meaning when used to describe how the work of Christ made it possible for Gentiles to be reconciled to God (see Romans 15:9).

The reason for this praise is given in Psalm 57:10. The qualities anticipated in 57:3—**love** and **faithfulness**—were experienced in David's rescue and found to be unlimited in scope. Not only do they stretch from heaven to earth, they link heaven and earth—that is, God with His people. The words of the refrain ring out even more powerfully. Let God be glorified in heaven and on earth, for both are filled with His love and faithfulness.

ENDNOTES

[1]Psalm 57:8c.

[2]Marvin E. Tate, *Psalms 51–100,* Word Biblical Commentary, vol. 20, eds. David A. Hubbard and Glenn W. Barker (Waco, Texas: Word Books, 1990), p. 79; see Psalm 16:9; 30:12 for other instances of **glory** referring to human faculties.

56

"THERE IS A GOD WHO JUDGES"[1]

Psalm 58:1-11

I t is difficult to read Psalm 58 without cringing at the psalmist's cries for revenge.[2] These imprecatory psalms should not be avoided, however, for they have much to teach about God and the Christian's attitude toward inequity.

The psalm opens abruptly with a rhetorical question to the wicked rulers (58:1-2): **Do you rulers indeed speak justly . . . Do you judge uprightly . . . ?** They most certainly do not! In their hearts they plot evil and carry it out with their hands. **Mete out** is literally "weigh out," as with a scale. Ironically, their wickedness employs the very device which implied (and still implies) honest impartiality.

The description of the just rulers continues, but now it is addressed to everyone. Their wickedness, intrinsic to their nature (**from the womb** [58:3]), is dangerous like the poisonous **venom of a snake.** The serpent is a fitting symbol—cunning, yet deadly. Worse still, these men are uncontrollable (see 58:4-5). The **cobra** could be mastered by the swaying of the charmer's pipe; to find oneself in the company of a snake that would not be charmed was a picture of disaster (see Jeremiah 8:17) which no amount of skill could avert.

Facing such a danger, the psalmist turns to God in a prayer which asks that the enemy be disarmed and dismissed (see Psalm 58:6-8). Let them be like toothless lions ("all bark and no bite"; 58:6). May they disappear like water in dry soil (58:7a) and find their arrows blunted and ineffective (58:7b). Let them disappear even as they go about their business. This draws on the popular belief that the slimy trail left by the **slug** is its own dissolution (58:8a).[3] **May they not see the sun** (58:8b).

It may be significant that the confident words with which this psalm concludes are spoken after the prayer of verses 6 through 8 and not after the address to the wrongdoers or to others. Verses 9 through 11 describe God's intervention on behalf of the righteous. That divine judgment will be swift and sure is unmistakable, however difficult verse 9 is to translate. The vindication of the righteous, denied at the hands of the rulers, will finally come, to the delight of those vindicated. To **bathe their feet in the blood of the wicked** (one's enemies, that is) is a metaphor of ultimate triumph in battle, not unlike similar statements in Revelation (see Revelation 19:2, 13).

God has reversed the situation with which the psalm began. Those who were deprived justice (see Psalm 58:1) now experience vindication at God's hand (58:11). The **earth**, where the wicked **mete out violence** (58:2), is now the arena of God's ongoing judgment (58:11). There is only one conclusion to be drawn: **Surely there is a God who judges the earth** (58:11). It is to His heavenly court that all cases of injustice can be taken. Where recompense lies beyond our reach, be assured—it does not lie beyond His.

ENDNOTES

[1]See Psalm 58:11.

[2]For more on imprecatory psalms, see the introduction to this commentary.

[3]A. Cohen, *The Psalms,* Soncino Books of the Bible, ed. A. Cohen (London: Soncino, 1950), p. 184.

57

MY STRENGTH, MY FORTRESS, MY LOVING GOD

Psalm 59:1-17

The title for this psalm indicates David wrote this when King Saul tried to trap and kill him in his home (see 1 Samuel 19:11-17). Psalm 59 pleads for help in the face of a fearsome enemy, but concludes with a rousing assertion of confidence.

Protect (59:1) is the verb form of the noun translated **fortress** in verses 9, 16 and 17. Since David's home was not his castle but a death trap, only God could be his safe haven. David asserts that all of this happened in spite of his innocence (59:3-4a), therefore, God should **arise** and intervene (59:4b-5). He heaps up names for God in verse 5a to emphasize his loyalty and strengthen his appeal.

Since **nations** (59:5, 8) usually describes non-Israelites and these were not involved in Saul's jealous rampage against David, some suggest this psalm was altered in a time of international conflict. **Traitors** (59:5b) translates a word which can mean wicked (for example, Proverbs 2:22), something undependable (like a lame foot; see Proverbs 25:19), or someone who fails to keep a promise (Judges 9:23; Habakkuk 1:13). This word can also be used to describe a person who betrays a relationship, whether between humanity and God (Jeremiah 3:20), husband and wife (Exodus 21:8), extended family (Jeremiah 12:6), or friends (Lamentations 1:2). If David wrote this psalm after escaping an attempt on his life by his father-in-law, the last meaning may fit best. If so, **nations** may be used here ironically: "My own family has betrayed me, treating me like a foreigner" (see Psalm 54:3). Whoever they are, the

185

psalmist wants them punished. He particularly asks God not to show them mercy, for God has a tendency to do so.

In Psalm 58, the enemy was compared to snakes; here they are like **dogs** that snarl and prowl **about the city** (59:6-8). These are not gentle house pets but vicious canines out for a kill (59:6). Foaming from their mouths (**spew out**) are **swords**—that is, words both destructive and blasphemous (59:7). **Who can hear us?** is meant to mock not only people but God himself. It is Yahweh who has the last laugh, however (59:8) for, as in Psalm 2, He mocks the mockers.

Bolstered by divine laughter, the psalmist breaks out in a confident chorus, repeated with some alteration in 59:17. **God,** not the strong men, is the psalmist's strength (**fierce** [59:3] and **strength** [59:9] translate very similar words). In the metaphor of loving **fortress** is found the comforting combination of rock-solid security with paternal affection.

It is to this loving and powerful God that David appeals for vindication (see 59:10b-13). He is confident that God will **go before** him or "come to help" him, depending on whether a combat or rescue motif is in view. When He does come, David asks that His judgment on the wicked be gradual and not immediate so that the psalmist's **people** (perhaps his fellow Israelites) will learn the value of obedience (59:11). The unrighteous will be trapped by their own words (59:12) while the righteous are safely shielded by God (59:11). When God **consumes** the enemy (repeated to emphasize his urgency), all will know that God rules (59:13).

Verses 14 and 15 return to a description of the unrighteous as dogs, but this time it is to contrast the wicked with the righteous psalmist (59:16; **They** [59:14] and **I** [59:16] are emphasized in the original Hebrew). They howl in dissatisfaction at night but David, full of God's strength and love, sings in the morning. Again sounds the refrain (59:17), in which we can join, praising God who is our strength and loving fortress.

58

A NATIONAL CRY FOR HELP

Psalm 60:1-12

As observed earlier, not all the psalms are individual expressions. This psalm communicates a corporate plea in the face of a national calamity. From the title it appears that Israel, while fighting the Syrians in the north, had been attacked by Edom in the south, resulting in national humiliation for Israel. The psalm's title indicates how King David met this challenge. The differences which exist between the historical accounts of David's struggles with Syria and Edom and what is learned from this psalm can be reconciled.[1]

This is the only psalm which contains **For teaching** in its title. Some think it was taught to laity or temple singers, although it remains unclear why this and not other psalms was in the curriculum. More likely, it was taught to troops preparing for the battle against Edom.[2]

Defeat had devastated the nation (see 60:1-5). The verb translated **burst forth** (60:1) can describe something being broken through, like a wall, or it can picture an unexpected attack; this is probably what is intended here. Defeat had shaken them as if by an earthquake, a phenomenon not uncommon to this area. Edom's invasion is described in catastrophic terms because it represented God's rejection of Israel (see 60:1). It was their own God who handed them the cup of wine (see 60:3).

The New International Version translates verse 4 as an expression of confidence. The sight of a raised and unfurled **banner** would fill Israel's heart with hope. If **banner** is taken as a sign of retreat rather than advance (see Jeremiah 4:6), Psalm 60:4 continues the tone of despair which characterizes 60:1-3. Whether confident or despairing, Israel knew where to turn for deliverance (see 60:5).[3]

An answer comes in 60:6-8, although it is unclear whether David or God is speaking. Those who see these as David's words point out that some of the territory mentioned in verses 6 through 8 was claimed by Saul's son and would-be king of Israel, Ish-Bosheth (see 2 Samuel 2). This land was then taken by David when he became monarch. They also observe that the verb which lies behind **in triumph** (Ps. 60:6) is never used in the Old Testament with God as the subject.

The New International Version is probably correct in translating 60:6-8 as God's encouragement to Israel. God is the landowner who parcels out His possessions to earthly tenants. The choice of these particular locations would remind David that God had allotted him the kingdom of Saul, the land of Judah, and other nations.

The **washbasin** (60:8a) was a dirty vessel, used for bathing or even toilet purposes.[4] To **toss my sandal** (60:8b) alludes to taking possession of land—in this case, **Edom. Philistia** is called to shout over God (60:8c; not the other way around as in the NIV), which is probably a summons to proclaim God king.

Assuming 60:6-8 represents God's promise to him of victory, David responds with two questions: **Who will bring me to the fortified city?** and **Who will lead me to Edom?** (60:9). The fortified city is probably Petra, which according to Obadiah 3, was considered impregnable. David is no longer worried about just protecting his southern boundary, he seeks the conquest of **Edom,** the realization of the promise in Psalm 60:8b.

For this to happen, however, God must stop rejecting them (60:10; see 60:1). He must go before them into battle (v. 9) for human aid is **worthless** (60:11). The psalm closes with confidence that God will bring **victory** (60:12). **He** receives special emphasis in the Hebrew and, just as was promised in 60:8, God's foot is placed on Edom (**trample down our enemies** [60:12]). To see His foot on our enemies requires the eyes of faith. We must fear God (60:4) enough to trust Him through what appears to be defeat, confident that He loves us and will therefore deliver us (60:5).

ENDNOTES

[1]For attempts to harmonize the passages involved (see Psalm 60, 2 Samuel 8:13 and 1 Chronicles 18:12), see F. Delitzsch, *Psalms,* Commentary on the Old Testament, vol. V, translated by James Martin (reprint, Grand Rapids, Michigan: Wm. B. Eerdmans Publishing Co., 1978), p. 193; A. Cohen, *The Psalms,* Soncino Books of the Bible, ed. A. Cohen (London: Soncino, 1950), p. 189; and

Derek Kidner, *Psalms 1–72,* Tyndale Old Testament Commentaries, ed. D.J. Wiseman (Downer's Grove, Illinois: InterVarsity Press, 1973), p. 215.

[2]For a fuller explanation, see Delitzsch (p. 192) who even titles this "Drill Psalm After a Lost Battle."

[3]Verses 5 through 12 are also found in Psalm 108:6-13.

[4]Marvin E. Tate, *Psalms 51–100,* Word Biblical Commentary, vol. 20, eds. David A. Hubbard and Glenn W. Barker (Waco, Texas: Word Books, 1990), p. 102.

59

SECURE IN GOD

Psalm 61:1-8

lthough we know little of David's struggle, Psalm 61 reveals a man in need of protection. His prayer, repeated in three stanzas (61:1-3, 4-5, 6-8), is for God-given security. There is a boldness in his opening words (61:1) that suggests a "covenant confidence" in God:

> **Hear my cry, O God;**
> **listen to my prayer.**

If David wrote this psalm, one wonders when he found himself at **the ends of the earth** (61:2a), that is, at a distant place against his will? One commentator suggests the Aramean campaign (referred to in Psalm 60),[1] while another points to Absalom's rebellion.[2] The Old Testament contains numerous accounts of God's people being far from home in a foreign land, where other gods were worshiped.

Not only was David far away, but he had grown too weak (61:2b) to return home or even to find refuge. For this reason he asked God to lead him to a **rock** of safety (61:2c). The rock was not merely **higher than** David but inaccessible to him ("Lead me to the rock that stands far out of my reach" [NJB]). Unless God brings him there, David will never find the security he needs. He drew the confidence to make such a striking request from his past experiences of God as **refuge** (61:3).

In the second stanza the psalmist seeks security in a more personal place, the presence of God (see 61:4-5). He desires to dwell in God's **tent** forever, a reference to the tabernacle (61:4a). The **wings** under which he seeks **shelter** are most likely those of the cherubim which stood over the ark of the covenant (61:4b). In both stanzas the psalmist has requested access to the inaccessible—the rock out of reach and the Holy of Holies.

As the first request for security concluded with a reason for God to intervene (61:3), so the second request ends with such a reason (61:5). The pronoun **you** in **for you have heard my vows** (61:5a) is emphasized, while the whole phrase reflects an ongoing familiarity with God. **You have given me the heritage of those who fear your name** (61:5b) refers to God's gift of the land; these are poignant and personal words in light of the psalmist's present circumstances (61:2a).

In the third stanza (61:6-8) the psalmist again appeals for security, this time by asking for the long life that such security would bring and that verse 2b suggests is sorely needed. For the Israelite, a long life was "the most precious gift and the most marvelous blessing that God could give."[3] **Increase the days of the king's life,** and **his years for many generations** may mean granting the king's dynasty as many future generations as his remaining years of life.[4] To insure his longevity, two bodyguards would be appointed: **Love** *(chesed)* is the term for God's covenant kindness; **faithfulness** (or firmness) insured unshakable stability (see Proverbs 20:28). No earthly king, including David, was **enthroned in God's presence forever** (Ps. 61:7). It is not surprising, therefore, that after the monarchy ended in 586 B.C. the Jews applied this phrase to the Messiah[5] and that the church saw the role fulfilled in Jesus.

What follows the third request for security is not a reason (as earlier) but a statement of what would happen when the request was granted. Promised was continual **praise** (to correspond to the king's continual reign) during which he would, day after day, **fulfill my vows** (61:8). These are not two activities (as the NIV suggests) but one. The God who heard him from a distance and restored him to home and health will be repaid with lifelong praise.

Since the Messiah is now **enthroned in God's presence forever,** we can be confident that those same bodyguards—**love and faithfulness**—will still be on duty to protect God's people (61:7). We can join the psalmist as he sings praise to God's name and fulfills his **vows** daily (61:8).

ENDNOTES

[1]A. Cohen, *The Psalms,* Soncino Books of the Bible, ed. A. Cohen (London: Soncino, 1950), p. 192.

[2]F. Delitzsch, *Psalms,* Commentary on the Old Testament, vol. V, translated by James Martin (reprint, Grand Rapids, Michigan: Wm. B. Eerdmans Publishing Co., 1978), p. 202.

[3]Hans-Joachim Kraus, *Theology of the Psalms,* translated by Keith Crim (Minneapolis: Augsburg Press, 1986), p. 164.

[4]Cohen, p. 193.

[5]Marvin E. Tate, *Psalms 51–100,* Word Biblical Commentary, vol. 20, eds. David A. Hubbard and Glenn W. Barker (Waco, Texas: Word Books, 1990), p. 115.

60

FAITH UNDER FIRE

Psalm 62:1-12

This is a psalm about faith. Six times a small Hebrew word appears, translated variously as **alone** (62:1-2, 5-6), **fully** (62:4), and **but** (62:9). For all its size—only two letters in Hebrew—it is full of faith, for it is a word that affirms the truth while under attack. The emphasis on faith comes from more than just this word, however. The psalm expresses confidence in God, challenges opponents, encourages rest and provides insight into what really matters, all the time under fire from a deceitful enemy (see 62:3-4).

The psalm begins confidently with the psalmist asserting his trust **in God alone** (62:1-2). With God providing security, he **will never be shaken** (made to stumble, stagger, reel, or tip over and fall). Some translate this line "I shall not be greatly moved" (ASV) rather than **I will never be shaken,** suggesting that some shaking might occur but with no serious consequences.

According to verses 3 and 4, destructive shaking is precisely what the enemy sought to do. First in questions addressed to his enemies (62:3), then to others about the enemies (62:4), David confronts their attempts to destroy him. The description of himself as a **leaning wall** and **tottering fence** (v. 3b) does not contradict the stability he possesses in verse 2b (the word for "as" is not translated by the NIV). The enemy only perceives the psalmist as unstable; he is, in fact, as solid as his God (see 62:2a). The **lofty place** (62:4) from which the enemy seeks to topple him is taken to support the view that King David is the author.

Next the psalmist offers himself (his **soul**) some words of counsel (62:5-7). The essence of verse 1 is repeated in verse 5, although what was a statement becomes a command and **salvation** is changed to **hope.** Verse 6 repeats verse 2 almost word for word, except that **never be shaken** becomes **not be shaken.** He who shook a little in verse 2 is now rock solid. Verse 7 develops the theme of verse 6, pointing out that the psalmist's glory does not depend on retaining his lofty place but on God alone.

Advice is now given to others (62:8-10): **Trust in him at all times** and nothing else. If the final line of verse 7 (literally, "my refuge is in God") is taken with what follows, then verse 8 begins and ends with God as **refuge,** a God who desires the trust of His people and longs to have them **pour out** their hearts to Him. Secure within this refuge one can, like Hannah in the Tabernacle (see 1 Samuel 1:15), honestly "tell him all your troubles" (TEV).

The two things in which many place their trust—other people and money—are singled out with warnings. Do not rely on people, for they are "lightweights" (**nothing** [Ps. 62:9]). Put any person on a scale—put everyone there—and (literally) "they will go up." How could it be otherwise when their combined weight is less than a breath? **Do not trust** in money or what it can purchase (62:10). No reason is given, but since the word for **take pride** is the verb form of the noun translated **breath** in 62:9, the meaning is clear: Money is too easily blown away to put one's faith in it.

The final statement of confidence (62:11-12) was originally spoken by God (62:11a) and is now addressed back to Him. These verses do not primarily identify a quality of God (as the NIV suggests) but indicate what God possesses—that is, strength (**You, O God, are strong**) and love (**You, O Lord, are loving**). Because God possesses strength, He is capable of protecting the righteous and punishing evildoers. Because He possesses love, He will use His strength for what is best. Having Him, one has all that is needed; wealth or the favor of others is unnecessary. That God will vindicate His people is put beyond doubt by the emphasis, in the Hebrew, of the pronoun **you** in the phrase **You will reward each person** (62:12b). What a comfort to remember that the God who possesses strength and love also possesses knowledge; He will bring justice for all.

61

A LOVE BETTER THAN LIFE

Psalm 63:1-11

To be away from home and unable to return is a distressing experience, as Psalm 63:1 reveals. As the psalm continues, however, one senses the psalmist drawing closer to God and more confident in spite of his difficulties; by 63:11, his song of joy returns. The **dry and weary land** where the psalmist searches for God (63:1) describes the Desert of Judah, identified in the title as the place where David wrote this psalm. If written while he was king, this psalm fits the time of Absalom's rebellion (see 2 Samuel 15:23, 28; 16:2; 17:16).

To translate "I seek thee early" (NEB) rather than **earnestly I seek you** (63:1) creates a word play with **night** in v. 6 and furthers the theme of the psalm. With soul and flesh longing for God, David is as dry and weary as the land he inhabits (see 2 Samuel 16:2, 14). In Psalm 63:2, he describes his former times of worship in the **sanctuary.** There he experienced (the Hebrew word is stronger than **beheld**) a clearer understanding of God's **power** and **glory.** One might expect such a memory to deepen David's discouragement, but the opposite occurs. Verses 2 through 4 seem to say, "As I praised you in the good times (63:2), so I will praise you once again, even in these difficulties." Standing between his past and future experiences of God lies the truth which makes this attitude possible. God's **love is better than life** (63:3), therefore, it is possible to praise Him in all circumstances. His love is limitless and so will be David's **praise** (63:4). God's love makes life a feast (63:5), a striking metaphor when contrasted with the dryness of 63:1.

David searched for God in the early morning and was still contemplating him through the three **watches of the night** (63:6). While in the sanctuary, he would have worshiped beneath the **wings** (figuratively) of the cherubim which stood over the ark of the covenant. Discovering by faith that those wings shade him even in the wilderness, he sings for joy (see 63:7). Verse 8 provides a beautiful picture of what God intends for the divine-human relationship, for as the psalmist holds tightly to his God, he finds that God is holding on to him. There is comfort in knowing that my grip on God is not my only security.

Something of what this "upholding" means is described in verses 9 through 11. Those who seek to destroy the king will themselves be shattered in the process. To descend to the **depths of the earth** (63:9) meant premature annihilation. Jackals were the final scavengers who ate what larger animals left; to be their food meant one was deprived burial, a horrible thought for the Jews.

The king, however, will be vindicated along with all the righteous (see 63:11). While focusing on the honesty of the speakers, the psalm closes with a description of the judgment of the wicked. Those who **swear by God's name** (that is, those whose words are honest before God) will be honored by God (rather than **will praise** God). Those whose speech is marked by deception (**liars**) will be silenced. Aside from reminding us of the importance of our words, these verses affirm the psalmist's confidence: God's love will vindicate His people.

62

SUDDEN DESTRUCTION

Psalm 64:1-10

The picture of the enemies in Psalm 64 is one of the most frightening in the Psalter. Their attack, pernicious and aggressive, posed a real threat to the psalmist, whom the title identifies as David. Little wonder he called on God to protect his life (see 64:1) from enemies who plot his destruction (64:2).

Those who object that words are not potent weapons have yet to be wounded by them as David had been. The enemies did not openly accuse, but ambushed by anonymous innuendos. Even more unjust, the target of their gossip was a blameless man. All of this was carried out without fear of man or God; they boasted that no one could foil their plot (see 64:4c-5).

Although verse 6 is difficult to translate, the New International Version provides as good an effort as any. The psalm pivots on this verse, which represents the boast of the enemies and summarizes their plans and claims. The observation, **Surely the mind and heart of man are cunning** (64:6c), reflects God's assessment of the wicked and sets the stage for His assault (64:7-9).

Throughout verses 7 through 9, the psalmist repeatedly contrasts God's attack of the enemies with their attack on the righteous. As they had shot arrows at the blameless (64:3), so God shoots arrows at them thus vindicating the righteous person. They attacked suddenly (64:4); so does God (64:7). The very weapons they employed (64:3) are turned against them (64:8) and the **perfect plan** which they hatched over time is ruined **suddenly.** They admired themselves as **cunning** (64:6) but are publicly humiliated (64:8). Their weapons of secrecy (64:2, 4, 5) are openly destroyed (64:8). So complete is the disaster that **all who see them will shake their heads in scorn** of the wicked (64:8).[1]

Not only will this destruction vindicate the righteous, it will bring two other results. First, **all mankind will fear** God (64:9a). The proper reverence that the enemy lacked (64:4) will become, at their devastation, the possession of all. The second result will be praise of God. Ironically, the same word is used to describe the deeds of the evildoers (64:2) and the **works** of God (64:9). The one brought disaster; the other, praise.

The last two verbs in verse 9 seem out of order; one would expect **ponder** to precede **proclaim.** The New Jerusalem Bible makes good sense of the current order:

> Everyone will be awestruck,
> proclaim what God has done,
> and understand why he has done it.

As if to echo the plea in verses 1 and 2, the psalm closes with a summons to praise Yahweh and **take refuge in Him** (64:10). Violent enemies may employ secret weapons against the righteous (see 64:2, 4-5), but there is a place where His people can be safe and rejoice in God.

ENDNOTE

[1]By adding **in scorn,** the New International Version has accurately reflected the "malignant, mocking astonishment" (F. Delitzsch, *Psalms,* Commentary on the Old Testament, vol. V, translated by James Martin [reprint, Grand Rapids, Michigan: Wm. B. Eerdmans Publishing Co., 1978], p. 223) implied in the phrase "to shake the head."

63

SAVIOR, LORD, PROVIDER

Psalm 65:1-13

For Israel, with agriculture as its lifeblood, natural disasters like drought were devastating. Not only did they bring economic hardship, but they also created a theological problem: Why is God not blessing His people? Psalm 65 may reflect the people's response when God delivered them from such a natural disaster.

The tone of gratitude which pervades this psalm is sounded in its opening announcement: **Praise awaits you, O God, in Zion** (65:1) or perhaps better, "praise is rightfully yours" (NJB). The Psalter speaks frequently of promises of praise made to God in times of disaster. These are now to be fulfilled (see 65:1) since God has heard their prayer and intervened.

Because verses 3 and 4 praise God for forgiveness, the drought was apparently understood as the result of sin. There are times when sin affects society, but this passage should not be used to teach that all disasters are caused by sin. Although the Hebrew of verse 3 is difficult to translate, David's point is clear: Sin which overpowers humans can be overcome by God. How relevant this truth remains today!

Forgiveness of sin brought the opportunity to fellowship with God. Israel was especially privileged to be chosen as the place where God established His House. The Temple was a place of good (65:4b; **things** is added). Best of all, to be in his **courts** meant one was **near** Him (65:4a).

Verses 5 through 8 speak not primarily of creation, but of the universal rule of God. All the earth will put their trust in the One who demonstrates His sovereignty with **awesome deeds of righteousness** (65:5), deeds which are enumerated in verses 6 and 7.

In the ancient Near East, mountains were more than formidable works of creation; they represented the homes of the gods (see 121:1-2).

To David, God's creation of the **mountains** (65:6) reflects His superiority over all other "gods," against whom he has **armed** himself **with strength** (65:6).

The seas (65:7) represented chaos, the force that the Old Testament and other ancient Near East documents describe as opposing the created order (see 89:9). This too lies under God's control as do the tumultuous **nations** (65:7). God rules over all, from the rising to the setting of the sun (65:8).

The final section (65:9-13) "puts every harvest hymn to shame as plodding and contrived. Here we almost feel the splash of showers, and sense the springing growth about us."[1] It is possible (see the NIV footnote in 65:9) that God is being described as a farmer who prepares the land, irrigates the crops (65:9b-10), and whose "carts overflow" with the **bounty** of the harvest (65:11). Verses 12 and 13 picturesquely describe the **hills, meadows,** and **valleys** clothing themselves with **gladness. Flocks** and **grain,** in order to join in the celebration, **shout for joy and sing** (65:13). Deprivation was an ever-present danger for Old Testament believers, yet they knew where to go in difficulty and whom to praise in abundance. Are we, who live so much more securely, as quick to look up?

ENDNOTE

[1]Derek Kidner, *Psalms 1–72,* Tyndale Old Testament Commentaries, ed. D.J. Wiseman (Downer's Grove, Illinois: InterVarsity Press, 1973), p. 229.

64

PROMISES KEPT TO A GOD WHO KEEPS PROMISES

Psalm 66:1-20

C learly, Psalm 66 was written to express thanks to God for deliverance and to promise that offerings would accompany this thanks. What is not clear is whether this promise is expressed by an individual or the nation (as Psalm 65). First-person plural pronouns (**our, us,** and **we**) appear in 66:8-12 and first person singular (**I, my,** and **me**) from verse 13 to the end. Possibly the worshipers who gathered at the Temple sang verses 1 through 12 while one person, perhaps the king or his representative, sang the rest.

The initial call to praise (66:1-4) summons **all the earth** to join in the celebration of God's deliverance. Israel's role as "light to the nations" (Isaiah 49:6) was a part of God's original plan as revealed to Abraham (Genesis 12:3). Not always embraced by Israel, the New Testament authors found this plan a way to explain the mission to the Gentiles (Galatians 3:8). Since universal worship was yet to come, the verbs in Psalm 66:4 should be translated they "will bow down" and "will sing praise."

The summons to **come and see what God has done** is followed by a poetic description of Israel's exodus from Egypt and entry into Canaan (66:5-7). **Waters** should be "rivers"; this is a reference to the crossing of the Jordan.[1] The gift of the Promised Land provides reason to praise God's sovereignty (see 78:54-55): "There (in the land He gave us) let us praise Him who rules forever by his power (shown by giving us the land)" (see 66:6b-7a).

The Exodus from Egypt and conquest of Canaan become the backdrop against which to read a description of the community's current experience (66:8-12). Although God had kept them from stumbling (66:9) and helped them (66:10-12a), He let them be humiliated and be tested by **fire and water** (66:12). This phrase could mean "from one extreme to another" (see Isaiah 43:2) or could refer to a purification process known from Numbers 31:23. Finally God provided relief by allowing them to pass into a **place of abundance** where they could "breathe again" (66:12 NJB).

In gratitude for this deliverance, the vows promised in the time of difficulty will now be fulfilled (see 66:13-20). Only a portion of the vow offering was burnt or given to the priests; the rest served as the main course for a fellowship meal. Here, however, the whole offering (see 66:13) is given to God, signifying the extent of the people's gratitude.[2]

Echoing the summons to all nations in verse 5, another call is sounded, this one to **all you who fear God** (66:16). Those who respond are told of the psalmist's deliverance (see 66:17-19). He emphasizes that, even in trouble, praise was on the tip of his tongue and his heart was pure. Those who await deliverance from the promise-keeping God, should wait with a clean heart and a readiness to praise.

ENDNOTES

[1]This term, however, is not used elsewhere in the Old Testament for the Jordan. Some (as the New International Version) suggest that the term here has its less common meaning and is another reference to the Sea of Reeds.

[2]Derek Kidner, *Psalms 1–72*, Tyndale Old Testament Commentaries, ed. D.J. Wiseman (Downer's Grove, Illinois: InterVarsity Press, 1973), p. 235.

65

BLESSED TO BLESS OTHERS

Psalm 67:1-7

When God called Israel to be His people, it was not for their benefit only but that through them He might bless all the world. What is alluded to in Psalm 66:4 becomes the theme of Psalm 67: Israel's desire to be blessed, not as an end in itself, but so that the **ends of the earth** would **fear him** (67:7).

The first stanza (67:1-2) prays God's blessing on Israel in language very similar to the priestly benediction of Numbers 6:24-26. The shining of God's face represents His favor, even life itself, much as the shining of the sun enables growth and harvest. The result of this blessing would be that God's ways and salvation would become known to all nations (see Psalm 67:2). This prayer for blessing leads naturally into the refrain of verse 3. God, by blessing Israel, would reveal His ways to all peoples, prompting them to praise Him. This progression is more evident if we translate verse 3 as "Peoples will praise Thee."

Verse 4, standing in the middle of the psalm, is its pivotal verse. It builds on the promise of revelation and the prediction of praise in verses 1 through 3. When the nations realize what God has done, they will **be glad and sing for joy** (67:4). God's **ways** and **salvation,** left general in verse 2 are made more specific here:

> **... for you rule the peoples justly**
> **and guide the nations of the earth** (67:4).

Guide translates a word which can mean "lead" in a general sense (see Numbers 23:7; Proverbs 18:16) or "disperse" (Job 12:23; 2 Kings 18:11). In at least one passage, it means simply "protect" (Job 31:18).

Here it means to lead in a protective or beneficent sense, as a shepherd would lead his flock (Psalm 23:3) or as God led Israel through the wilderness (Psalm 78:14, 53). Commentator Derek Kidner points out the beautiful combination in 67:4b of perfect fairness with shepherd-like concern.[1] The reappearance of the refrain (see 67:5) is fitting; with such a just and caring God, why would the nations not praise Him?

In the final stanza, God is thanked for the past harvest and appealed to for further blessings (67:6-7). Agricultural abundance would show the nations Israel's blessing and draw them to worship Israel's God (see Jeremiah 33:9; Isaiah 60:3). With this psalm's emphasis on the international implications of Israel's blessings, **God, our God** draws attention to her privileged role.[2]

The psalm concludes by again sounding its theme: God's blessing on Israel will bring **all the ends of the earth** to fear Him (67:7b). In her better moments, Israel remembered why she was blessed, thanks in part to passages like this. Who could have imagined, however, that God would carry out the ultimate realization of His plan and reveal His glory to the nations using a Jewish baby boy?

ENDNOTES

[1]Derek Kidner, *Psalms 1–72,* Tyndale Old Testament Commentaries, ed. D.J. Wiseman (Downer's Grove, Illinois: InterVarsity Press, 1973), p. 237.
[2]Ibid.

66

"MAY GOD ARISE"[1]

Psalm 68:1-35

Of all the psalms, this one may be the most difficult to interpret, for the meaning of many words and phrases remains uncertain. For all its difficulties, "the 'disconnectedness' of the psalm . . . is transformed into a 'connectedness' by its concentration on God and his praise."[2] God appears by name in nearly every verse and by no less than seven different names. This psalm appears to have been written to accompany the procession of the ark of the covenant into God's Tabernacle (see 2 Samuel 6). It also asserts His superiority over the gods of Israel's neighbors, His chief rivals for Israel's affections.

The psalm opens with the words to be repeated whenever the ark of the covenant set out from the camp of Israel (see Numbers 10:35). Psalm 68:2-3 describes the result; the enemy is suddenly destroyed and the righteous rejoice at their own vindication. Having arisen, God marches from Egypt to Jerusalem (68:4-18). He showed His concern for the helpless (vv. 5-6) most clearly when He rescued Israel from Egypt, the **sun-scorched land,** a phrase which may intimate God's superiority to Egypt's sun god. To refer to God as **him who rides on the clouds** (68:4) almost certainly asserts God's superiority to Baal, the Canaanite storm god.

Verses 7 through 14 poetically describe the conquest of Canaan. The thunderstorm (see 68:8a) alludes to a time when God used a storm to defeat the Canaanites (see Judges 4:15; 5:4, 21). He beats Baal at his own game then sends gentler rains to water the crops (see Psalm 68:9).

It is not always easy to understand what is being referred to in 68:11-14, which Bible commentator Derek Kidner called a "tumble of swift images and excited snatches of description."[3] The enemies who possessed the land have been defeated and plundered. The Lord announced the victory and many heralds went off to proclaim it (see 68:11). **Sleep among the campfires** appears to be a quotation from

Judges 5:16, referring to Reuben's unwillingness to go to battle. His failure to receive any of the spoils was intended to remind David's hearers to participate in God's victories and claim His blessings. The dove (see Psalm 68:13) has been variously explained but probably refers to Israelite women wearing the spoils of war (see 2 Samuel 1:24).[4] **Snow . . . on Zalmon** (Ps. 68:14) may be a poetic description of the enemy in flight or may reflect the idea that snow and ice are weapons in God's arsenal (see Job 38:22-23).

Jerusalem's selection by God is celebrated in Psalm 68:15-18. His choice of Mount Zion causes much taller mountains to gaze on her with envy. As Zion is greater than they, so Zion's God is greater than their gods. This is brought out more clearly when the phrase **majestic mountains** is translated, literally, "mountains of gods." In verses 17 and 18, God ascends Zion, stepping directly from Sinai into the sanctuary to show the close connection between God's law and His sanctuary.

Verses 19 through 31 describe the procession of worshipers to the sanctuary. Compared to the gods who need to be carried in processions (see Jeremiah 10:5), what a privilege to have a God who **daily bears our burdens** (Ps. 68:19)! A Savior from death (68:20) is greater than the Canaanite god of death. The enemies brought from **Bashan** and **the depths of the sea**—that is, from highest heights and lowest depths, will receive their due (68:21-23).

The procession (68:24-27) includes singers in the lead, musicians coming behind with maidens all around them singing the words of verse 26. Also in the procession are several Israelite tribes. Benjamin and Judah may be mentioned first and second because these tribes produced the first and second kings of Israel. The other two probably represent the northern tribes.

God enthroned will be worshiped by all, including Israel's perpetual nemesis, Egypt (68:28-31), the **beast among the reeds** (68:30). By bringing God tribute (68:30), she acknowledges that Yahweh is greater than the gods of Egypt. Cush (located south of Egypt and representing the remote regions of the world) and the **kingdoms of the earth** (68:32) must come to God's throne where He sits—majestic, powerful, and awesome.

The early church used this psalm to commemorate Pentecost, for on that day the exalted Christ poured out on the church the gift of the Holy Spirit (see Acts 2:33).[5] Let the earth worship, for God has indwelt His Temple, the body of Christ—the church.

208

ENDNOTES

[1]See Psalm 68:1.

[2]Marvin E. Tate, *Psalms 51–100,* Word Biblical Commentary, vol. 20, eds. David A. Hubbard and Glenn W. Barker (Waco, Texas: Word Books, 1990), p. 184.

[3]Derek Kidner, *Psalms 1–72,* Tyndale Old Testament Commentaries, ed. D.J. Wiseman (Downer's Grove, Illinois: InterVarsity Press, 1973), p. 240.

[4]Ibid.; Kidner also mentions other possibilities.

[5]The Greek term that *Pentecost* comes from means "fiftieth" or "the fiftieth day" and is literally the fiftieth day after the end of the Passover. It is also known as the Jewish Feast of Weeks; the day is part of the Jewish observances, and was the beginning of the offering of first fruits.

67

CRY OF A WOUNDED SOUL

Psalm 69:1-36

Desperate, unjustly accused, humiliated, and forced to wait for God's intervention, the writer of Psalm 69 presents a picture among the most despairing in all the Psalter. New Testament writers found this fertile soil from which to draw insights into the life of Jesus (see Matthew 27:48; John 2:17; 15:25; Acts 1:20; Romans 15:3). While the emotions of this psalm may be raw, its structure is delicately balanced.[1] The title attributes it to David, but several details within the psalm fit a later time (especially Psalm 69:30-36). If David wrote Psalm 69, it was probably revised later in a time of national disaster.

The strongly evocative cry for help and description of distress in verses 1 through 4 indicate that David has experienced cruel and undeserved treatment. The enemies' method and motive are explored in verses 5 through 12. While David acknowledged folly and guilt (69:5), he did not consider himself responsible for his troubles. Contrary to the accusations, God knew the real truth about him (**you** is emphatic in verse 5).

David was primarily concerned that his suffering would tarnish God's reputation and shake others' confidence (see 69:6-7). He appeals to God's reputation by using three different names for God in verse 6 and reminds Him that he suffered on God's behalf (see 69:7). If David is the author, **zeal for your house** (69:9) could refer to the price he paid to establish God's house in Jerusalem (see 132:1). To be rejected by one's siblings (69:8), to be ridiculed while grieving (69:10-11), and to be publicly mocked (69:12) were among the worst indignities one could know.

His request for God's help (69:13-18) echoes his cry in 69:1-4. Although his cries had gone unanswered (69:3), he continued to pray (69:13; **I** is emphatic). Whether the **time of your favor** refers to when to pray ("at the time for prayer") or to the goal of prayer ("when you decide to intervene"), David's confidence was founded on God's love (69:13, 16). The threat of death lies behind the psalmist's fear of descending to the **pit** and sinking in its **mire** (69:14-15).

Although the word order is rearranged in the New International Version, the psalmist carefully crafted 69:16-17 to express the heart of his request for help. Verse 16 begins with "answer me," and verse 17 ends with "answer me quickly." God's good love (69:16b) contrasts with the seriousness of the psalmist's difficulty (69:17b). The two phrases in the center express his chief desire positively (**in your great mercy turn to me** [69:16c]) and negatively (**do not hide your face from your servant** [69:17a]).[2]

The psalmist sought more than deliverance; he desired vengeance (69:19-28). As verses 13 through 18 echoed verses 1 through 4, this passage parallels verses 5 through 12. The psalmist is scorned (69:7, 9, 10, 19, 20), slandered (69:11, 12, 26), and mocked when suffering (69:10-12, 20-21). Both sections attribute the ultimate cause of the psalmist's suffering to God (69:7, 26). To prepare for his prayer for judgment, David again describes his disgrace (69:19-21). Gall was a poisonous plant (see Hosea 10:4), but the word could also be used to express bitterness or deadly poison, like the venom of a snake (see Deuteronomy 32:33; Job 20:16).[3]

David's prayer for God to punish his enemies (see Psalm 69:22-28) reflects their persecution of him. Because they poisoned his meal, he asks that their table become a **snare** (69:22). May the **eyes** (69:23) which gloated over him go blind. **Backs** (69:23) is literally "loins," a term used for the waist (see 2 Samuel 20:8) and for the place where pain would be most keenly felt (1 Kings 20:31). It also means the seat of strength (Deuteronomy 33:11; 1 Kings 12:10), the connotation here: Let them be weakened as repayment and so they could inflict no further harm. David prays that they would not be forgiven but become increasingly guilty (see Psalm 69:27). To **not be listed with the righteous** (69:28) refers to physical death; the idea of eternal life awaited a future day. Verse 29 begins with David's distress (the theme of 69:21-28) and moves toward his vindication or salvation (69:30-36).

This salvation, either miraculously experienced or confidently anticipated, would produce many favorable results (69:30-36). Praise would be given, a sacrifice more pleasing to God than one with **hoofs** (that is, ritually pure) and **horns** (that is, full-grown rather than immature). The poor—perhaps the vulnerable onlookers in verse 6—

would be encouraged (69:32-33) while all would know of God's power over His enemies (69:34-36).

As argued in the introduction to the commentary, imprecatory psalms (like Psalm 69) can be used by the Christian. Such psalms reveal the depth of human sin, the gravity of human pain, and how confidence in a faithful God can provide strength in one's bitterest moment.

ENDNOTES

[1]For more on imprecatory psalms, see the introduction to this commentary.

[2]L.C. Allen, "The Value of Rhetorical Criticism in Psalm 69," *Journal of Biblical Literature,* vol. 105 (1986), pp. 577–98, as cited by Marvin E. Tate, *Psalms 51–100,* Word Biblical Commentary, vol. 20, eds. David A. Hubbard and Glenn W. Barker (Waco, Texas: Word Books, 1990), p. 190.

[3]Derek Kidner, *Psalms 1–72,* Tyndale Old Testament Commentaries, ed. D.J. Wiseman (Downer's Grove, Illinois: InterVarsity Press, 1973), p. 247.

68

"COME QUICKLY, GOD"[1]

Psalm 70:1-5

The five verses of Psalm 70 appear, with only minor changes, in Psalm 40:13-17.[2] The presence of both psalms in the Psalter is not accidental, for each serves a slightly different purpose. Both are cries for help, but Psalm 70 seems to have had a more specific use in Israel's worship. Its title identifies it as a **petition** or, more literally, "for a remembrance." It may have been sung to accompany the memorial portion of an offering (see Leviticus 2:2)[3] or to remind God of the needs of His people. If Psalms 70 and 71 were to be read together, as seems likely, the use of the same Hebrew verb in 71:16 (**proclaim**) suggests that the call to remember could be directed at the worshipers.

There is no consensus as to which of the two psalms came first. Some think Psalm 40 is a modification of Psalm 70 because the latter forms a "complete unity," beginning and ending with a call for God to hurry. Others believe that Psalm 40 is the original since it is more "full-toned and soaring."[4]

When the two psalms are read side by side, Psalm 70 appears more abrupt and urgent. Verse 1 lacks the phrase, "be pleased" with which 40:13 begins. To **turn back** the enemy implies greater gravity than "let them be appalled" (40:15). Since the underlying verbs differ by only one letter, the change may be accidental. The same is true of the verb used in 70:5 and 40:17. **Come quickly to me** is more urgent than "think of me" but differs only slightly in the Hebrew. Whether standing alone or incorporated into another psalm, these verses ring with confidence in God. They remind us that God deserves our trust and that we can confidently remind God when we need His help.

ENDNOTES

[1]See Psalm 70:1, 5.

[2]See the discussion of Psalm 40 for an exposition of those verses.

[3]F. Delitzsch, *Psalms,* Commentary on the Old Testament, vol. V, translated by James Martin (reprint, Grand Rapids, Michigan: Wm. B. Eerdmans Publishing Co., 1978), p. 288.

[4]Marvin Tate (*Psalms 51–100,* Word Biblical Commentary, vol. 20, eds. David A. Hubbard and Glenn W. Barker [Waco, Texas: Word Books, 1990], p. 204) accepts the first view. Delitzsch (p. 288) supports the second, as does Craigie, but for different reasons (Peter C. Craigie, *Psalms 1–50,* Word Biblical Commentary, vol. 19, eds. David A. Hubbard and Glenn W. Barker [Waco, Texas: Word Books, 1983], p. 314).

69

THE CRY OF AN AGED HEART

Psalm 71:1-24

Psalm 71 allows a greater glimpse into the life of the psalmist than most of the psalms do. Here is an aged saint, struggling against powers beyond his strength. In his old age—a time to be honored and respected—he is ridiculed and slandered (see 71:11). In spite of his years of faithfulness to God, he experiences **troubles, many and bitter** (71:20), and God seems distant (71:12). Yet instead of bitterness or resentment he speaks frequently of God's limitless righteousness (71:2, 15, 16, 19, 24). Through the years he has learned (71:17) that God is faithful, always does what is best, and always vindicates the cause of the just. It is to this God that he goes for relief. He does not wish merely to be rescued; he wants to enjoy unbroken fellowship with his rescuer (71:3, 6, 8, 14, 15, 24). That his praise will be wholehearted is suggested by the repetition of the organs of praise (71:8, 15, 23, 24). His frequent allusions to other psalms show how he maintains his loyalty for God.[1]

He cries for God (71:1-4) to vindicate and protect him, then supports his cry with reasons why God should intervene (71:5-8). He has a long history of reliance upon God, beginning at birth (71: 5-6). He also seeks God's help because he has become **a portent to many** (71:7). The word translated **portent** is sometimes rendered miracle or confirming sign, (see 1 Kings 13:3, 5; Isaiah 8:18; 20:3) but these are hardly appropriate here. In Deuteronomy 28:46, the term is used to describe the symbolic effect of God's judgment on disobedience. At least in the eyes of his enemies, the psalmist has come to symbolize God's displeasure; his suffering is taken as evidence of divine punishment (see Psalm 71:11). **But you are my strong refuge** (71:7b) is the psalmist's answer to this false perception. Even in his difficulty, he continues to praise God all day long (71:8).

Another call for help is sounded (71:9), followed by another reason for God's intervention (71:10-13): Fierce enemies deny him any hope of rescue (71:11c). Nevertheless, the psalmist is convinced God will hear and answer his prayers (71:12-13). When God intervenes (71:14-18), the psalmist will praise God abundantly for His abundant grace (71:14-16)[2] until the psalmist's vindication becomes public knowledge (71:16-18). Such news will answer those who saw him as a symbol of God's punishment (71:7). Of course, this news will only spread if he is spared (71:18).

The psalmist concludes with words of confidence in God's "sky-high" righteousness (71:19-24). Although troubles have come, God will restore him from the place of death, **the depths of the earth** (71:20-21). The honor and comfort he lacked during his time of affliction will be abundantly supplied (71:21).

Again he promises praise for his coming restoration (71:22-24). Stringed instruments as well as the human voice will carry the note of thanks to the **Holy One of Israel** (71:22). This name for God, used often in Isaiah but only three times in the psalms, speaks both of God's perfection and His covenant with Israel. With such a perfect and personal God who has shown His love by rescuing the psalmist, praise can only be continual (71:24). His confidence in the righteousness of God in spite of difficulties, his eager expectation of the fullness of God's blessings in spite of the "reality" which age can bring, and his reliance upon God's Word provide a model for Christians of any age.

ENDNOTES

[1]Verses 1 through 3 are found in 31:1-4. Verses 5, 6, and 17 echo 22:10-11. Verse 12 echoes 22:1, 11, 19 and 40:13. Verse 13 is similar to 35:4, 26 and 109:29. Verse 18 echoes 22:30-31; verse 19 is similar to 36:6; and verse 24 echoes 35:28 (see F. Delitzsch, *Psalms,* Commentary on the Old Testament, vol. V, translated by James Martin [reprint, Grand Rapids, Michigan: Wm. B. Eerdmans Publishing Co., 1978], pp. 290–96; and Derek Kidner, *Psalms 1–72,* Tyndale Old Testament Commentaries, ed. D.J. Wiseman [Downer's Grove, Illinois: InterVarsity Press, 1973], p. 252).

[2]The Hebrew contains a word play between **tell** and **measure** (71:15). Both words are built on the same Hebrew root.

THEY WILL FEAR HIM DAY AND NIGHT, FOREVER

Psalm 72:1-20

W hen good people are afflicted and oppressed, they need a defender, someone who will bring about justice. The one in Israel who, more than any other, was entrusted with this task was the king. Psalm 72 asks God to bestow on the king the capacity to administer justice and then describes the resulting blessings. Because it describes the king in language too large for life, it has come to be interpreted as messianic.

The opening verse entreats God to grant the king the ability to rule with His justice as His representative on earth. The granting of this request would bring the blessings described in 72:2-17. In the kingdom where God's justice is experienced among God's people (72:2), the land will prosper (72:3). There is a play on words in the Hebrew, for the verb can be translated either **bring** or "bear" (as in producing fruit). The mountains will proclaim the prosperity of the God-blessed land by their fruitfulness (72:16) when justice prevails.

A just kingdom is a long-lasting kingdom, according to 72:5-7. The New International Version's choice to follow the Septuagint in verse 5 rather than the Hebrew text is unnecessary, since the Hebrew provides a sensible reading: "They (either the oppressors or all the king's subjects) shall fear you, day and night, forever."[1] Prosperity again is promised (72:6-7) but this time with greater emphasis on the success of the **righteous** person who will **flourish** like a field watered abundantly and when most needed.

219

Not only a long reign but an extensive one is promised to the just king (see 72:8-11). The boundaries described in verse 8 are those predicted for the Messiah in Zechariah 9:10. Prosperity (**tribute** and **gifts**) and security (**bow before him, lick the dust,** and **will serve him**) will accompany this righteous reign (72:9-11). **To the ends of the earth** (72:8) probably refers to southern Spain and the islands off the Mediterranean coast. **Sheba** could refer to a wealthy country in southeast Arabia[2] while the identity of **Seba** is unclear. The specific locations are less important than that this king will rule forever over the world.

The length and breadth of this reign depend, however, on the measure of its justice (see 72:12-14). The **for** which begins verse 12 suggests that those nations which submit in verses 10 and 11 do so, not because they must but because of the winsomeness of this just society. **Rescue** (72:14) translates the Hebrew for "to redeem" or "to act as kinsman." God instituted a system whereby a person's well-being became the responsibility of his or her next of kin. This might require a financial bail-out and the continuation of a person's lineage (see Ruth 1–4) or revenge for bloodshed (see Numbers 35). The king, as God's representative, was to act as kinsman for His people by taking up their cause. What served as a noble aspiration for Israel's kings, became the cause of death for the King of Kings.

May such a king reign long in luxury is the cry of Psalm 72:15-17. Indeed, the king who hears his subjects' cries for help would become the object of their prayers and blessings. His land would be so prosperous the crops would even grow on top of the mountains, and the people (the **fruit** of verse 16) would "blossom out of cities like the herbs of the earth."[3] Verse 17 sounds very much like God's original promise to Abram (see Genesis 12:2-3).

What follows in Psalm 72:18-20 was written by those responsible for gathering the psalms into collections. Verses 18 and 19 form the closing doxology for Book 2, followed by the double **Amen** to be pronounced by those who heard it read. Verse 20 is difficult because there are additional psalms later in the Psalter which are said to come from David. This note originally could have marked the end of an anthology of David's psalms that remained after this collection was incorporated into the Psalter.[4] We serve a King who perfectly fulfills this psalm. Perfect in His judgments and faithful to the needy, His reign is wider than the earth and eternal in its duration. **Praise be to his glorious name forever** (72:19a).

ENDNOTES

[1]F. Delitzsch, *Psalms,* Commentary on the Old Testament, vol. V, translated by James Martin (reprint, Grand Rapids, Michigan: Wm. B. Eerdmans Publishing Co., 1978), p. 301; see also the New International Version footnote. The Septuagint is the Greek translation of the Hebrew Bible prepared around 200 to 300 B.C.

[2]Marvin E. Tate, *Psalms 51–100,* Word Biblical Commentary, vol. 20, eds. David A. Hubbard and Glenn W. Barker (Waco, Texas: Word Books, 1990), p. 221.

[3]Delitzsch, p. 298.

[4]For other explanations, see *Psalms 1–72* by Derek Kidner, Tyndale Old Testament Commentaries, ed. D.J. Wiseman (Downer's Grove, Illinois: InterVarsity Press, 1973), p. 254; and *The Psalms* by A. Cohen, Soncino Books of the Bible, ed. A. Cohen (London: Soncino, 1950), p. 30.

Part Three

BOOK 3

Psalms 73:1–89:52

B ook 3 of Psalms contains only seventeen psalms, all of which are attributed to someone. The first eleven are ascribed to Asaph (Psalms 73–83), the most attributed to any one person in Book 3. Asaph prefers to refer to God as Elohim. The rest of the authors—David (Psalm 86), the Sons of Korah (Psalms 84–85, 87–88), Heman the Ezrahite (Psalm 88), and Ethan the Ezrahite (Psalm 89)—prefer Yahweh. Book 3 ends with the doxology, **Praise be to the LORD forever! Amen and Amen** (Psalm 89:52).

"TILL I ENTERED THE SANCTUARY"[1]

Psalm 73:1-28

It is no accident that Book 3 begins with a psalm whose theme and purpose are similar to those of Psalm 1. At the near midpoint in the Psalter, we are again reminded that the proper posture for praise is righteousness. This psalm is more realistic than Psalm 1, granting that the wicked do prosper, but is no less certain about the outcome. In Psalm 1 the wicked are like chaff; here they are only a bad dream (see 73:20).

The opening note of confidence (73:1) sets the tone for the psalm, emphasizing that the heart of the matter, for God, is the matter of one's **heart,** not one's possessions.[2] While the word **surely** leaves no questions about the psalmist's confidence, the next section (73:2-16) reveals that such confidence was only produced after a time of doubt. The psalmist's struggle—a struggle as wrenching as his eventual confidence is solid— arises from his envy of the wicked (73:2-3). His **feet had almost slipped** (73:2) off God's high road and into the embrace of a practical agnosticism because he saw the **prosperity of the wicked**.

This **prosperity** (73:4-12) included a life so free from struggle that even death came easily. The New International Version alters the Hebrew of verse 4 because a reference to death seems premature (see the NIV footnote). To die without a struggle, however, indicates the extent of their peace, and contrasts with the psalmist's inner wrestling (see 73:2). They not only die without a struggle, they live without any (73:5) and thus are proud and clothed with **violence** (73:6). The New English Bible captures the thought of verse 7: "Their eyes gleam through folds of fat, while vain fancies pass through their minds."

The chief weapons of the wicked are their words. They **scoff,** slander, and **threaten oppression** (73:8). Their boasts are so big they extend to heaven and spread over the earth (73:9). Verse 10 suggests there are many willing to follow the proud, drinking at the fountain of their arrogant boasts. Worst of all, they mock God, suggesting He is too blind to see what they are doing (73:11). Yet, in spite of their effrontery, they continue **carefree,** making money hand over fist (73:12).

This is too much for the psalmist. When he compares the untroubled arrogant and their cheery entourage with his own efforts at godliness, he determines he has been righteous **in vain** (73:13-14). The wicked are without burdens all day long and experience no chastisement, while the psalmist is "under a hail of blows all day long" and is "punished every morning" (NJB). He can say nothing for fear that others would abandon God's way and seek refreshment at the fountain of the arrogant (73:15; see 73:10).

His perspective changes when he enters the Temple (**the sanctuary of God** [73:17]). There he remembers that wickedness has no place with a holy God. The Temple, established within Israel as an act of God's mercy, reminds him of God's love. In God's holy place, he encounters One who does all things perfectly, including the administration of justice.

With this new perspective he can see that the wicked will be suddenly, completely destroyed, leaving no more behind than a bad dream (73:18-20). This perspective enables the psalmist to see the futility of his doubt (73:21-22). He had become **senseless,** like **a brute beast,** unable to draw the right conclusions from the facts. Had he the sense, he would have known that God was always with him, even when everything seemed wrong (73:23). He would have understood that God was supporting and guiding him (73:23-24a) and that God would one day vindicate him.[3]

The wicked set themselves up as the occupants of **heaven** and **earth** (73:9), but the righteous know that only God is in heaven and He is all they need on earth (73:25). Even when prosperity fails and death approaches, his security is solid because it depends on God (73:26). The closing verses sharply contrast the wicked and the righteous (73:27-28; see 1:6). While those far from God will perish, God will be good to those who remain near Him. To remain near Him is to take **refuge** (73:28) in Him. It means to accept Him as one's portion (73:26), being content with God when one has nothing else. To remain near Him is not entirely our doing, for He is holding us by the hand (73:23). His presence may not always be noticeable, but it is always enough.

ENDNOTES

[1]See Psalm 73:17.

[2]**Heart** occurs six times: verses 1, 7, 13, 21, and 26 (twice).

[3]This, rather than the promise of heaven, was originally in the mind of the psalmist.   Later it became clear that God can and may reserve this final vindication until after death.

72

A CRY FROM THE SACRED RUINS

Psalm 74:1-23

P salm 74 mourns the Temple's destruction at the hands of the Babylonians in 586 B.C. The psalmist understood that God had permitted this because of Israel's sin; the psalmist knew why destruction had come. His question was, **How long** (74:10) before God intervened on behalf of His people? Each of the stanzas in the psalm (74:1-9; 10-23) begins with a question, followed by appeals for God's aid.

The Temple ruins testified that God's anger continued to smolder against Israel. Would God relent (see 74:1)? Verses 2 through 9 appeal for God to do just this. The psalmist asks God to **remember** His past dealings with Israel, particularly the Exodus (74:2). Counting on the pathetic sight to stir Him to action, he summoned God to survey the ruins of the sanctuary (see 74:3). The peace of the Temple had been shattered by the roaring of the enemies, a term used elsewhere to refer to the roaring of lions and the sound of thunder. God's holy place had been defamed with the symbols of enemy triumph, **standards as signs** (perhaps military insignias; 74:4).[1] The interior is smashed, the building is consumed in flames, and the place of God's name is desecrated (see 74:5-7). All that can be seen are the enemy's signs; God has left them with none of His own (the same Hebrew word is used in verses 4 and 9). All that is heard is the enemy's roaring; God's voice through the prophets is silent. Worst of all, no one knew how long this would go on.

How long before God tires of this mockery against His name, removes His hand from His garment and, with one blow, destroys His enemies (74:10-11)? In contrast to the bleak picture which constituted the psalmist's first appeal (see 74:4-9), verses 12 through 17 are full of confidence. God is the conquering King who has ruled over Israel **from of old** (74:12). These verses blend myth with history to demonstrate God's sovereign power. Creation (74:16-17) and the Exodus (74:13, 15) are described in the language of Canaanite myth where Baal defeated Taninim (the **monster in the waters**) and **Leviathan,** two creatures belonging to Baal's rival, Yam, the Sea God. Why would the psalmist use myth to express God's sovereignty? "What Baal had claimed in the realm of myth, God had done in the realm of history—and had done for His people, *working salvation.*"[2] To know that while Yahweh did not prevent the devastation of His mountain He yet remained superior certainly would bring confidence to the Israelites. That God's power and concern for His people are beyond question is seen in the multiple use of the pronoun **you** in verses 13 through 17 and in God's control over time (**day**, **night, sun, moon, summer, winter**[3]) and space (**boundaries of the earth** [74:17]).

The recognition of God's power makes the psalmist more confident that He will intervene. God is asked to remember the mocking of the enemy (74:18, 22, 23), the suffering of His people (74:19, 21), the devastation of the land (74:20b) and the promises He had made (74:20a). **The uproar** of the enemy is continually rising (74:23); may it not be long before God himself rises to intervene.

History reveals that God did answer. He restored the Israelites to their homeland beginning in 538 B.C. and allowed them to rebuild the Temple, just as He promised He would (see Ezra 1:1). The increasing confidence they showed in this psalm is honored. Ours is a God who hears and answers prayer.

ENDNOTES

[1]Derek Kidner, *Psalms 73–150,* Tyndale Old Testament Commentaries, ed. D.J. Wiseman (Downer's Grove, Illinois: InterVarsity Press, 1975), p. 266.

[2]Ibid., p. 268; see Marvin E. Tate, *Psalms 51–100,* Word Biblical Commentary, vol. 20, eds. David A. Hubbard and Glenn W. Barker (Waco, Texas: Word Books, 1990), p. 251.

[3]The seasons were understood to be Baal's doing (Tate, p. 252).

73

GOD HAS ARRIVED

Psalm 75:1-10

While we cannot know with certainty when this psalm was originally composed, it appears that the final editors of the Psalter deliberately placed it after Psalm 74. The very question which pervaded Psalm 74 is answered in Psalm 75. God's intervention remains in the future, but on the authority of God himself, it is certain to come.

The opening verse expresses the gratitude of God's people for His **wonderful deeds** (75:1). God's name, subjected to ridicule in Psalm 74, now draws near, bringing with it confidence. As if to demonstrate this drawing near, God himself speaks in 75:2-5, emphatically asserting that He will designate a day for judgment when He will execute justice fairly (see 75:2). Verse 3 may express the paradox of God working out His unshakable will in a tottering world (see Romans 8:28; as in Psalm 75:2, the **I** is emphatic). This would have been a comfort in the pre-exilic days when the psalm probably originated but especially in the days after the fall of Jerusalem. How reassuring to know that God is in charge, holding firmly the pillars of the wildly spinning world.

God speaks again, this time to the proud and wicked (**the** arrogant) whom He compares to oxen (75:4-5). Boasting and rebellion must cease. Instead of raising their **horns** and stretching their **neck,** they should submit themselves to God's yoke.[1] In verses 6 through 8, the psalmist warns his hearers against the dangers of such pride. God alone has the capacity to exalt or humiliate. The end of verse 6 can be rendered **no one . . . from the desert can exalt a man** or "not from the desert of the mountain-heights." Both translations make sense of the passage but the evidence leans toward the rendering preserved by the New International Version.

The praise offered by an unnamed host in verse 1 is now taken up as the psalmist's own: **I will declare . . . I will sing** (75:9; **I** is emphasized in the Hebrew). He will **praise . . . the God of Jacob** (79:9) who had accomplished **wonderful deeds** (see 75:1) of vindication for Israel through their history. The last word in this psalm appears to be God's (see 75:10) who does what, according to 75:6-7, only He can do. God promises to **cut off the horns of all the wicked** but exalt the **horns of the righteous** (75:10). **Horns,** used four times in Psalm 75, often means "strength" (see 1 Samuel 2:1, 10) and derives this sense from the dangerous horns of oxen (see Deuteronomy 33:17; 1 Kings 22:11). It can stand for the person who epitomizes strength—the king (Psalm 89:17; 132:17; 148:14). **Horns** can also be used for the results that strength brings, such as security (Psalm 18:2), dignity (Psalm 112:9), and even an abundance of sons (1 Chronicles 25:5). According to Psalm 75:10, God will cut off the **horns** of the wicked leaving them powerless and humiliated (see Jeremiah 48:25; Lamentations 2:3), but He will exalt the strength and glory of the righteous. God's final word reminds us that "the LORD has a day of vengeance" (Isaiah 34:8); He can be counted on to right our wrongs for us.

ENDNOTE

[1]Derek Kidner, *Psalms 73–150,* Tyndale Old Testament Commentaries, ed. D.J. Wiseman (Downer's Grove, Illinois: InterVarsity Press, 1975), p. 272.

74

A GOD TO BE FEARED

Psalm 76:1-12

P salm 76, like Psalm 46, presents God as a universal ruler with a local address. He has taken up residence in Jerusalem (76:1-3), but His power extends over mighty armies (76:5-9) and **the kings of the earth** (76:12). This celebration of God's dominion may have been written after the miraculous defeat of the Assyrian army during the days of Hezekiah (see 2 Kings 19; Isaiah 37).[1]

The opening verses celebrate God's greatness as revealed in military victory (76:1-3). The battle occurred in Jerusalem (**Salem** or **Zion**) where God had taken up residence. **Tent** and **dwelling place** (76:2) can refer to the Tabernacle or to God's "battle-quarters" (NEB). They can also be translated "lair" and "den"; the psalmist compares God to a lion guarding its home. Verse 3 makes clear that God not only defeated His enemy but also rendered further warfare impossible.

This victory is celebrated in 76:4-12 with God's **majestic** character (76:4) in triumph over His enemies (76:5-6) resulting in reverence (76:7-9), praise (76:10), and devotion (76:11-12). Verse 4a pictures God as glorious **light,** but verse 4b is difficult to translate. The New International Version suggests a comparison of God's majesty to **mountains rich with game,** that is unspoiled abundance. Others see an allusion to God, the lion, devouring his prey (see the NJPS). Still others follow the Septuagint and describe God as "more majestic than the everlasting mountains" (RSV).

Verses 5 and 6 take us on a tour of the battlefield which provides proof of God's majesty. The mighty **warriors** who invaded the land seeking spoils have themselves been **plundered.** They sleep the sleep of death, unable any longer to lift a finger in their own defense. Even the mighty weapons of warfare lie ruined. What was the means whereby God

233

wrought this mighty destruction? His word of **rebuke,** capable of rolling back the sea (see 2 Samuel 22:16) and shaking heaven (see Job 26:11), has silenced the enemy.

The effects of this victory are felt around the world (see Psalm 76:7-12). God has proven that He **alone** (76:7a) should **be feared** rather than the attacking armies (the **neighboring lands** [76:11]), or the gods of those nations. Though His anger is terrible (76:7b), His judgment restores a stable and secure society where the **afflicted** find mercy (76:8-9). The New International Version's footnote on this verse may translate verse 10 best:

> Surely the wrath of men brings you praise,
> and with the remainder of wrath you arm yourself (see Isaiah 59:17).

Human anger brought the enemy army against Judah, allowing God to show His power. The victory wrought by this power prompts praise.

The fear of God, especially a God capable of working good through both divine and human anger (see Psalm 76:7-10), should produce loyal allegiance—**Make vows to the LORD your God and fulfill them**—the theme of the remaining verses (76:11-12). Israel's dependence upon God should be demonstrated by making and fulfilling **vows** (76:11a). Other countries should show their fidelity with tribute (76:11b; see 2 Chronicles 32:23) for God's majesty extends beyond Jerusalem over all **the kings of the earth** (Ps. 76:12). It extends even to our own time and place, summoning us to kneel before Him, and Him alone.

ENDNOTE

[1]The Septuagint mentions the Assyrians in the title; see *Psalms* by F. Delitzsch (Commentary on the Old Testament, vol. V, translated by James Martin [reprint, Grand Rapids, Michigan: Wm. B. Eerdmans Publishing Co., 1978], p. 343) for other similarities between this episode and Psalm 76.

75

CRY FROM THE DARK VALLEY

Psalm 77:1-20

P salm 77 portrays the psalmist's agonized search for God. Ironically, although the language is personal (**I** and **my**) and the tone quite intimate, the problem which lies behind this psalm is national. The first half of the psalm, describing the psalmist's struggle (see 77:1-9), begins with him crying out to God (see 77:1-4). Whether verse 2 refers to outstretched hands (NIV), weeping eyes (Tanakh/NJPS) or perspiring body (NEB), the psalmist pours out his heart to God in continual prayer. This is too serious a concern to be soothed by platitudes; this requires divine intervention.

Yet God does not answer. This silence, incubated in the agony of his soul, keeps the psalmist from even remembering God without groaning and growing still fainter (see 77:3). Not only is God silent, He appears to be worsening matters by depriving the psalmist of sleep and the ability to speak (see 77:4).

Finding no success in prayer, the psalmist turns to reflecting on the old days when, even in his struggles, God gave him **songs in the night** (see 42:8). But now there is no song, only long sleepless nights praying to a God who does not answer. Again he **mused** (77:6) on God but with no greater success than before (see 77:3). In fact, while earlier thoughts had left him speechless (see 77:4), now they prompt him to question.

The six questions in 77:7-9 are not addressed to God but reflect the troubled, even despairing, meditations of the psalmist who wonders if the Lord has rejected His people forever. Perhaps it was the Babylonian exile, or the breakup of Solomon's kingdom into Israel and Judah, or the fall of the northern kingdom to Assyria in 722 B.C. that caused the psalmist to wonder if God's **unfailing love** *(chesed)* had failed (77:8).[1]

Most commentators regard verse 10 as the key verse, but for different reasons depending in part on how they translate **appeal** and **years.** These would literally be "my sickness" and "years," a seemingly incompatible combination. The New International Version must slightly alter the first word to get **appeal** but leaves us with a line that makes sense. Some versions alter the second word to "change" and produce translations like "What hurts me most is this—that God is no longer powerful" (TEV). Commentator F. Delitzsch retains both words with some success: "My decree of affliction is this, the years of the right hand of the Most High."[2] That is, God has determined that he must suffer but not forever.

The key element of verse 10 is the final clause, **the right hand of the Most High.** Remembering this turns the psalm from lament to praise. This phrase is found three times in the song which the Israelites sang to celebrate the victory over the Egyptians at the Red Sea. Twice in Exodus 15:6 and once in 15:12, God's right hand is said to have brought the victory. That later Israelites continued to view the Exodus as the work of God's **right hand** is evident from its frequent mention in the psalms in this and related contexts (see 17:7; 20:6; 44:3; 60:5; 78:54).

Once again the psalmist **meditates** (77:12; translated **muse** in 77:3, 6), this time on God's **miracles** and **works,** and once again it is *to* God (77:11b) rather than *about* Him. His musings reveal that God's ways are **holy**—that is, perfect (77:13-14). There is no God like Him for He is "the God doing miracles" (a literal translation of verse 14a).

For the Israelites, the greatest demonstration of God's perfect power was when He became the Redeemer for His kinsmen (**your people** [77:15]). Again the Exodus becomes the focus of the psalmist's meditation (see 77:15-20). The waters, personified, fled in agony from the sight of God. A ferocious thunderstorm, complete with rain, thunder, lightning and either wind or the rumbling of the thunder, burst on the scene (see 77:17-18). God, like a shepherd, then led His people **through the mighty waters . . . by the hand of Moses and Aaron** (77:19-20). His footsteps, though invisible, were very real. Although verse 20 appears almost anticlimactic, it is a reminder that this mighty miracle was done so that God could lead His flock to safety.

The psalm, lacking an appeal for God to use His great power on behalf of the psalmist, testifies to quiet trust in the face of unresolved difficulty. This trust may have resulted from seeing God's power in history and nature (77:15-18) and from the recognition that God's ways, while invisible (77:19), are still perfect (77:13). The psalmist's questions (77:7-9) appear to be answered by the awareness that God sometimes leads His flock through deep valleys (77:19-20). Recognizing the power of God, the inscrutability of His ways and the constancy of His love can lead us through our valleys as well.

ENDNOTES

[1]Cohen suggests the first (A. Cohen, *The Psalms,* Soncino Books of the Bible, ed. A. Cohen [London: Soncino, 1950], p. 246) and Delitzsch the second (F. Delitzsch, *Psalms,* Commentary on the Old Testament, vol. V, translated by James Martin [reprint, Grand Rapids, Michigan: Wm. B. Eerdmans Publishing Co., 1978], p. 350), but the third is also possible and would account for the specific mention of northern tribes in Psalm 77:15.

[2]See *Psalms* by F. Delitzsch, Commentary on the Old Testament, vol. V, translated by James Martin (reprint, Grand Rapids, Michigan: Wm. B. Eerdmans Publishing Co., 1978).

A LESSON FROM THE PAST

Psalm 78:1-72

B ible commentator Derek Kidner suggests subtitling this psalm
"From Zoan to Zion" since it describes Israel's journey from
Egyptian slavery to life in the Promised Land.[1] For the Jews,
history was much more than the story of the past; it offered guidance for
the future.[2] Relating these episodes warned Israel against unfaithfulness
and revealed the faithfulness of God.

The didactic function of the psalm is demonstrated in the summons to
hear **teaching** (*torah;* 78:1-4). This word can refer to the Law of Moses
(see 78:5) or prophetic preaching, but here it means the insightful
retelling of Israel's history. It is further qualified by the terms **parables**
and **hidden things** (78:2; see 49:4). More than the bare recitation of
facts, this psalm has a practical goal (affecting the future choices of God's
people) and a divine source (which reveals what may not be obvious).

The psalmist begins with the giving of the Law (see 78:5-8) since
God's commands were the standard against which Israel was judged.
This Law was to have passed from parent to children in an unbroken
exchange so that Israel would **trust . . . not forget his deeds** and **keep
his commands** (78:7). In this way, Israel would not be **a stubborn and
rebellious generation** (78:8), the same adjectives used in Deuteronomy
21:18 to describe an unmanageable son. The following verses show,
however, that Israel became just such a son.

The first detailed retelling of Israel's unfaithfulness (see Psalm 78:9-
16) begins with a puzzling verse. **The men of Ephraim** is probably
used in verse 9 for all Israel or the northern tribes in particular who,
although well-prepared to do so, failed to follow God (see 78:67). The
Israelites did the opposite of what God had required (see 78:7). Instead

239

of trusting God, they turned back, **refused to live by his law,** and **forgot what he had done** (78:10-11), specifically that God had delivered them from slavery and led them through the wilderness (78:12-16). **Zoan** is the city of Tanis located in the northeastern portion of the Nile Delta at or near the city of Ramses.[3]

The psalm continues to document the ongoing pattern of Israel's rebellion and God's responses. God answered their complaints (78:17-20) with discipline (78:21-22, 30-31) but also with gracious provision (78:23-29). Because they were unfaithful to His covenant, they again came under God's judgment and ended their days in **futility** (literally, "breath"; 78:32-37). There is mercy even in judgment, however, for God remembered they were only **a passing breeze** and showed compassion (78:38-39).

Israel failed because of a short memory. It forgot God's power, even its greatest demonstrations: deliverance from Egypt (78:42-51), guidance through the wilderness (78:52-54), and the conquest of Canaan (78:55). From Egypt, God redeemed His people (see 77:15) using ten plagues, six or seven of which are explicitly mentioned (see 78:44-48), with the rest implied in 78:49. God led His flock through the wilderness, drove the Canaanites from Palestine, and **settled the tribes of Israel in their homes** (78:55).

Once in the land of Canaan, however, Israel's forgetfulness sent it drifting into idolatry (see 78:56-58) which God punished by rejection (see 78:59-64). The rejection may be described in 1 Samuel 4, where God **abandoned** His appointed meeting place (Ps. 78:60) and **the ark,** which represented His presence (78:61). The **priests** (78:64) are probably Hophni and Phinehas, Eli's sons, while the widow who could not mourn was Phinehas's wife. From the capture of the ark the psalm moves quickly to God's choice of Judah, Jerusalem and David (see 78:65-72). This transition reflects a main theme of 1 and 2 Samuel. There the departure of God's glory (symbolized by the loss of the ark) is resolved by the return of that glory when David brought the ark to Jerusalem (see 2 Samuel 6).

When **the Lord awoke** (Ps. 78:65)—a poetic description for the end of God's inactivity on Israel's behalf—He brought victory and **chose the tribe of Judah** (78:68-69) rather than **Ephraim**—that is, the Northern Kingdom of Israel (78:67). He chose Jerusalem rather than Shiloh for His dwelling place. He chose **David** as king rather than other candidates, including Joshua and Samuel, both Ephraimites. The psalm ends with God's flock led by worthy shepherds (see Psalm 77).

Although Israel's history revealed a tragic story of past mistakes, it also reveals a God who is full of mercy and quick to forgive. Our pasts may be full of mistakes, but God's grace is abundant.

ENDNOTES

[1]Derek Kidner, *Psalms 73–150,* Tyndale Old Testament Commentaries, ed. D.J. Wiseman (Downer's Grove, Illinois: InterVarsity Press, 1975), p. 280.

[2]A. Cohen, *The Psalms,* Soncino Books of the Bible, ed. A. Cohen (London: Soncino, 1950), p. 250.

[3]James M. Weinstein, "Zoan," *Harper's Bible Dictionary,* gen. ed. Paul J. Achtemeier (San Francisco: Harper, 1985), pp. 1166–67.

77

A CRY OF FAITH FROM THE ASHES

Psalm 79:1-13

The agony, bewilderment, and indignation which resulted from Babylon's destruction of Jerusalem in 586 B.C. leave the reader in respectful silence. Just as powerful is the evidence of Israel's faith. The loss of king, capital, Temple, and land raised questions about that nation's relationship with God. Did this mean the end of their special status? Had God abandoned them forever? Even in the face of such questions, they still prayed for God's help with humble confidence in the love of God.

The psalm begins by describing the process of devastation from invasion, to defilement of the Temple, to the destruction of Jerusalem, to the wholesale slaughter and enduring scorn (see 79:1-4). Twice in these verses the dead are described as unburied, a tragic fate revealing a society without the capacity to exercise the merest decency.[1] Along with the theme of utter devastation, these verses make it clear that God also had become the victim. It had been His **inheritance** and His **holy temple;** these were His **servants** and His **saints** (79:1-2).

Such a scene raises the question: **How long, O LORD? Will you be angry forever?** (79:5). As with Psalm 74, Israel did not wonder why God had permitted such a tragedy, but whether His anger was permanent. The ashes of Jerusalem may have ceased to smolder, but would God's jealous anger never cool? No divine reply is given, but the psalmist's next words reveal his confidence that God had not forsaken His people.

In this confidence, the psalmist calls upon God to punish the attackers: **Pour out your wrath on the nations** (79:6-7; repeated almost exactly in Jeremiah 10:25).[2] The phrases **that do not acknowledge you . . . that do not call on your name** clarify that these are God's enemies and not merely Israel's. Those who had left the dead to be devoured by birds and animals (79:2) are devouring Jacob themselves (79:7), further intensifying their guilt and making punishment more necessary. God should **pour out** His wrath (79:6) on those who had **poured out** (Israel's) **blood like water** (79:3).

The psalmist summons God to show mercy to Israel and provides Him with several reasons to do so (79:8-13). The Hebrew which lies behind **the sins of the fathers** (79:8) can also be translated "former sins." Both fit the context, but the New International Version echoes similar language in Lamentations 5:7. The psalmist appeals for fairness; must his generation bear the guilt of its fathers?

He next appeals to **the glory of your name** (Ps. 79:9-10). Since God's reputation had suffered as a result of this disaster, He should "set the record straight" by vindicating the righteous. As well, God's name implied His special relationship with Israel. To act for His name's sake meant reaffirming that relationship by vindicating Israel (see 79:10). To intervene while they are still around to see it (**before our eyes**) would answer the enemy's taunting question, **Where is their God?** (79:10).

In verse 11, the psalmist seeks to arouse God's pity by referring to those imprisoned and **condemned to die**. The latter phrase is literally "sons of death" and could refer either to those about to die (as the NIV) or to those suffering the "living death of exile."[3] Again appeal is made to God's reputation (79:12) which had been slandered by the neighboring nations (79:4) who, for this reason, deserve the full measure of punishment (**seven times**). If God answers their prayer, Israel will respond with eternal praise (79:13), for God's flock (77:20; 78:70-72) had been called to this very task. The promise of praise was not a bribe but a reminder that, once vindicated, Israel could return to this God-given mission.

In the Hebrew, the words **your praise** bring this psalm to an end. What a cry of faith from the ashes! If the time ever comes when we must stand amid the ashes of all that gives life meaning, may our prayers be full of such faith and praise.

ENDNOTES

[1]Derek Kidner, *Psalms 73–150,* Tyndale Old Testament Commentaries, ed. D.J. Wiseman (Downer's Grove, Illinois: InterVarsity Press, 1975), p. 287. "In death, nothing was worse than to lie exposed on the field . . . a prey to animals" (Othmar Keel, *The Symbolism of the Biblical World: Ancient Near Eastern*

Iconography and the Book of Psalms, translated by Timothy J. Hallett [New York: Seabury Press, 1978], p. 66).

[2]This psalm seems to borrow heavily from other Old Testament passages; see *Psalms 51–100* by Marvin E. Tate, Word Biblical Commentary, vol. 20, eds. David A. Hubbard and Glenn W. Barker (Waco, Texas: Word Books, 1990), pp. 299–300.

[3]A. Cohen, *The Psalms,* Soncino Books of the Bible, ed. A. Cohen (London: Soncino, 1950), p. 262.

78

"RESTORE US, O GOD"[1]

Psalm 80:1-19

D istress had struck the nation of Israel and Psalm 80 is its cry for help. The particulars of the difficulty are uncertain. The diet of **tears** (80:5) and the metaphor of **the vine** (80:8-16) hint at a natural disaster such as a drought. It could instead have been military defeat by a strong army; early interpreters suggest an attack by Assyria in the eighth century B.C.[2]

The opening stanza, summoning God's attention (80:1-2), describes God as **Shepherd of Israel** whom he leads **like a flock** (a metaphor found in the previous three psalms). This close, intimate relationship is balanced by the reference to God as the One who sits **enthroned between the cherubim** (80:1), that is, the ark of the covenant. The mention of **Joseph . . . Ephraim, Benjamin and Manasseh** may suggest this prayer was originally written by or about the Northern Kingdom, Israel. This particular triad (**Ephraim, Benjamin, and Manasseh**) could have been mentioned because these were the tribes instructed to follow the ark when it moved in the wilderness (see Numbers 2:17-24; also Psalm 80:1).[3]

Psalm 80:3 serves as a refrain which appears two other times (see 80:7, 19) with slight variation. The heart of this prayer is for God's **face**—representing His gracious favor—**to shine** on His people (see 67:1; Numbers 6:25) and produce restoration and salvation. In the words of a Gaelic proverb, "During distress God comes: and when he comes it is no more distress."[4]

Having secured God's attention (see Psalm 80:1-2), the next stanza asks **how long** before God again shows His favor. His people have prayed but have received no answer. Divine silence could not be due to weakness in God, for He is the **LORD God Almighty.** Therefore, it must be God's smoldering **anger** which prevents their prayers from being heard (see Lamentations 3:44). God's silence subjected Israel to a diet of **tears** (Ps. 80:5), which implies deep sorrow and a bitter existence, and to the scorn of her neighbors (see 79:4). The chorus reappears in 80:7 with the addition of the title, **Almighty** which suggests increased confidence in God and which prepares the way for the verses which follow.

God's past relationship with Israel, described by the metaphor of God as farmer and His people as the **vine,** is the theme of verses 8 through 13. This passage emphasizes God's efforts: He secured the vine, cleared a place, planted it, and cultivated the soil to insure its growth. The vine quickly grew to fill the land, to cover the mountains, to shade the mighty cedars of Lebanon, and to stretch out in every direction. This great growth meant usefulness (**shade**) and fruitfulness.

God's earlier activity on behalf of this vine contrasts sharply with His breaking down the vineyard wall (see 80:12). The vine's vast size has dwindled, and its fruitfulness feeds only wild **boars** and **creatures of the field** (80:13). What a paradox that animals devour this abundance while Israel consumes only **tears by the bowlful** (80:5)!

Verses 14 and 15 are not another occurrence of the refrain, but are similar enough to suggest that the author consciously develops its themes. While there is no explicit reference to salvation, the verses which follow describe Israel's plight and summon God's help. Because the vine has been cut down and burned at "the rebuke of God's face" (a literal translation; see 80:16), it must be His hand which restores it (80:17). The nation—**son of man** (80:17)—planted by God's **right hand** now needs God's hand to "rest upon it," implying both honor and protection. When again restored to the status of most favored nation, turning back would be unthinkable (see 80:18).

The psalm closes with the refrain, this time addressed to the LORD **God Almighty,** stressing Israel's confidence in God (80:19). In their knowledge of God as Shepherd and the One **enthroned between the cherubim** (80:1), they found the faith to call on Him, even when their difficulties were from His hand. He who remains the Shepherd and King of His people can still be found faithful.

ENDNOTES

[1]Psalm 80:3a; see 80:4, 7, 19.

[2]There is nothing in the psalm to contradict the Septuagint's mention of

Assyria in the title (Marvin E. Tate, *Psalms 51–100,* Word Biblical Commentary, vol. 20, eds. David A. Hubbard and Glenn W. Barker [Waco, Texas: Word Books, 1990], p. 304; F. Delitzsch, *Psalms,* Commentary on the Old Testament, vol. V, translated by James Martin [reprint, Grand Rapids, Michigan: Wm. B. Eerdmans Publishing Co., 1978], p. 383).

[3]John J.S. Perowne, *The Book of Psalms,* 2 vols. (Andover, Massachusetts: Warren F. Draper, 1885), p. 84.

[4]As quoted in *The Treasury of David* by C.H. Spurgeon, vol. 4 (New York: Funk and Wagnalls, 1882), p. 25.

79

CELEBRATION AND CONSECRATION

Psalm 81:1-16

Just as we have certain hymns especially appropriate to specific holidays, this psalm seems to have been written for the Feast of Tabernacles. One of the three festivals at which all Jewish men were to be present in Jerusalem, it was celebrated from the fifteenth to the twenty-second of the seventh month (roughly mid-September to mid-October). It was a joyous holiday which commemorated Israel's journey through the wilderness and celebrated the just-completed harvest; the common element was God's abundant provision. As well, the law was to be read at this festival every seven years (see Deuteronomy 31:10-13).[1]

Appropriate to this festive setting, the psalm begins with a call to celebrate God's blessings on Israel (see Psalm 81:1-5). Songs and shouts were to mingle with the beat of the tambourine and music of the stringed instruments. The shofar or **ram's horn** was used for signaling in battle or, as here, to announce times of worship. **New Moon** (81:3) refers to the seventh month, and full moon to the opening day of the Feast.[2]

After the people drew near, God addressed His congregation (see 81:5c-16); very likely, these words were spoken by a priest or prophet as God's representative. **Where we heard a language we did not understand** (81:5c) has been variously interpreted. Some have suggested that the unknown language is Egyptian; others that it is God's voice, alluding to His resumption of communication with Israel through Moses.[3] Israel is admitting her reluctance to listen in the past (see 81:8, 11, 13)—as if God spoke in a foreign tongue—but is promising to listen now.[4]

The essence of God's sermon is "obey me." That He deserves their obedience is proven by His faithfulness in the Exodus (see 81:6-7) when

He lifted the basket of oppression from their shoulders. **Basket** carrying in the ancient Near East was "the most tedious, strenuous, and common form of labor. Mud was hauled in baskets; finished bricks were carried in baskets." This metaphor could also be used to describe service to one's god; even kings could be pictured this way.[5] Perhaps God is pointing out that He is more willing to liberate His people and serve them (see 81:10, 16) than to be served by them.

That God has clearly shown them how to obey Him is evident from verses 8 and 9, which refer to the giving of the Law. This was given not for Israel's salvation, but to show them how to live as God's people. It was essential, then, that their loyalties be undivided: **You shall have no foreign god among you** (81:9). So that there could be no possibility for confusion, God made himself clearly known to them: "I, Yahweh, am your God" (see 81:10). With such a rescuing and providing God, what need had they for another? At this festival celebrating God's provision, He reminds them that all they must do is **open wide your mouth** in humble dependence upon Him, and He **will fill it.**

In spite of all God had done to make obedience easy, Israel failed to obey. God said,

> **So I gave them over to their stubborn hearts**
> **to follow their own devices** (81:12).

The Jewish rabbis expressed the thought, "All is in the hands of God except the fear of God,"[6] while Paul elaborates on the psalmist's words in Romans 1.

"Giving them up" was not God's last word on the subject. Seeking to woo back His people, He makes further offers (see Psalm 81:13-16). If they will obey, He will defeat their enemies "at one stroke" (81:14 [NJB]). He promises to provide for their needs in the most beneficent manner (see 81:16). Not only will He give wheat of the finest quality, but He will even give "honey from the rock" (richest food from least likely places).[7]

God longs for the fellowship of His people now as He did then. His objective is not what we can bring to Him, however, but what He can do for us. He would rather serve us than be served by us (see 81:16). The Cross proved that.

ENDNOTES

[1]This feast is sometimes called Sukkot (literally "booths"), in which the celebrants were to reside during the Feast to commemorate their travels in the wilderness (see Leviticus 23:34-43; Numbers 29:12-39; D. Freeman, "Tabernacles, Feast of," *New Bible Dictionary,* rev. ed. [Wheaton, Illinois: Tyndale House Publishers, 1982], p. 1161).

[2]Derek Kidner, *Psalms 73–150,* Tyndale Old Testament Commentaries, ed. D.J. Wiseman (Downer's Grove, Illinois: InterVarsity Press, 1975), p. 293.

[3]A.F. Kirkpatrick, *The Book of Psalms,* The Cambridge Bible for Schools and Colleges, ed. A.F. Kirkpatrick (1902; reprint, Cambridge: Cambridge University Press, 1910), p. 491; see the New Jerusalem Bible:

> I heard a voice unknown to me,
> "I freed his shoulder from the burden." . . .

[4]M.D. Goulder, *The Psalms of the Sons of Korah,* Journal of the Study of the Old Testament, supplement 20 (Sheffield: JSOT Press, 1982), p. 111, as cited by Marvin E. Tate, *Psalms 51–100,* Word Biblical Commentary, vol. 20, eds. David A. Hubbard and Glenn W. Barker (Waco, Texas: Word Books, 1990), p. 319; see Job 42:3, 5.

[5]Othmar Keel, *The Symbolism of the Biblical World: Ancient Near Eastern Iconography and the Book of Psalms,* translated by Timothy J. Hallett (New York: Seabury Press, 1978), pp. 271–72.

[6]A. Cohen, *The Psalms,* Soncino Books of the Bible, ed. A. Cohen (London: Soncino, 1950), p. 269.

[7]Tate, p. 326; see Deuteronomy 32:13-14.

80

JUDGE OF THE JUDGES

Psalm 82:1-8

P salm 82 provides another example of the appeals for justice heard frequently in the psalms, but with a difference. The setting of this psalm is the court where God gathers those appointed to judge and scolds them for failing to judge justly.

The scene opens with God presiding (literally, standing to decide a significant matter) in the **great assembly** (82:1), not for advice but to judge the judges. Who are these **"gods"** to whom God speaks? It is not likely that they are angels or demons, for they die like humans (see 82:7). They are probably humans entrusted by God with the solemn duty of providing justice on the earth. They can be called "gods" (see Exodus 21:6; 22:8; 1 Samuel 2:25) because they act as His representatives. With this title, the psalmist portrays human judges in all the grandeur of their office.[1]

God's speech to these judges (see Psalm 82:2-7) begins with a question: **How long** will you judge unjustly? The defenseless—the weak, fatherless, poor, oppressed, and needy—were being tyrannized by the wicked (see 82:3-4). Instead of being chastised for such oppression, the wicked were given special treatment (see 82:2). These judges cannot acknowledge or understand God's passion for justice, because they are blinded by corruption (see Exodus 23:8). While some might minimize the seriousness of injustice, God says it rocks the earth to its very foundation (see Psalm 82:5b).

God himself (**I** is emphatic in 82:6) had honored them with the power to judge, but their faithlessness brought dishonor. Although appointed as **"gods"** and **sons of the Most High** (82:6), they will die because their actions do not reflect their namesake and Heavenly Father. Since the psalmist has described these judges in grand terms, death may be a poetic description of how far they have fallen, or it may refer to execution as payment for allowing the innocent to be condemned.[2]

The psalm has shown that looking for justice from any source will eventually bring disappointment. There is only one exception: The One who controls all the nations is capable of judging justly. It is to this One that the psalmist finally turns for justice.

In a world so full of injustice, we must remember that God will vindicate His own. While His justice is not always immediate, someday it will be perfectly realized. He who built this world on the foundations of justice (82:5c) cannot do less.

ENDNOTES

[1] H. Niehr, "Gotter oder Menschen—eine falsche Alternative, Bemerkungen zu Psalm 82," *Zeitschrift fur die alttestamentliche Wissenschaft,* vol. 99 (1987), pp. 94–98, as cited by Marvin E. Tate, *Psalms 51–100,* Word Biblical Commentary, vol. 20, eds. David A. Hubbard and Glenn W. Barker (Waco, Texas: Word Books, 1990), p. 341.

[2] A. Cohen, *The Psalms,* Soncino Books of the Bible, ed. A. Cohen (London: Soncino, 1950), p. 271.

81

SURROUNDED, YET SECURE

Psalm 83:1-18

Israel was surrounded by enemies on every side. Throughout its history, nations to the north, south, east and west sought its overthrow and joined in league against it. Such a time drew forth the national lament recorded in Psalm 83. While no known historical incident directly corresponds to the array of enemies in 83:6-8, some have suggested this psalm originated when a similar confederation converged on King Jehoshaphat (see 2 Chronicles 20).[1]

The psalmist begins with an ardent cry for help (Psalm 83:1), pleading with God to intercede on Israel's behalf. God must speak up for His people because a coalition of nations is devising their destruction (83:2-8). The psalmist sees them gather and **rear their heads** in pride (83:2); he learns of their plot to utterly destroy Israel (83:3-4). God must act because the object of their animosity is His cherished treasure (83:3).

Verses 5 through 8 reveal more of this coalition. With one heart, they have made a formal **alliance** indicating their determination. The choice of wording—**form an alliance** (literally, "cut a covenant")—may be intended to remind God of His covenant with Israel. The list of nations here is striking for at least two reasons. First, it includes many nations who have kinship ties with Israel. Moab and Ammon are descendants of Abraham's nephew, Lot. Ishmaelites trace their lineage back to the half-brother of Isaac and the Hagrites may be descendants of Hagar, Ishmael's mother.[2] Esau is said to be the ancestor of Edom and the Amalekites. Few fights are as bloody as those between relatives.

What is also noteworthy is that this list describes the enemy on every border, beginning on the east and moving north, then Amalek in the

South, Philistia and Tyre on the west and Assyria in the north. Since no coalition this extensive was known to come against Israel, and since there are ten nations mentioned—a number symbolizing perfection—this list may signify the absolute isolation and desperate need of God's people.[3]

For this reason, God is called upon to destroy them (see 83:9-18). Two incidents from Israel's history are recalled as illustrations of God's power (see 9-12): Gideon's defeat of the Midianites (Judges 6-8) and Deborah's defeat of the Canaanites (Judges 4–5). Faith was to be found by looking back at God's work in the past. In both examples, God used weak instruments to accomplish great victories, a comforting fact to the beleaguered Israelites.[4] Because they sought to take God's pastureland, the psalmist asks that their corpses lie like dung on the earth.[5]

The anticipated victory is described using vivid natural metaphors: May they be blown away like the wind blows **tumbleweed** and **chaff** (Ps. 83:13), pictures of what is lightweight and dispensable. So that they trouble Israel no more, let them be pursued and consumed by God's **tempest,** a powerful and destructive thunderstorm (83:14-15).

What is the ultimate object for which the psalmist prays? It is not merely the defeat of the enemies nor is it ultimately security for Israel. The psalmist's goal is God's glory which cannot be fully realized until the enemy is defeated. At this time people will **seek God's name** (83:16)—that is, turn their loyalty to Him. Verse 18 elaborates, emphasizing the unique character of God and His absolute dominion over the earth. As for Israel, so for us: We may be surrounded by the enemy, but above us is the Most High God.

ENDNOTES

[1]See *The Psalms* by A. Cohen, Soncino Books of the Bible, ed. A. Cohen (London: Soncino, 1950), p. 272; F. Delitzsch (*Psalms,* Commentary on the Old Testament, vol. V, translated by James Martin [reprint, Grand Rapids, Michigan: Wm. B. Eerdmans Publishing Co., 1978], pp. 407–8) mentions that it was an Asaphite who interposed in Jehoshaphat's crisis.

[2]Marvin E. Tate, *Psalms 51–100,* Word Biblical Commentary, vol. 20, eds. David A. Hubbard and Glenn W. Barker (Waco, Texas: Word Books, 1990), p. 344. R.P. Gordon ("Hagrites," *New Bible Dictionary,* rev. ed. [Wheaton, Illinois: Tyndale House Publishers, 1982], p. 449) considers this improbable, suggesting instead that they are an Aramean tribe. If so, this too provides a family connection since Abraham was an Aramean. The Hagrites are mentioned in 1 Chronicles 5:10, 19-20; 11:38; 27:31 and were probably located east of the Jordan River.

[3]Derek Kidner, *Psalms 73–150,* Tyndale Old Testament Commentaries, ed. D.J. Wiseman (Downer's Grove, Illinois: InterVarsity Press, 1975), p. 300; Tate, p. 345. Gebal may be Byblos, near Tyre (see the New International Version footnote on this verse) but is more likely a city south of the Dead Sea (Kidner, p. 301; Delitzsch, p. 409; Tate, p. 344).

[4]Kidner, p. 301.

[5]Cohen, p. 273.

82

"HOW LOVELY IS YOUR DWELLING PLACE"[1]

Psalm 84:1-12

To the Old Testament believer, there was no place more special than the Temple. It was the embodiment of Jewish religious expression, for in the midst of this nation, God had taken up residence. To be able to visit Him there was a sacred duty and high privilege. Psalm 84, which celebrates the Temple as the visible expression of the presence of God, probably originated in connection with the Feast of Tabernacles, one of the three sacred festivals which all Jewish men were required to attend.[2] **Blessed** appears three times (84:4-5, 12); each use describes a larger circle where God's blessings fall: first, on those who dwell in God's house, second, on those who go there, and third, on all who trust in God.

The opening stanza extols the greatness of the sacred sight (84:1-4). **Lovely** (84:1) might be better translated "beloved"[3] which captures the psalmist's feelings toward the **dwelling place** of Yahweh Almighty, feelings he continues to express in verse 2. He deeply longs to be there and sings for joy (not **cry out** as translated by the New International Version) at the thought of fellowship with the **living God** (84:2). God's house is such a blessed place that even creation longs to be near Him there (84:3). The sight of sparrows fluttering, swallows flitting, and birds nesting near the sacred altars underscored the peace and security the Temple represented. Blessed are those who make their home in God's house (84:4)!

Because the Temple is such a blessed place, those who journey from their homes to take "refuge" (NEB) in its courts (84:5-9) are also blessed.

Even the ground on which the pilgrims travel is enriched by their footsteps (84:6). The NIV treats the **Valley of Baca** as a location, although unknown. It might instead refer to a place of weeping or to an arid location.[4] A combination of the latter two would suggest that the pilgrims can turn a dry, sorrowful place into fertile ground for rejoicing. There seems to be another word play in the last line of verse 6, for the Hebrew words for blessings and **pools** are almost identical (see the NIV note on this verse). The true source for blessings is evident in that the pilgrims uncover the **springs,** but it is God who sends the rain. Their journey, so blessed by God, is effortless, for the pilgrims proceed with ever-increasing strength (**strength to strength** [84:7]).

Some consider the **prayer** for the king in verses 8 and 9 to interrupt the flow of the psalm, but a prayer for the king's blessing would be very fitting here.[5] He is God's representative on earth (see 84:12) and his well-being directly affects the health of the nation.

From verses 10 through 12, it would appear that the pilgrims have arrived at their destination and are filled with praise for God's house. **One day** here is better than many anywhere else; to be a mere **doorkeeper** here is better than being a guest of honor among **the wicked** (84:10). This place is special primarily because God is here (84:11). The One who gave the rain (84:6) here provides the warmth and light of the **sun.** He shelters like a **shield,** brings "grace and glory" (Tanakh/NJPS), and grants every good thing to the pure in heart. The psalm concludes with a final word of blessing to the one who **trusts in** God. Faith is not a New Testament invention; God has always been accessible only through this door.

Christians do not have a Temple—we are the Temple, especially when we gather for worship (see 1 Corinthians 3:16). Our ardor for this fellowship—with God and with each other—should be no less than the Israelites for their Temple.

ENDNOTES

[1]Psalm 84:1a.

[2]See the reference to autumn rains in 84:6, which began shortly after (by Th. Booij, "Psalm LXXXIV, A Prayer of the Anointed," *Vetus Testamentum*, vol. XLIV (1994), pp. 433–41).

[3]Booij, p. 437.

[4]Ibid., p. 439; A. Cohen, *The Psalms,* Soncino Books of the Bible, ed. A. Cohen (London: Soncino, 1950), p. 276.

[5]Booij, p. 441.

83

A LAND AT PEACE

Psalm 85:1-13

A bout 50 years after Jerusalem's fall in 586 B.C., the king of Persia permitted the exiles to return home. With great joy and optimism they made the journey and began to rebuild. Before long, however, they realized that Israel would not regain its former greatness and their optimism faded (see Ezra 3:11-12). It was most likely during this time of disillusionment that Psalm 85 was written. Based on God's past faithfulness to Israel (see 85:1-3), the psalmist appeals to God for a full measure of restoration (see 85:4-9), eloquently described in verses 10 through 13.

Israel's history told the tale of God's faithfulness. While these mercies lie behind verses 1 through 3, probably uppermost in the psalmist's mind is God's recent act of kindness, allowing the Jews to return from exile. These are the **fortunes** which God restored. The **iniquity** and **sins** that He **forgave** and **covered** were those which caused the exile (85:2). Israel's return to her home was proof that God had turned from His anger (85:3).

Because God had been gracious to His people, they turn to Him in their present need (85:4-7). They were restored to their land; now they ask to be fully restored. All His wrath had been set aside; may it be put away again (85:4-6). Verse 6 is arguably the key verse in this psalm. The psalmist appeals to the covenant (**your people**) and once more returns to the image of restoration, using the same verb root as in verses 1, 3, and 4. He refers to God's willingness to "turn from His wrath, and men from their rebellion . . . and situations be revolutionized."[1] **You** is emphasized in verse 6a, as if to say, "Even if no one else came to Israel's rescue, God would come." His **unfailing love** *(chesed)* would bring Him, and with Him, salvation, for He is **God our Savior** (85:4, 7).

His question asked, the psalmist now listens for God's answer (see 85:8). Perhaps he sought the answer from a prophet or perhaps he

263

meditated on God's past revelations, but, because his hope was in God, he looked to Him for the answer. He was not disappointed. God would bring **peace to his people, his saints** (85:8). **Peace** *(shalom)* means much more than the absence of conflict; it speaks of fertile fields and happy hearts, of safety and justice and harmony, of life as God meant it to be lived. The **folly** that deprived them of their homeland must, of course, be abandoned. A hungry man will die, regardless of how many meals you prepare, if he refuses to eat them. But to those who **fear** God—that is, who willingly embrace His mercy—there is **surely** a glorious salvation ahead (85:9).

The beautiful picture that emerges from verses 10 through 13 does not describe the process of salvation but what it will look like when it arrives. There will be harmony on earth and between earth and heaven. Life will prosper under God's beneficent reign. In this tranquility, God can move about freely and wherever He is, there is peace. This is what God desires for His people, even now.

ENDNOTE

[1]Derek Kidner, *Psalms 73–150,* Tyndale Old Testament Commentaries, ed. D.J. Wiseman (Downer's Grove, Illinois: InterVarsity Press, 1975), p. 308.

84

A PATCHWORK OF FAITH

Psalm 86:1-17

P salm 86 is a patchwork of verses drawn from different psalms and other Old Testament passages, carefully combined to meet a pressing need. The reference to David as author may, then, refer to the Davidic source of its material.[1] Like a homemade quilt, this reworking of older material is a work of art with a pattern both complicated and simple. Suggested outlines for this psalm vary with each commentator, but all agree that God's sovereignty is the central theme.

Accompanying each appeal the psalmist makes in verses 1 through 4, is a reason for that request. He asks God to hear and answer because **I am poor and needy** (86:1). He prays to be guarded and saved because **I am devoted to you** (86:2). This appeal is based on their covenant relationship, just as the request of verse 1 appeals to God's compassion. Because he calls to God **all day long**—he calls continually—he wants to be shown **mercy** (86:3). He seeks gladness because he lifts up his soul—that is, he looks expectantly to God (86:4).

In verses 5 through 7, he continues his plea but changes the pattern. He inserts his **prayer** (86:6) between two assertions of confidence (86:5, 7), the first praising God's forgiveness, goodness and love (*chesed;* see Exodus 34:6) and the second declaring his confidence in God's answer.

Psalm 86:8-10 represents the key stanza in the psalm with verse 9 the key verse. The great God presented here is the reason the psalmist can pray with confidence in verses 1 through 7 and verses 13 through 17. Others may claim that their gods are supreme (86:8), but they are mistaken, for **you alone are God**—there is only one God (86:10). When **the nations,** who have been made by God, finally realize this, they will return to worship their creator (86:9). This verse "expresses the culminating hope in Jewish thought, the union of all mankind under the Sovereignty of God."[2] In fact, the psalm's middle verse explains why Israel was called and why Christ came: that through God's chosen nation and servant, all peoples would be reconciled to God (see Genesis 12:1-3; Acts 3:25; Galatians 3:8).

As the second stanza contained an appeal with two statements of praise, so does the fourth (see Psalm 86:11-13). Now the psalmist seeks wholehearted devotion to God so that he may fully reverence and **praise** God (86:11-12). In verse 7, the psalmist looks ahead to God's answer, while in verse 13 he looks back on God's rescue. Both are based on God's steadfast **love** (*chesed;* 86:5, 13).

Victory has not yet arrived, however. The prayer with which the psalm began now resumes with even greater intensity (vv. 14-17). Yet God's **love,** referred to earlier in this psalm, remains a source of steady confidence (86:15) as does the psalmist's past loyalty to God. This is what he implies by calling himself God's **servant** and the **son of your maidservant** (86:16): "We have a long tradition of service to you." Servanthood has been subtly sounded throughout the psalm by the use of the word for Lord. It is no sign of doubt that he asks for a sign of God's goodness; it reflects his confidence in God (86:17).

The lines of this prayer express fervent faith that is based on God's past goodness. Even the way this psalm was constructed—piecing together earlier passages—teaches this lesson. God's Word and works can provide something new, something beautiful, something comforting for difficult days.

ENDNOTES

[1]F. Delitzsch, *Psalms,* Commentary on the Old Testament, vol. V, translated by James Martin (reprint, Grand Rapids, Michigan: Wm. B. Eerdmans Publishing Co., 1978), p. 13. A partial list of borrowed passages from Psalm 86 includes the following:

86:1	Psalm 55:2; 40:17; 70:5
86:2	Psalm 25:20; 31:6;
86:3	Psalm 57:1-2
86:4	Psalm 25:1
86:7	Psalm 17:6
86:8	Exodus 15:11; Psalm 89:8; Deuteronomy 3:24
86:9	Psalm 22:28; 72:17

86:10	Psalm 72:18
86:11	Psalm 27:11; 26:3
86:13	Deuteronomy 32:22
86:14	Psalm 54:3
86:15	Exodus 34:6
86:16	Psalm 25:16; 116:16
86:17	Isaiah 26:11

[2]A. Cohen, *The Psalms,* Soncino Books of the Bible, ed. A. Cohen (London: Soncino, 1950), p. 281.

85

BORN IN ZION

Psalm 87:1-7

Israel, adorned in the mantle of divine appointment, anticipated that all the world would someday follow Yahweh. This, the message of Psalm 86:9, is more fully elaborated in Psalm 87. A different perspective is embraced by the translators of the New International Version, who read the psalm as a celebration of Israel's supremacy over all the other nations. Scholarly opinion—past and present, Jewish and Christian—however, consistently maintains that this psalm anticipates universal adherence to the God of Israel. The date when the psalm was written has proven elusive; almost every possibility has been suggested. If it arose during the later monarchy (as seems most likely), the psalm could have been composed for use at a festival (see **sing** in 87:7).

The psalm is full of "enigmatic and staccato phrases"[1] spoken by a narrator (see 87:1-3, 5-7) and by God (see 87:4) both to and about the city of Jerusalem. The first two verses identify Zion as established and sanctified by God because of His great love for it. The city is next informed: **Glorious things are said of you** (87:3), the essence of these glorious things being delineated in the verses which follow.

God's promise to **record** the true lineage of the nations (87:4) is echoed in verse 6. The first reference makes God's intention public while the second demonstrates its permanence (**the register**). **Rahab** refers to Egypt, the great national power to the south, while **Babylon** represented the great power to the north. Closer to home are Israel's perpetual enemies, **Philistia** and **Tyre,** the epitome of arrogance (see Ezekiel 28). The psalmist envisions a day when even these nations will be counted among God's chosen people. In the ancient Near East conquering kings asserted domination by publicly recording that conquered foreigners now belonged to their kingdoms.[2] Here God not only calls them citizens of His land, He has made the stranger native-born.

This one and that one (Ps. 87:5) may be better rendered "one after another."[3] The psalmist describes an unending list of people about whom it could now be said, **This one was born in Zion** (87:6). How can such a marvelous thing happen? **The Most High himself will establish her** (87:5).

To be part of something so wonderful was cause for celebration in song, presumably by Zion's new citizens (87:7). **Fountains** (translated "springs" in 84:6) could refer to the source for their new identity, for their songs of praise,[4] or for the life-giving nourishment which God provides. Perhaps the phrase is left ambiguous to accommodate all these and more.

What the psalmist anticipated, the early Church preached as accomplished in principle, for God had begun to reconcile the world to himself in Christ. Paul alludes to Psalm 87 in Galatians 4:26 and speaks specifically about universal reconciliation in Ephesians 2:12. Revelation 7:9 describes the innumerable multitude "from every nation, tribe, people and language standing before the throne." Christians have joined the throng of nations in Psalm 87:4 about whom God records, **this one was born in Zion.**

ENDNOTES

[1]Derek Kidner, *Psalms 73–150,* Tyndale Old Testament Commentaries, ed. D.J. Wiseman (Downer's Grove, Illinois: InterVarsity Press, 1975), p. 314.

[2]Marvin E. Tate, *Psalms 51–100,* Word Biblical Commentary, vol. 20, eds. David A. Hubbard and Glenn W. Barker (Waco, Texas: Word Books, 1990), p. 390.

[3]F. Delitzsch, *Psalms,* Commentary on the Old Testament, vol. V, translated by James Martin (reprint, Grand Rapids, Michigan: Wm. B. Eerdmans Publishing Co., 1978), p. 20.

[4]Medieval Jewish commentator David Kimchi as cited by A. Cohen, *The Psalms,* Soncino Books of the Bible, ed. A. Cohen (London: Soncino, 1950), p. 284.

86

SURROUNDED BY DEATH

Psalm 88:1-18

"There is no sadder prayer in the psalter,"[1] for no psalm descends to such a level of despair and remains there. It may have arisen as a national expression of hopelessness during Israel's lowest moment, the destruction of Jerusalem and exile into Babylon. The psalmist not only sings in a minor key, but in the shadow of death. Perhaps he was terminally ill (there is no mention of enemies), but whatever the cause, death seemed to lurk around every corner. Over and over, death appears; its horrible facets are exposed in turn. The many and varied expressions for death multiply its terrors and accentuate its immediacy.

The psalm does contain a glimmer of hope in the phrase, **the God who saves me** (88:1). God may be the cause of the problem and may delay its resolution, but He is still the source of hope. The cry by **day and night** is the cry of true faith (88:1-2). His help is desperately needed because the psalmist is on the verge of death (88:3-5). He has drawn so **near the grave** that he is already set aside among the corpses. **Whom you remember no more** (88:5) speaks of death as that realm where people are **cut off** from His **care** (literally, "hand").

Not only is the psalmist on the verge of death, God has brought him to this point (88:6-9; graphically portrayed in the frequent **you**'s). Verses 3 through 5 put the psalmist among those needing burial; verse 6 has God doing the burying. It is God's **wrath** which has brought this about (88:7) and God's doing which removed another source of support, **my closest friends** (88:8).

Several words in verses 4 through 7, usually used in a positive sense, are here used negatively. The verb behind **lies heavily** (88:7) normally means "lean, lay, rest, or support." **Set apart with the dead** (88:5) is literally "free in death," while **man without strength** (88:4) uses a term for man which often connotes human strength.[2] Perhaps the psalmist is expressing, in pained irony, that God *should be* bringing freedom and support but is not.

The psalmist continues to plead daily to God with hands outstretched, either in prayer or so that God can pull him from the pit (see 88:6).[3] He appeals first on the basis that if he dies, he will not be able to praise God (88:10-12). The psalmist appeals not to God's ego but to the purpose for which humanity was created, to praise God. Since death, as the Hebrews understood it, meant the end of praise, God must act. Dimming eyes (88:9) in this context means imminent death (see Psalm 6:7; 38:10; Lamentations 5:17), so God must act now.

Next the psalmist appeals to his continued faith in God (see Psalm 88:13-14). In spite of unanswered prayers, he has continued to cry out each day (**I** in verse 13 is emphatic). Finally, he pleads for help on the grounds that his problems are very serious and long-standing, **from my youth** (88:15-18). They have left him in **despair**, unable to act or even know what is best. Meanwhile the waters of God's wrath continue to rise. With friends and loved ones all gone, the **darkness** is his only companion (88:18).

Why would God permit such a testimony of despair in this book of praises? It shows that God's people are not always rescued from suffering and reminds us that this world is not our final destination. Meanwhile, God remains present even when He seems to be absent. To trust Him for salvation while surrounded by death evidences the brightest faith and the purest praise.

ENDNOTES

[1]Derek Kidner, *Psalms 73–150,* Tyndale Old Testament Commentaries, ed. D.J. Wiseman (Downer's Grove, Illinois: InterVarsity Press, 1975), p. 316.

[2]Francis Brown, *The New Brown-Driver-Briggs-Gesenius Hebrew and English Lexicon* (Peabody, Massachusetts: Hendrickson Publishers, 1979), pp. 149–50.

[3]Othmar Keel, *The Symbolism of the Biblical World: Ancient Near Eastern Iconography and the Book of Psalms,* translated by Timothy J. Hallett [New York: Seabury Press, 1978], p. 322.

87

WHERE IS YOUR FAITHFULNESS?

Psalm 89:1-52

The key to understanding Psalm 89 is recognizing the contradiction which existed between God's promise to David of a permanent dynasty (see 2 Samuel 7) and the disaster which befell Judah at the hands of the Babylonians. It was the "painful tension" between promise and reality which led to the questions that conclude Psalm 89.[1] The first 37 verses celebrate God's selection of David as His chosen king. As the psalmist expresses his determination to praise God (see 89:1-2), he uses three words which will each recur seven times throughout the psalm: **love** (*chesed;* 89:1, 2, 14, 24, 28, 33, 49), **faithfulness** (89:1, 2, 5, 8, 24, 33, 49), and **forever** (89:1, 2, 4, 28, 36, 37, 52).[2]

The establishment of God's covenant with David is the theme of verses 3 through 37, beginning with the announcement of this agreement (89:3-4). That God, not David, is the One being glorified is clear from verses 5 through 18, which praise Yahweh for His **faithfulness** (89:5-8), His **power** (89:9-13), His **righteousness** (89:14-17), and His covenant with the **king** (89:18). God's strength, emphasized by the repeated and emphatic use of **you** in verses 9 through 12 is demonstrated both in nature (**sea** [89:9]) and history (89:10). **Rahab** (89:10) can refer to the great sea creature of Babylonian literature or to the nation of Egypt (see 87:4). Standing between nature and history, perhaps it represents God's power over both. **Tabor and Hermon** (89:12) beautifully symbolize God's strong and exalted **hand** (89:13) since **Tabor** was the sight of Deborah's victory over Sisera (see Judges 4) and **Hermon** towers over nine thousand feet.[3]

This covenant is proclaimed in a second divine oracle (see Psalm 89:19-37). God has crowned (instead of **strength**) and **anointed** David, his servant (89:19-20). He promises to make his reign secure (89:21-23), extensive (89:24-25), intimate and **exalted** (89:26-27). The psalmist consciously portrays the human king as the embodiment of God himself. In verse 25, the king exercises dominion similar to God's in verses 9 and 10, becomes God's eldest son and is even called "Elyon," a title for God (89:27). This covenant will be permanent, like the heavens (89:28-37). Even the disobedience of the king's sons cannot alter it (89:30-34). On the authority of God's sacred promise, before a witness, David's **throne** will endure forever (89:35-37).

The following verses (89:38-51) present a most striking contrast with what preceded. The permanent covenant appears to have ended; God seems to be doing the opposite of what He promised (89:38-45). Instead of honoring the king, He has defiled him and subjected his people to shame. The throne which was to have been exalted (89:3-4, 28-29) is now thrown down (89:44). The enemy's **right hand,** not the king's (89:25), has been exalted (89:42); Jerusalem, not the enemy (89:23), has been crushed (89:40). With bitter irony the psalmist speaks of the king **cut short** in his youth (89:45); the word for **youth** *(aloom)* is almost identical to the word for eternity *(olam)*.[4]

The contradiction between what God promised and what happened left Israel with a dilemma: Should they turn away from God as unreliable or continue to trust in His love in spite of the contradiction? The psalmist chose to trust (89:46-51). God's anger must not burn long because mortality makes such combustible kindling (89:46-48). Even though all evidence is against him, he still calls God to honor the covenant and show love to His **anointed one** (89:49-51). This dilemma becomes ours as well when God's promises collide with reality. To trust in God's love, against all appearances, and to continue to call on God should be our commitment.[5]

ENDNOTES

[1]Derek Kidner, *Psalms 73–150*, Tyndale Old Testament Commentaries, ed. D.J. Wiseman (Downer's Grove, Illinois: InterVarsity Press, 1975), p. 319.

[2]Because 89:52 was added later, *olam* was only used six times in the original psalm. An additional use is suggested in 89:45 (see comments there).

[3]Kidner, p. 321.

[4]This word play may supply the missing use of *olam*. Kidner notes that this was literally fulfilled with King Jehoiachin, whose reign of three months ended at age eighteen. For the next thirty-seven years he was **covered** with **shame**— prison garments (pp. 324–35).

[5]Verse 52 was added later as the doxology which marks the conclusion to Book Three of the Psalter, a book which has spoken often of national disaster (Kidner, p. 325).

Part Four

BOOK 4

Psalms 90:1–106:48

Book 4 of Psalms opens with a psalm attributed to Moses (Psalm 90), which is appropriate since Moses' name is mentioned six times in Book 4 and only one time elsewhere in the Psalter (Psalm 77:20). Two psalms are ascribed to David (Psalms 101, 103) but most are not attributed to anyone, unlike the three earlier books. Some psalms have titles but no ascription of authorship (Psalms 92, 98, 100, 102). Yahweh is clearly the preferred name for God in Book 4.

God's reign as King, an important theme throughout the psalms, comes into special focus in Psalms 93 through 100. Book 4 ends with these words: **Praise be to the LORD, the God of Israel, from everlasting to everlasting. Let all the people say, "Amen!" Praise the LORD** (Psalm 106:48).

88

PRAYER FOR PERMANENCE

Psalm 90:1-17

P salm 90 begins Book 4—most of whose psalms are anonymous—of the Psalter (Psalms 90–106). The title attributes this psalm to **Moses, the man of God,** but many scholars doubt his authorship. Instead the psalm may have been attributed to Moses because it echoes Genesis 1 through 3 and Deuteronomy 31 through 33, both associated with Moses.

Psalm 90 opens with words of praise, most familiar to us in the paraphrased form given them by Isaac Watts:

> O God, our help in ages past,
> Our hope for years to come,
> Our shelter from the stormy blast,
> And our eternal home.

God is eternal, existing before creation, and almighty, having given birth to creation. Yet He is also personal, having been **our dwelling place throughout all generations** (90:1-2).

Humanity, on the other hand, is time-bound and weak (90:3-6). At God's command it returns **to dust** (see Genesis 3:19) while He continues on forever. **A thousand years** is to Him only **a day** or less (Ps. 90:4). Reference to the night watch leads to a picture of **sleep,** only this is the sleep from which one does not wake (90:5). Together, verses 5 and 6 portray bright promise which ends in disappointment.

Having contrasted the eternal and almighty God with temporary and fragile humanity, the psalmist now examines that transience from a human perspective (see 90:7-11). God's **anger** appears in the opening and closing verses of this stanza, symbolizing its inescapableness. God's wrath is continual because human sins are continually present before Him, even **secret sins** (90:8). A short life (especially when contrasted with verse 4), so full of trouble, ends with **a moan** (90:9-10).

Although the picture looks bleak, the psalmist does not accuse God of being unfair. He knows that transience comes as naturally to us as timelessness to God. He prays for **a heart of wisdom** to live as he must under such circumstances (90:12). Perhaps the requests which follow (see 90:13-17) flow from the hope he received in answer to this prayer.

Having seen human frailty and divine permanence, the psalmist recognizes that the only way to produce anything permanent is by dependence upon God. So he asks God to **relent**—that is, turn back and show mercy (90:13). Since God is full of **unfailing love** (*chesed;* 90:14), may Israel be filled with this **love** in **the morning** (contrast the emphasis on night in verses 4 through 6). Then **all our days** (90:14) will be full of joyous songs (contrast **all our days** passing in wrath [90:9], a marvelous reversal). As the world was God's offspring (90:2), may God's creative power be shown to Israel and its offspring (90:16).

With such demonstrations of God's favor ("the sweetness of the Lord" [Tanakh/NJPS]), Israel's work will be established (90:17; repeated for emphasis). To **establish** (90:17), meaning "firmly founded," is different from withering grass and other symbols of transience, and is instead like the mountains that God created (90:2) and the **dwelling place** (90:1) that He had been to them.

Whether in a flash or as a slowly dawning realization, most people come to recognize the transience of human existence. For some, this news brings despair. Others, like the psalmist, turn to God to find their permanence in Him. One's understanding of God makes the difference. If we know He is a God of love and joy, and if we know Him as **our dwelling place throughout all generations** (90:1), we will turn to Him.

89

IN THE SHELTER
OF THE MOST HIGH

Psalm 91:1-16

It is difficult to fathom the insecurity the Israelites faced. They had no insurance, no welfare, no pension plans. Their livelihood depended on the weather. Their nation, located on the land bridge between Asia and Africa, saw frequent military traffic, which often put their security in jeopardy. Into this frightening world, God speaks the promise of protection in Psalm 91.

Verses 1 and 2 are so laden with powerful and comforting images that it takes the remaining verses to explore them. God is described using four different names: **Most High, Almighty, LORD,** and **my God.** The first and second portray His power, the third His covenant relationship with Israel, the last His intimacy. Four terms are used to describe the place of safety: **shelter, shadow, refuge,** and **fortress.** The first suggests a place of secrecy; the second, shade; the third, shelter; and the fourth, a fortress or stronghold of God's power.

In verses 3 and 4, the psalmist compares God's people to birds; while hardly a flattering comparison, it makes clear Israel's dependence upon God. It is not enough that He saves from the net of the bird catcher (**fowler's snare** [91:3]), but He even becomes like a mother bird who shelters with her wings (91:4). The imagery changes to that of warfare, where God's **faithfulness** ("constancy" [NJB]) becomes a **shield** (large enough to cover the entire body) and a **rampart** (91:4). The latter word, used only here in the Old Testament, may refer to a portable wall used for protection during battle.[1] The combination of these images—the soft protection of a mother bird's wing with the hard shield—is doubly comforting.

Such protection eliminates **fear,** even in the face of ominous enemies (91:5-6). While the enemies' exact nature is unclear, together they constitute a serious threat from human forces (**terror** and **arrow**) and fatal illness (**pestilence** and **plague**). Just as these foes represent significant opposition, so they attack around the clock: **night, day, darkness,** and **midday.** From all of this and at all times, however, the one who trusts in God will be safe, even if many thousands succumb (91:7). Protection is surpassed by vindication, for the wicked will be punished by stronger hands than ours (91:8). After reaffirming the need for trust (91:9) and restating the promised protection (91:10) the secret to such security is revealed. God has commanded His **angels** to protect His people, even to carry them lest they stumble over stones. Here again, protection brings victory (91:13).

An oracle from God confirms the certainty of these blessed promises (91:14-16). Those who trust are described as those who love Him, know Him (91:14), and **call upon** Him (91:15). To speak of protection under divine wings was not uncommon among Israel's neighbors. However, this protection is not limited to a privileged few but is available to all who trust.[2] Those who see here the promise of a trouble-free existence should note Jesus' commentary on it. He answered Satan's quotation of these words (see Luke 4:10-12) by showing that faithfulness meant taking up a cross, not claiming angelic conveyance over the rough terrain of life.

Protection is only the beginning of God's answer (see Psalm 91:8, 13). To this He adds His presence, honor, long life and, finally, the opportunity to see **salvation** (91:15-16). All of this is available in the shelter of the Most High.

Even as civilization has resolved many uncertainties, it remains insecure. The pathway to peace does not lie in human accomplishments but belongs to those for whom trust in God is enough.

ENDNOTES

[1]Othmar Keel, *The Symbolism of the Biblical World: Ancient Near Eastern Iconography and the Book of Psalms,* translated by Timothy J. Hallett [New York: Seabury Press, 1978], p. 222.

[2]Wings are found as a picture of divine protection throughout the ancient Near East (Keel, pp. 191–92, 352–53).

90

SONG FOR THE SABBATH DAY

Psalm 92:1-15

Although most of the psalms were used in Israel's worship, Psalm 92 is one of the few identified for such use in the title: **For the Sabbath Day.** What is the connection between the Sabbath and Psalm 92? In Genesis 2:2-3, God designates the seventh day for rest, setting it apart from the other six and highlighting His activities in creation (see Exodus 31:17). References in Psalm 92 to God's work (see 92:4-5) and to trees flourishing in God's house (see 92:12-14) strike the chord of divine creativity.

God also created the Sabbath to make a statement about His lordship. The Israelites were to rest on that day as a weekly reminder that their possessions came from God's hands, not their own. Sabbath violation meant rebellion against God's sovereignty (see Numbers 15:32-36). This lordship is celebrated by the seven uses of the name Yahweh in Psalm 92.

The Sabbath also anticipated the day when God's lordship would be universally evident in prosperity and righteousness. Every seventh day Israel's sights were to be lifted from the mundane to the eternal rest which was to come (see Psalm 95:11; 132:14; Isaiah 56:4-8; 58:13-14). References in Psalm 92 to God's vindication and blessing serve this purpose well.

It is good to praise the LORD (Ps. 92:1), both because God is praiseworthy and because it benefits the one praising (92:1-3). The praise is melodious, employing stringed instruments (92:1, 3), and it is continual, both **morning** and **night** (92:2). **Night** is plural in the Hebrew, perhaps to emphasize the appropriateness of praise during difficult times. Praise should exalt God's name and should concentrate on His **love** *(chesed)* and **faithfulness.**

Verses 4 through 15 announce that praise is appropriate because joy comes from considering the marvelous works and profound thoughts of God. Contrary to the New International Version, it is the greatness of God which the **senseless man** and **fool** do not understand (92:5-6).[1] The **wicked** may **spring up like grass,** but their prosperity will be short lived. They will be eternally destroyed (92:6-7) while God, in His eternal Sabbath rest, will be **exalted forever** (92:8). Verse 9 sounds like a piece of Canaanite poetry, dated about a half-century before David and written in honor of Baal.[2] If the psalmist is writing with that poem in mind, he is implicitly pointing out the superiority of Yahweh, for it is not Baal, the god of fertility, but Yahweh who produces the perpetual flourishing pictured in verses 12 through 14.

Not only God (92:8) but also God's people know exaltation (92:10). To lift up the horn of the oxen means strength and victory. To be anointed with **fine oils** pictures gladness and honor. As in Psalm 23:5, the anointing is accompanied by victory which the psalmist is able to witness (92:11).

Life under the lordship of God brings blessing like a thriving tree (92:12-14). The **palm** is the picture of graceful beauty, the **cedar** of strength and majesty.[3] The **righteous,** planted in the courtyard of the Temple, are always fruitful and verdant, even in old age: "Their healthy green proclaims Yahweh's power of blessing."[4] The contrast between the righteous and the wicked (92:7) is unmistakable.

The psalm closes with praise, showing that rest is not our doing but flows from God's character as upright, permanent, and pure (92:15). For the believer, **it is good to praise the Lord** (92:1), for we enjoy a Sabbath rest under His lordship and prosper in His presence, even in the darkest night.

Endnotes

[1]See the New Jerusalem Bible on 92:5-6:

> How great are your works, Yahweh,
> immensely deep your thoughts!
> Stupid people cannot realize this,
> fools do not grasp it.

[2]Derek Kidner, *Psalms 73–150,* Tyndale Old Testament Commentaries, ed. D.J. Wiseman (Downer's Grove, Illinois: InterVarsity Press, 1975), p. 336.
[3]Ibid., p. 337.
[4]Othmar Keel, *The Symbolism of the Biblical World: Ancient Near Eastern Iconography and the Book of Psalms,* translated by Timothy J. Hallett [New York: Seabury Press, 1978], p. 135.

91

THE LORD REIGNS AMONG US

Psalm 93:1-5

This psalm begins a series of psalms (93–100) with the enthronement of God as their theme.[1] This theme is sounded, trumpet-like, in the very first line: **The LORD reigns.** Robed in grandeur and strength, He stands before His people. By His majestic power (93:1a), He established the **world** (93:1b); in fact, the world's stability depends on the stability of God's rule. Because this throne is not begun in time, it will not end in time (see Psalm 90:2).[2]

In 93:3-4, the psalmist continues to celebrate the rule of God, but does so by focusing on one dimension of that rule, His sovereignty over nature. **The seas** may crash and roar, but Yahweh is mightier still. **Mightier** here implies glory and magnificence as well as power.[3] Note how each of these verses ascends, line by line, then comes crashing down just like the waves in the sea.

The psalm closes by referring to God's law lasting forever (93:5). God's **statutes,** His royal decrees, stand firm. God's palace, the Temple, is beautified by His **holiness.** His firm decrees and holy house will endure, like His throne, forever.

The God who established His glorious, eternal, and supreme reign over the earth has also chosen a people and taken up residence among them forever. Perhaps this was in John's mind when he wrote, "In the beginning was the Word, and the Word was with God, and the Word was God. He was with God in the beginning. . . . The Word became flesh and made his dwelling among us. We have seen his glory, the glory of the One and Only, who came from the Father, full of grace and truth" (John 1:1-2, 14).

ENDNOTES

[1] A. Cohen, *The Psalms,* Soncino Books of the Bible, ed. A. Cohen (London: Soncino, 1950), p. 307.

[2] F. Delitzsch, *Psalms,* Commentary on the Old Testament, vol. V, translated by James Martin (reprint, Grand Rapids, Michigan: Wm. B. Eerdmans Publishing Co., 1978), p. 75.

[3] Cohen; A.F. Kirkpatrick, *The Book of Psalms,* The Cambridge Bible for Schools and Colleges, ed. A.F. Kirkpatrick (1902; reprint, Cambridge: Cambridge University Press, 1910), p. 564.

92

LET THE RIGHTEOUS JUDGE ARISE

Psalm 94:1-23

Throughout the Old Testament, God reveals himself as just. When dealing with humanity, His fairness was assumed (see Genesis 18:25). In detailing His expectations for human judgment, He demanded even-handed justice, making certain that the rights of the powerless were protected (see Exodus 22:21-24). The psalmist prays Psalm 94 because he knows that "God is a righteous judge" (Ps. 7:11) who demands justice on earth. The psalmist does not specify the nature of the injustice he is experiencing. It may be international (see Nehemiah 4) or internal (see Amos 2:6-7). Because injustice is thriving, however, God must arise.[1]

The opening verses (Psalm 94:1-3), addressed to Yahweh as **the God who avenges** and **Judge of the earth,** call for Him to **shine forth** and **rise up.** The psalmist seeks vindication, not selfish interest. Since God is neither blind (94:7) nor **corrupt** (94:20), justice is only a matter of time (**How long?** [94:3]).

Perhaps to impress upon God the seriousness of the situation, the oppressors are described (see 94:4-7). They speak arrogantly (see 94:4), which connotes a boastfulness against God as well. **Pour out** is too mild for the Hebrew (see the same verb in 59:7); perhaps "rant" or "gush out" (NJPS) would be better. They murderously oppress God's people (see 94:5-6). The helpless among God's inheritance, those He singled out for special care, are singled out for attack by the enemy. They have interpreted God's silence as deafness and assume He is either unaware or unconcerned about what is happening, for He **pays no heed** (94:7).

But God does know what is happening and is concerned; therefore, these senseless ones had better **take heed** (94:8-11; the same verb is used in verses 7b and 8a). They betray their senseless folly (see 92:6) by missing the obvious truth that if God created the means to communicate, He cannot go blind and deaf. The One who has revealed His will is both capable and willing to enforce it. The New International Version may be correct in referring to the futility of human thoughts in 94:11. It is also possible that **they** refers to humanity. The meaning would then be that God, knowing human weakness,[2] will bring justice to the rescue.

God shows justice, not merely by punishing the wicked but by rewarding the righteous. This reward is pronounced and described in 94:12-19. The Hebrew word translated **discipline** (94:12) can also be rendered "instruct" (see Proverbs 31:1; Isaiah 28:26), a meaning that seems to fit better here. By His **law** (Ps. 94:12), God tells His people what He requires and, most importantly, reveals himself as a God of justice. The confidence to call for God's justice and the patience to wait for it arose from an understanding of God's Word. Eventually—as soon as the wicked have finished digging a pit big enough to fall into (see Psalm 9:15)—justice will come. Until then, God grants **relief** (94:13), "inward quietness in face of outward troubles."[3]

Such relief is inevitable, for Yahweh is faithful (94:14-15). He will come to the aid of His people and His inheritance (94:14; see the same terms in verse 5) and will restore justice to its place on the foundation of **righteousness** from which it had been toppled (94:15). The psalmist describes his own experience of vindication in verses 16 through 19. The situation was grave, but God's **love** (*chesed;* 94:18) was greater; His mercies (**consolation**) were more numerous than the reasons for worry (94:17-19).

The closing verses (94:20-23) summarize the psalm by contrasting the wicked and the righteous. The wicked may have the seat of honor and authority (see Ecclesiastes 3:16; Proverbs 9:14; Nehemiah 5:7) from which they dispense misery and death. The righteous, however, find God a safe refuge in trouble (94:22) and a sure recourse for justice (94:23).

ENDNOTES

[1]Because God has "established his throne for [righteous] judgment" (Psalm 9:7-8), Psalm 94 belongs with Psalms 93 through 100, a collection which takes God's kingship as its theme (see 93:2).

[2]See Psalm 39:5-6, 11; 62:9; 144:4 where human insignificance is used positively as a reason for God to help.

[3]Derek Kidner (*Psalms 73–150,* Tyndale Old Testament Commentaries, ed. D.J. Wiseman, [Downer's Grove, Illinois: InterVarsity Press, 1975], p. 342) cites Isaiah 7:4 as an example.

93

REST IN THE GOD OF THE ROCK

Psalm 95:1-11

ncluded in the collection of psalms that explore the theme of Yahweh's kingship (see Psalms 93–100), Psalm 95 describes the foundation on which His kingdom is based (95:3-5, 7). As well, the sobering concluding verses summon the reader to the obedience that should characterize God's loyal subjects.

The opening call to praise (95:1-2), noteworthy for its exuberance (**sing for joy** and **shout aloud** [95:1]), is followed by the reasons for praise (95:3-5). Glory belongs to Yahweh, for He is **the great God, the great King above all gods** (95:3). This is neither a reference to angels nor an admission that other gods actually exist (see Psalm 96:5). Instead the psalmist asserts that all the forces of nature, deified by Israel's neighbors, lie within the hands of Yahweh (95:4). He holds title to the whole earth because He created it (95:4-5). This connection is even clearer in commentator Artur Weiser's translation of verse 5: "The sea is his, for he made it, and the dry land, for his hands formed it."[1]

Each of these—depths, heights, and sea—was thought by Israel's neighbors to possess supernatural associations. The depths were the domain of the dark powers, and the mountaintops the abode of the gods.[2] Many of Israel's neighbors associated the sea with the deadly monster of Chaos, identifying its defeat with creation and its continual stirring as the threat of a new invasion.[3] Yet Yahweh not only controls these realms but, because He created them, removes them entirely from the dreaded domain of the supernatural.

A second call to praise and reason is issued in verses 6 and 7. The Israelites must worship God, for He is not only their **Maker,** but He is their God and they are His people. This is the language of the covenant, God's bond of unity with Israel. The **great King above all gods** (95:3) has become their Shepherd, and they are the **flock under his care** (literally, "flock of His hand"; 95:7). This flock is controlled, protected, and led by the same hand which created and controls the universe.[4]

After the jubilant tone of the first two stanzas, the words of warning in 95:7b-11 are striking, though not out of place. The rule of Yahweh necessarily elicits both celebration and a summons to loyal obedience. Note that the warning is addressed to the Israelites of the psalmist's day (**you**). Because they were part of God's covenant people, the actions of their forefathers were, in some way, their actions as well. God himself counsels the Israelites not to make the same mistake they had made at **Meribah** and **Massah** (95:8) There they forgot God's miracles of deliverance, questioned whether God was really among them, and blamed Moses for their troubles (see Exodus 17:1-7). Their hard hearts (see Psalm 95:8) "disgusted" God (95:10 TEV) who solemnly forbade their entry into Canaan (95:11).

By calling it **my rest,** God implies more was at stake than just entry into the Promised Land. Israel missed the opportunity to participate in God's Sabbath rest, "the enjoyment of His finished work not merely of creation but redemption."[5] This is why the psalmist can hold open the possibility of **rest** (95:11) even to those already in possession of Palestine, and why the writer of Hebrews (in Hebrews 3–4) can use these verses to call Christians to that rest.

Then and now, rest requires obedience—loyal hearts and an acknowledgment of God's ways (see Psalm 95:10). Then as now, obedience is easier when we remember that **the great King above all gods** (95:3) is also our Shepherd.

ENDNOTES

[1]Artur Weiser, *The Psalms—A Commentary,* translated by Herbert Hartwell, The Old Testament Library, gen. eds. G. Ernest Wright, John Bright, James Barr and Peter Ackroyd (Philadelphia: Westminster Press, 1962), p. 625.

[2]See Isaiah 5:14; Psalm 68:15-16; 89:12; Weiser, p. 626; Othmar Keel, *The Symbolism of the Biblical World: Ancient Near Eastern Iconography and the Book of Psalms,* translated by Timothy J. Hallett [New York: Seabury Press, 1978], p. 71.

[3]See Psalm 74:13-15; Habakkuk 3:8-15; also Keel, pp. 47–56.

[4]F. Delitzsch, *Psalms,* Commentary on the Old Testament, vol. V, translated by James Martin (reprint, Grand Rapids, Michigan: Wm. B. Eerdmans Publishing Co., 1978), p. 87.

[5]Derek Kidner, *Psalms 73–150,* Tyndale Old Testament Commentaries, ed. D.J. Wiseman (Downer's Grove, Illinois: InterVarsity Press, 1975), p. 346; see discussion on Psalm 92.

94

SING TO YAHWEH A NEW SONG

Psalm 96:1-13

This psalm stands among Israel's most noble expressions. When first called to be God's chosen people in the person of Abram, they were commissioned as a source of blessing to all the nations (see Genesis 12:1-3). By summoning the **families of nations** (Ps. 96:7) to glorify Yahweh, Psalm 96 reflects a partial, yet sincere effort to fulfill that calling. The summons is issued in two stanzas, each beginning with a call to worship followed by reasons to praise God.

The first calls the reader to praise God as Creator (see 96:1-6). **Sing to the Lord** is repeated three times with increasing intensity. It must be a **new song,** not in the sense of never before being sung, but with a vigor as fresh and alive as its theme (96:1-2).[2] It is to be sung by **all the earth**; the Hebrew makes clear that this refers to all earth's inhabitants ("all men on earth" [NEB]). **His salvation, his glory,** and **his marvelous deeds** are to be proclaimed not only within Israel, but among all **nations** and **peoples** (96:2-3).

Israel's God is praiseworthy (96:4-6), greater and more awesome than all other gods (95:3). They are worthless,[3] but He has created the heavens to reflect His **splendor and majesty**. Yet God has also revealed His **strength and glory** in a more personal way: in His **sanctuary,** among His people (96:6).[4]

In light of Yahweh's all-surpassing glory, the nations are invited to acknowledge Him as their God by turning from their worthless deities (96:7-8). After the triple use of **ascribe to the Lord** (meant to echo the triple **sing to the Lord** in verses 1 and 2), the call to worship continues. The nations are to bring tribute to their new Sovereign and worship this awe-inspiring, holy God.[5]

The three affirmations of verse 10 all point in the same direction: **The LORD reigns.** Two pillars—creation and judgment—support His throne. He has proven His lordship by creating the world (see 96:5b) and will exercise that lordship in righteous judgment.[6]

The thought of Yahweh coming to reign brings all creation to its feet (96:11-13a). **Heavens, earth, sea,** and **fields** are chosen to represent all of nature (see 95:4-5). Particular attention is given to the joyous expressions of the **trees of the forest** (96:12-13a; see Isaiah 55:12). More than once the righteous person is compared to a tree which flourishes in the fertile soil of God's presence (see Psalm 1:3; 92:12-14; Jeremiah 17:8). Here humanity flourishes and bears fruit under God's blessed rule.

The second call to worship begins in Psalm 96:7 and continues into 96:13, where the reason for praise appears: God is coming to judge. All nations will stand before the throne of Him who is altogether right and true. That He is coming adds urgency to the summons. There is also joy in knowing that justice is on the way.

After many years, God did come in the person of Jesus, whose words and deeds revealed God's kingdom already begun in Him. The summons to yield to God's lordship is extending to, and being embraced by, all **families of nations** (96:7). When the King returns, He will—perfectly and finally—**judge the world in righteousness and the peoples in his truth** (see Revelation 19:11-16).

ENDNOTES

[1]Although the origin of this psalm is not specified, it appears as part of a larger song in 1 Chronicles 16.

[2]Derek Kidner, *Psalms 73–150,* Tyndale Old Testament Commentaries, ed. D.J. Wiseman (Downer's Grove, Illinois: InterVarsity Press, 1975), p. 348.

[3]The psalmist employs a word play here: **gods** is *elohim,* while **idols** is *elilim.* The latter refers to what is good-for-nothing (F. Delitzsch, *Psalms,* Commentary on the Old Testament, vol. V, translated by James Martin [reprint, Grand Rapids, Michigan: Wm. B. Eerdmans Publishing Co., 1978], p. 91).

[4]These two terms are ascribed to the ark of the covenant in Psalm 78:61.

[5]Some take **holiness** (96:9) to describe the worshiper ("worship the LORD in holy array" [RSV]) or as a reference to the holy place (the sanctuary; Loretz, as cited by Marvin E. Tate, *Psalms 51–100,* Word Biblical Commentary, vol. 20, eds. David A. Hubbard and Glenn W. Barker [Waco, Texas: Word Books, 1990], p. 511). That the worshipers **tremble** (96:9) before God supports the New International Version's translation.

⁶See *The Psalms—A Commentary* by Artur Weiser, translated by Herbert Hartwell, The Old Testament Library, gen. eds. G. Ernest Wright, John Bright, James Barr and Peter Ackroyd (Philadelphia: Westminster Press, 1962), p. 630.

95

THE KING HAS COME

Psalm 97:1-12

A s Psalm 96 announces the coming of the divine King (see 96:13), Psalm 97 describes His arrival and rule in cataclysmic terms. The opening pronouncement of Yahweh as king is followed by a portrait of His rule (97:1-6). It is a time for joy, a time to **let the earth be glad** (97:1; see 96:11a). Even those on **distant shores** (97:1)—that is, the "remote areas and nations, distant shores at the limits of the earth"— have reason to rejoice.[1]

God's arrival is described in the language of a fierce storm (97:2-6; see Psalm 29). **Clouds and thick darkness** (97:2a) pictures the mystery with which God chooses to surround himself. Israel's neighbors considered the solemn climax of their sacred ceremonies to be the unveiling of the image of their god. Here, as at Sinai (see Deuteronomy 4:11) and elsewhere in the Old Testament, God "reverently maintains the mystery of his nature and impressively indicates the threateningly serious character of his appearing."[2] Paradoxically, God is both hidden and revealed. The **righteousness and justice** which support His throne (Ps. 97:2) speak of God's revelation of himself through the Law. They speak of a God whose righteousness can be proclaimed and whose glory can be seen (see 97:6, 8).

The storm rages with consuming fire and terrifying displays of power (97:3-4). Even the mountains, considered the most permanent part of creation, **melt . . . before the LORD** (97:5). Such a cataclysm has as its goal not destruction but the revelation of God's **righteousness** and **glory** (97:6).

This glory having been revealed, the psalmist portrays three responses to that glory (see 97:7-9).

First, those who worship other gods are **put to shame** (97:7). As in Psalm 96:5, the psalmist makes a word play with **idols** *(elilim)* and **gods** *(elohim)*. The New International Version translates the Hebrew verb for **worship him** in 96:7c as a command, although it can also be translated as a statement: "All gods worship Him." The latter meaning explains that the shame of those who serve idols comes from seeing their gods bow to Yahweh.

Second is the **glad** reaction to God's **judgments** in **Zion** (Jerusalem) and the surrounding Judean villages (97:8).

Third, the psalmist responds (97:9) by praising God in words that unite the themes sounded in 97:2-7. God is both **the Most High over all the earth** (God's power over nature) and **exalted far above all gods** (see 97:7).

This description of the coming of God's rule was intended not only to elicit praise but also to produce righteousness among God's people (see 97:10-12). The description of these people as "lovers of Yahweh" (a literal translation; 97:10) is meant to contrast with "servers of idols" (a literal translation of 97:7). God desires His people to show their love for Him by hating what He hates—**evil** (97:10). He shows His love for them by becoming, literally, "the keeper of the souls of his faithful ones" (see 97:10). For those who share in His righteousness, God scatters His light as seeds (97:11; **shed** is literally "sown"), dispersing the darkness that surrounds Him (see 97:2) and revealing himself more clearly. To know Him is to be filled with joy that overflows in praise of His **holy name** (97:12).

ENDNOTES

[1]Marvin E. Tate, *Psalms 51–100,* Word Biblical Commentary, vol. 20, eds. David A. Hubbard and Glenn W. Barker (Waco, Texas: Word Books, 1990), p. 516.

[2]Artur Weiser, *The Psalms—A Commentary,* translated by Herbert Hartwell, The Old Testament Library, gen. eds. G. Ernest Wright, John Bright, James Barr and Peter Ackroyd (Philadelphia: Westminster Press, 1962), p. 632.

96

PRAISE FOR THE PAST AND FUTURE

Psalm 98:1-9

P salm 98 is so similar to Psalm 96 that some have suggested that one is a variation of the other or that both came from a common hand. The resemblance extends beyond sharing very similar opening and closing verses. They are structured alike, and both elicit praise for Yahweh's reign.

The opening line of the first stanza of Psalm 98 (see 98:1-3) is identical to that of Psalm 96. As there, a **new song** refers to the song's vigor, not its age. While Psalm 96 continues its call to praise for several verses, Psalm 98 turns immediately to the reason for praise, God's **salvation** (98:2). Salvation is used here in a sense that is broader than redemption from sin. It represents God's intervention in history that accomplished both victory for the righteous and defeat for the wicked.[1]

The psalmist first speaks generally of this salvation (**marvelous things** [98:1b]) and then portrays the means by which it was brought about, **his right hand and holy arm** (98:1c; see 44:3).[2] God's powerful **right hand** is capable of creating (89:13), blessing (16:11), strengthening (18:35), protecting (63:8), punishing (21:8), and delivering (Exodus 15:6). His **holy arm** refers to His "power exercised in a holy cause."[3]

A second call to praise rings out in Psalm 98:4-6. The command to **shout for joy** to Yahweh, coming at the beginning and end of these verses, sets an exuberant tone that is intensified by the way the psalmist builds on his words in 98:4-5 (**music . . . music . . . harp . . . harp**). The New International Version has tamed the abrupt phrases in verse 4b, which could be translated more literally "burst, shout joyfully, sing praise." Praise from the **harp, trumpets,** the **ram's horn,** and the human voice in jubilant **song** and **shout** would create the distinctive sound for which

Temple worship was known.[4] Because God revealed His salvation to all the earth (98:2-3), praise is to come from all peoples and not just Israel (98:4).

Nature itself is summoned to praise God (98:7-9a). The **sea,** often described ominously in the Old Testament, roars its praise to God. The earth and its inhabitants join in, **the rivers clap their hands,** and the giant **mountains** joyously **sing together.** The glorious euphony of Temple worship is repeated in creation.

As with Psalm 96, the psalmist extends the second call to praise nearly to the end of the psalm before giving the reason for praise: God comes to "judge the world with saving justice and the nations with fairness" (98:9 NJB).[5] Psalm 98 calls God's people, then and now, to praise Him both for His actions in the past (98:1-3) and in the future (98:9). All nations, even all creation, are summoned to praise God, for He is the Lord, Redeemer, righteous Judge, and King.

ENDNOTES

[1]Derek Kidner, *Psalms 73–150,* Tyndale Old Testament Commentaries, D. J. Wiseman, ed. (Downer's Grove, Illinois: InterVarsity Press, 1975), p. 352.

[2]The Hebrew may be better translated,

> his right hand has brought him victory,
> even as has his holy arm

(Marvin E. Tate, *Psalms 51–100,* Word Biblical Commentary, vol. 20, eds. David A. Hubbard and Glenn W. Barker [Waco, Texas: Word Books, 1990], pp. 522–23).

[3]A. Cohen, *The Psalms,* Soncino Books of the Bible, ed. A. Cohen (London: Soncino, 1950), p. 320.

[4]The **harp** (more properly, lyre, since the strings were even in length) was a portable instrument often associated with worship. **Trumpets** were fashioned of metal and had a range of less than a half-dozen notes. The **ram's horn** *(shofar)* was not a musical instrument but a means of signaling for worship (see Psalm 81:3) or battle (Judges 3:27). "The noise of temple worship was legendary" (Tate, p. 525; see 2 Chronicles 29:25-30; Ezra 3:10-13).

[5]The wording of 98:9 is almost identical with 96:13, except the latter has an additional "for he comes" and ends with "his truth" rather than **with equity.**

97

"FOR THE LORD OUR GOD IS HOLY"[1]

Psalm 99:1-9

One is reminded by the opening pronouncement—**The LORD reigns** (see Psalms 93, 97)—how central the rule of God was to the psalmist. It undergirds each of the psalms and emerges as the dominant theme in Psalms 93 through 100. The triple mention of God's holiness (see 99:3, 5, 9; also Isaiah 6:3) sets a lofty tone for Psalm 99. The repetition of the refrain in 99:5, 9 indicates that the psalm should be divided into two stanzas. The first elicits praise for God's just rule over all nations (99:1-5), while the second focuses on His gracious rule over Israel (99:6-9).

Verses 1 and 2 alternate between announcement and reaction. That **the LORD reigns** causes the nations to tremble. Because God is seated on His throne **between the cherubim,** the earth shakes. God's greatness results in praise for His "name, great and awesome" (99:2 NJB). From verse 3 on, the psalm shifts back and forth from speaking about God to speaking to God (see 99:4, 8), which suggests its use in Israel's worship.

The cherubim which flank Yahweh's throne (99:1; see 1 Samuel 4:4; 2 Samuel 6:2) are not the cuddly angels associated with Valentine's Day. When encountered outside Eden with flaming swords (Genesis 3:24), on the ark of the covenant with their wings spread from wall to wall (Exodus 25:18-20), and in terrible glory in Ezekiel's visions (Ezekiel 1:4-28; 10:1-22), they evoked awe, not "warm fuzzies." Their descriptions are not always identical, but they appear to have been part animal, human and bird, combined for greatest strength, wisdom and speed.[2]

God's rule, celebrated in earth-shaking terms in Psalm 99:1-3, is most clearly realized in Israel (see 99:4; Amos 3:2). There His strength provides what His heart desires.[3] The psalmist emphatically affirms that God has **established equity** (by emphasizing **you**) and **justice** (by repeating the same Hebrew word twice in Psalm 99:4).

Verse 5 serves as a refrain which will reappear, slightly altered, in verse 9. Since God is already exalted (the same Hebrew root word, **exalt,** is used in verse 2), this call is to acknowledge His exaltation. Israel is to **worship** (or "bow down" as in Genesis 18:2) **at his footstool** (Psalm 99:5). God's footstool has been identified as the earth (Isaiah 66:1); Jerusalem (Lamentations 2:1); the Temple (Psalm 132:7) and the ark of the covenant (1 Chronicles 28:2). Given the association of footstool with the cherubim (Psalm 99:1), the ark is probably in view in 99:5.

The historical summary which begins the second part of the psalm verifies that God has treated His people fairly (see 99:6-7). **Moses and Aaron** and **Samuel** are singled out as exemplars of intercession and obedience. The hero of this account, however, is God who **spoke to them from the pillar of cloud.**[4]

As in Psalm 95, past history becomes the basis for the psalmist's message to his listeners (99:8). God demonstrated the fairness of His rule in His treatment of Israel[5] by answering their prayers, forgiving their sins and punishing them when necessary. In this He also revealed His character as a loving, attentive father. While this paternal portrayal contrasts sharply with that of 99:1-3, both pictures lead to worship, as demonstrated by the reappearance of the refrain in 99:9.

The third reference to God's holiness (see 99:9) is expanded to emphasize Israel's covenant relationship. In this expression—**for the LORD our God is holy**—the two pictures of God converge. In His holiness, He is **great and awesome** (99:3) and worthy of exaltation (99:5), but He is also **our God,** the one who hears and answers our cries.

<h2 style="text-align:center">ENDNOTES</h2>

[1]Psalm 99:9c; see 99:5c.

[2]It is not uncommon for kings in the ancient Near East to be pictured seated on thrones composed of cherubim (Othmar Keel, *The Symbolism of the Biblical World: Ancient Near Eastern Iconography and the Book of Psalms,* translated by Timothy J. Hallett [New York: Seabury Press, 1978], pp. 170–71). In the Old Testament, they not only protect Yahweh's throne, but they also transport Him as His chariot (see 2 Samuel 22:11; Psalm 18:10).

[3]Verse 4a is very difficult to translate as evidenced by the many options:

"You are a king who loves justice" (NJB); "Mighty King, you love what is right" (TEV); "Mighty King, who loves justice" (Tanakh/NJPS). The New International Version makes good sense of the Hebrew.

[4]Although only Moses and Aaron heard from the cloud in the wilderness, Samuel's inclusion is appropriate because of his encounter with God (see 1 Samuel 3) and his role as intercessor.

[5]The New International Version has supplied **Israel** where the Hebrew has only "them." Whether one follows the New International Version or treats "them" as referring to Moses, Aaron and Samuel, the end result is the same.

98

WORTHY WORSHIP

Psalm 100:1-5

It is fitting that a group of psalms dealing with God's rule should conclude with Psalm 100. Both the summons to worship (100:1-4) and the reasons for it (100:5) have a perspective as broad as it is deep. This psalm was originally written to accompany the thank offering in the Temple, the only offering the Rabbis believed would continue after the need for sin offerings had ceased.[1]

The call to worship summons the whole heart and the whole world to celebrate. The exuberance of **shout for joy** (100:1) and **joyful songs** (100:2) is balanced by service for God (**worship** [100:2]).[2] Worship must not only be exuberant, extensive and devoted, but it must be grounded in the affirmation that God is supreme. **Know that the LORD is God** (100:3) might be better rendered, "acknowledge that Yahweh, He is God." Such a faith commitment would be sorely needed in a polytheistic culture (see 1 Kings 18:39) in which all nations claimed supremacy for their deities. It is still needed in the present culture which sees little need for God at all.

God is to be praised, not only for being supreme but also because of His special relationship with Israel. **He . . . made us** (Ps. 100:3) refers not to the creation of the universe, but to the formation of Israel as a nation (see 95:6-7; Isaiah 29:23; 43:1; 44:2; Deuteronomy 32:6, 15). They belong to Him (**we are his**) as the **sheep of his pasture** (Ps. 100:3), a metaphor encountered in Psalm 95:7 and elsewhere (see 77:20; 78:52).

The call to worship continues with an invitation to pass through the Temple **gates** and into God's **courts** (100:4). Note that they are *His* courts, a reminder of the honor of being invited to God's house. Nothing less than abundant **thanks** (the same word is used twice in verse 4 and once in the psalm title) will suffice, given the blessings of knowing God as Creator, Shepherd and Host.

In the final verse (100:5), the psalmist describes Israel's God using three phrases—profound yet brief—which came to be almost an Old

Testament creed.[3] To call Yahweh **good** is not merely to speak of His character but identifies Him as the source of all which is worthwhile in life, such as **love** and **faithfulness.** **His love** *(chesed)* and **his faithfulness** can never end, for they are essential qualities of His eternal character. The first speaks to His merciful willingness to unite himself with humanity, the latter describes the constancy of that love.[4] Both find their clearest expression in Christ.

ENDNOTES

[1]A. Cohen, *The Psalms,* Soncino Books of the Bible, ed. A. Cohen (London: Soncino, 1950), pp. 324–25.

[2]The word used here is not the same word translated worship in Psalm 99:9. It can refer to physical labor (see Exodus 5:18); here it suggests the service which worship requires.

[3]The expression "Give thanks to the LORD, for he is good; his love endures forever" is used in 1 Chronicles 16:34; 2 Chronicles 5:13; 7:3; Ezra 3:11; Jeremiah 33:11; and Psalm 106:1; 107:1; 118:1, 29 (Marvin E. Tate, *Psalms 51–100,* Word Biblical Commentary, vol. 20, eds. David A. Hubbard and Glenn W. Barker [Waco, Texas: Word Books, 1990], p. 538).

[4]F. Delitzsch, *Psalms,* Commentary on the Old Testament, vol. V, translated by James Martin (reprint, Grand Rapids, Michigan: Wm. B. Eerdmans Publishing Co., 1978), p. 106.

99

A MODEL OF JUSTICE

Psalm 101:1-8

J ustice was an essential component in the society God established among the Israelites. The leaders, especially the king, were to conduct themselves with honesty, integrity and equity. Psalm 101 reflects the king's promise to rule justly, perhaps spoken publicly at a ceremony in Jerusalem. By following Psalms 93 through 100, with their emphasis on God's rule, it displays how much responsibility for justice God places in human hands.

The opening verses celebrate God's **love** *(chesed)* and **justice** (see Psalm 99:4) with a song of praise (101:1) and a promise of obedience (101:2). The king should glorify God's rule, for that rule reflects the perfect blend of mercy and fairness. Not only the king but all God's people are to show these same qualities (see Micah 6:8). By praising God's justice in Psalm 101:1, the king affirms that this is the model for his own rule.

Between the king's praise of God's rule (101:1-2a) and his promise to reflect that rule (101:2c-8), is the question: **When will you come to me?** (101:2b). Some take this to mean that the king is in trouble; by promising justice he bargains for God's help. This is unlikely, for although the psalms contain such bargaining, they do not usually encompass entire psalms as here.

Others, seeing David as the author, take verse 2b to reflect his longing for the day when God's ark will come to Jerusalem. God's hatred of evil became evident when, at David's first attempt to bring in the ark, Uzzah was struck dead. Therefore, the city must first be purified; this psalm reveals that process.[1] More likely, this question represents the king's admission that he must have God's help to administer justice against the strong tide of human evil.

The promise of obedience made in the first line of verse 2 is expanded in the rest of the psalm. Significantly, the king begins in his own palace (**house**). At home, where holiness is hardest, he will walk with **blameless heart** (101:2). He will avoid not only wickedness but worthlessness as well. In all his dealings, the king will maintain pure eyes (101:3a), pure hands (101:3b), and pure associations (101:4). The qualities he hates are the subtle sins of slander, deception and pride, qualities often thought essential to success (101:5-7). No one who does such things will be permitted in his company or his employ.

As verse 1 makes clear, God's justice is founded on **love.** This love is revealed not simply in His hatred of evil but in His blessing on the righteous. The king's justice, modeled on God's, is also characterized by care for the **faithful in the land** (101:6). They will dwell securely with the king, just as Israel lived in peace because of Yahweh's love (see Deuteronomy 7:9-26). Their security was based, not only on the king's justice, but on his appointment of just ministers to carry out his decrees (see Psalm 101:6-7). Note the repetition: As the king will be blameless in his house (101:2), only those who are blameless will dwell in his house (101:6-7); as no evil will be set before his eyes (101:3), so no deceiver will stand before him (literally, "before my eyes"; 101:7b).

He begins with a promise of righteousness at home in his heart, commits himself to pure associations, and concludes with a promise to exercise justice throughout **the land** (101:8). As he **put to silence** the slanderer (101:5), so will he **put to silence** all the wicked (101:8). There will be no laxness in judgment, for every morning, court will convene. Jerusalem is singled out because it was the **city of the LORD,** the righteous King after whose rule the king's justice was modeled.

While much has changed from the psalmist's day to ours, God has not. He still cares about justice. Our relationships ought to reflect the same purity of heart, association, and actions of which the psalm speaks. If justice is God's passion, His people must be forces for loving and fair justice in society.

ENDNOTE

[1] A. Cohen, *The Psalms,* Soncino Books of the Bible, ed. A. Cohen (London: Soncino, 1950), p. 326.

100

"YOU REMAIN THE SAME"[1]

Psalm 102:1-28

ts title identifies Psalm 102 as the **prayer of an afflicted man,** but its content (especially verses 13 through 22) reveals a nation's lament. Probably written in the exilic period, this psalm expresses Israel's grief and pleads for divine intervention, although many afflicted individuals have also found comfort in its lines. Here, too, are predicted the sufferings of one afflicted man—Jesus—according to Hebrews 1:10-12 and 13:8.

The psalmist begins by asking God to listen and end his sense of alienation (102:1-2). His suffering, described in verses 3 through 11, consumes him, body and soul. He burns with fever and cannot eat. As if a fire smoldered within him, his life is going up in **smoke** (102:3). Although the specific birds mentioned in verses 6 and 7 cannot be identified with certainty, the message is clear: The psalmist feels utterly alone.

He cannot escape this loneliness. At night it robs him of sleep (102:7) while by day he feels it in the ridicule of his enemies (102:8). What fans the consuming flames is the thought that God is bringing this suffering (102:9-10) in spite of his heartfelt sorrow (evidenced by his **tears** and **ashes** [102:9]) and imminent end (102:11).

In sharp contrast to his transient life (the **I** in verse 11 is emphatic) is the eternal nature of God (the **you** is emphatic in verse 12). This realization marks the turning point of the psalm[2] and begins a bold statement of confidence which lasts through verse 22. For the psalmist, God's eternal nature is no theological abstraction but an affirmation that God is always sovereign, always deserving of glory and capable of intervening at any time.

In verses 13 and 14, God's character is further defined as loving (the **you** is emphatic in verse 13). He is known as compassionate and willing **to show favor**, the latter phrase referring to the mercy due a faithful servant by his master.[3] God cares about what Israel loves (102:14); His love permits the boldness of verse 13b.

The combination of God's eternal nature and love is expressed in His name, Yahweh—a name used seven times in Psalm 102. By this name—which means "I am who I am" or simply "I am"—God revealed himself to His covenant people. A God who is both loving and eternal is a God both willing and able to intervene on behalf of His people.

Intervention is precisely what the psalmist envisioned. Unquestionably, Yahweh will rebuild Jerusalem (102:15-16) in response to the prayers of His people (102:17, 19-20).[4] This will result in universal adoration (102:15, 18, 21-22), where not only Israel but **the nations** (102:15) will come to worship God. Verse 18 describes the worshipers as a people "to be created" (better than **not yet created**), perhaps envisioning the one new people God created in Christ (see Ephesians 2:15).

The psalmist's complaint which appears in Psalm 102:23 seems out of place after the confidence of verses 12 through 22. It is not out of place, however; the psalmist, though confident, still suffers. Even with his confidence, he remains realistic. What is different in this final stanza (102:23-28) is how suffering and God are placed in proper perspective. After brief mention of human transience (102:23-24), the focus quickly returns to God's nature as eternal and loving. As eternal, He brought the universe into being and will remain after it wears out (102:25-27). His love is so great that even the end of the universe will not keep Him from blessing His people (102:28) and helping those who suffer.

ENDNOTES

[1]Psalm 102:27a.

[2]Derek Kidner, *Psalms 73–150,* Tyndale Old Testament Commentaries, ed. D.J. Wiseman (Downer's Grove, Illinois: InterVarsity Press, 1975), p. 361.

[3]Leslie C. Allen, *Psalms 101–150,* Word Biblical Commentary, vol. 21, eds. David A. Hubbard and Glenn W. Barker (Waco, Texas: Word Books, 1983), p. 9.

[4]The certainty of the psalmist in 102:16-17 is displayed in his use of the "prophetic perfect" where the verb tense usually translated as past action is rendered by the future ("will").

101

"PRAISE HIS HOLY NAME"[1]

Psalm 103:1-22

The four psalms with which Book 4 ends (Psalms 103–106) appear to have been purposefully sequenced. Psalm 103 speaks of God's blessings to an individual while Psalm 104 shows how God blessed nature. Psalm 105 points out how God blessed Israel with an inheritance while Psalm 106 acknowledges Israel's guilt and appeals for national restoration to the land after exile.[2]

Psalm 103 has been called "one of the finest blossoms on the tree of biblical faith."[3] It pronounces all God's benefits praiseworthy, but singles out God's love as its theme. The psalmist's experience of forgiveness, verified by God's past actions, has confirmed that **from everlasting to everlasting the Lord's love is with those who fear him** (103:17).

Usually, a call to praise is addressed to others. Here, however, the psalmist summons himself (**my soul** [103:1-2]). This is not because he needs encouragement but because of the personal nature of the **benefits** (103:2). These benefits, most prominently forgiveness, proceed from God's **holy name** (103:1). It seems incongruous to speak of being forgiven by God's holy name. After all, Israel was warned against profaning such a sacred name (see Leviticus 20:3; 22:2, 32) and punished for doing so (see Ezekiel 36:20-23; Amos 2:7). God's holiness, however, means more than absolute purity and hatred of sin. His **holy name** is a source of blessing and salvation for His people (Psalm 106:47; 111:9; 145:21; Ezekiel 39:7-8). God's holiness is as evident in His limitless love as it is in His hatred of evil.

Psalm 103:3-19 provides reasons for this praise, first given briefly (103:3-5), then in more detail (103:6-19). The brief recounting emphasizes not what he has received but the character and ongoing

313

activity of God. He is the God who forgives, heals, redeems, crowns and satisfies. In only three verses, one is lifted from the pit of destruction to soar on eagles' wings.

The specific description of God as one who vindicates the oppressed (103:6) is followed by what was then the greatest example of such vindication—the Exodus (103:7). God's treatment of Israel in the Sinai wilderness is a marvelous illustration of 103:8-10. With three comparisons, God's mercy is described: His **love** *(chesed)* is immeasurably high (103:11), His forgiveness is infinitely wide (103:12), and His **compassions** are intensely personal (103:13).

Such love may be difficult to accept, perhaps due to feelings of unworthiness. God knows that we are made of dust and are as temporary as a flower, and yet He loves us (103:14-16).[4] In fact, despite their brief and apparently insignificant existence, God's love for those who fear Him is eternal (103:17-18). To be loved by Him whose **kingdom rules over all** (103:19) is to know a love which cannot cease (see Romans 8:38-39). In the unending love of the Lord, one becomes eternally significant.

To fully praise such love requires help. Perhaps for this reason, the summons rings out to successively wider circles: first to **angels** and **mighty ones** (Ps. 103:20), then to all **heavenly hosts** and **servants** (103:21), and then to **all his works** (103:22a). God does not merely love the universe, however, He loves individuals and therefore, wants praise from each of us. For this reason, the psalm concludes as it began, summoning the soul—and each one of us—to bless the LORD (103:22b).

ENDNOTES

[1]See Psalm 103:1.

[2]The connection between Psalms 105 and 106 is strengthened if we take the **Praise the LORD** (or "Hallelujah" in the Hebrew), which ends Psalm 104, and place it at the beginning of Psalm 105 as in the Septuagint (Leslie C. Allen, *Psalms 101–150,* Word Biblical Commentary, vol. 21, eds. David A. Hubbard and Glenn W. Barker [Waco, Texas: Word Books, 1983], p. 28); see Derek Kidner, *Psalms 73–150,* Tyndale Old Testament Commentaries, ed. D.J. Wiseman (Downer's Grove, Illinois: InterVarsity Press, 1975), p. 373.

[3]Artur Weiser, *The Psalms—A Commentary,* translated by Herbert Hartwell, The Old Testament Library, gen. eds. G. Ernest Wright, John Bright, James Barr and Peter Ackroyd (Philadelphia: Westminster Press, 1962), p. 657.

[4]**He** is emphatic in 103:14.

102

I SING THE MIGHTY POWER OF GOD

Psalm 104:1-35

Psalm 104 rings with praise to Yahweh for His work as Creator and Sustainer of the world. Its magnificent imagery has inspired such well-known hymns as Robert Grant's "O Worship the King" and Isaac Watts' "I Sing the Mighty Power of God." The psalmist based this hymn on Genesis 1, which he elaborates with rich imagination.[1] The psalmist also wished to assert that it was Yahweh alone who created and sustains. Throughout this psalm Yahweh is exalted over the gods of Israel's neighbors.[2]

After the psalmist summons himself to praise (104:1a; see 103:1), he begins to describe God's glory in imposing language. Nature serves God's purposes—clothing, habitation, transportation, communication; nature is not itself divine (104:1b-4). The Canaanites considered Baal, the storm god, to ride upon the clouds, but here it is Yahweh at the reins (104:3). The psalmist "paints a picture with colors borrowed from the palette of Canaanite lore, to the greater glory of the true God."[3]

In verses 5 through 18, the focus shifts from heaven to earth which is securely established by God. **Waters** cover the earth (see Genesis 1:2) but, unlike ancient Near Eastern myths, those waters are placed there by God and recede at His command (see Psalm 104:6-9). By taming the torrent, Yahweh shows He is sovereign. The ancients feared these waters would return and flood the earth with chaos, a fear put to rest when God set a **boundary** the waters **cannot cross** (104:9). Something of the imagination with which the psalmist treats the Genesis account can be seen in verse 7. God's directive, "Let there be an expanse between the waters" (Gen. 1:6), becomes God's **rebuke** (as a parent might scold a disobedient child; see Proverbs 13:1) through a lightning storm which

sends the floods scampering in fear.[4] The God who **set** both earth
(Ps. 104:5) and waters (104:9) in their places is clearly in charge.

God's power accomplishes what His wisdom dictates, for once
properly placed, the waters cease to threaten and begin to bless (104:10-
13). All living things, from **the wild donkeys** to humankind (104:11-18),
drink at the well of God's provision.

The psalmist focuses again on the heavens, especially on the celestial
bodies as markers of time and season (104:19-23). **The sun,** ascending
and descending on command, is clearly under God's authority. In the
light of **the moon,** nighttime activities reflect divine control, for even the
ferocious **lions roar** to God, requesting **their prey** like house pets. While
sunrise brings a new cast of characters, here too, God is in charge.

Mention of human **work** (104:23) prompts praise for God's many
works, each one reflecting His **wisdom** (104:24). The marine world is
offered as an example (104:25-27), perhaps because of the dread it fostered
in the ancient Near East (104:9). The sea is not a force opposed to God but
part of His good creation. As with the earth (104:20-23), the sea is the
sphere of animal (**leviathan**) and human activity (**ships** [104:26]).

All look to you to give them their food at the proper time (104:27);
all refers to every creature in sea and on land. In God's hand they find
food, in His smile they find joy, and in His frown, fear. In their death,
God rules, for it is He who takes **away their breath** (*ruach;* 104:29) and
to His earth they return as dust. It is God who recreates, supplying His
Spirit (*ruach;* 104:30) and renewing **the earth.**

Because such a Sovereign deserves praise, the psalm closes with a
summons to glorify God (104:31-35). The psalmist requests others to
always honor God for His marvelous creation (104:31-32); then he
offers his own promise of perpetual praise (104:33-34). His wish that
the wicked be punished is not out of place, for the Creator and Sustainer
is also the God of justice; inequity mars the perfection of God's world.
Having spanned heaven and earth, time and eternity, the psalmist
returns to his own soul (104:35b), the soil where each of us must
proclaim Him Lord.

ENDNOTES

[1]For a treatment of the parallels, see Derek Kidner, *Psalms 73–150,* Tyndale
Old Testament Commentaries, ed. D.J. Wiseman (Downer's Grove, Illinois:
InterVarsity Press, 1975), p. 368.

[2]This psalm resembles an earlier Egyptian hymn to the sun god, Aten. The
psalmist may have patterned his hymn on this Egyptian model in order to

redirect all praise to Yahweh, the sun's creator (Kidner, p. 368; Leslie C. Allen, *Psalms 101–150,* Word Biblical Commentary, vol. 21, eds. David A. Hubbard and Glenn W. Barker [Waco, Texas: Word Books, 1983], p. 29).

[3]Allen, p. 33.

[4]There is a play on the Hebrew word *kol,* which can mean "voice" or "the sound of thunder."

103

"HE REMEMBERED HIS HOLY PROMISE"

Psalm 105:1-45

First Chronicles 16:8-22 identifies Psalm 105:1-15 as the song sung when David took the ark into Jerusalem.[1] Whatever its origin, Psalm 105 is primarily a celebration of Israel's blessings as God's chosen people (see Psalm 78). A secondary purpose emerges in the closing words: to call Israel to obey the covenant (105:45a). Such a hymn, with its emphasis upon the Exodus and giving of the land, would have been appropriate at the Feast of Tabernacles.

The call to worship in 105:1-5 contains many of the elements which characterized Israel's worship, including thanksgiving, jubilant song, and remembrance. **Make known among the nations what he has done** (105:1b) reflects Israel's calling to provide the means whereby all the world will be reconciled with God. The **strength** (105:4) to which they ought to look may refer to an attribute of God, or to the ark of the covenant as in Psalm 78:61.

Psalm 105:6-7 serves as a hinge between the call to worship and the historical recollection (105:8-45); those summoned to praise are heirs of the promises given to the patriarchs.[2] God's covenant with Abram, reaffirmed with his descendants, involved more than just the promise of Canaan (105:9-11). It is the land, however, which is the psalmist's chief focus. The patriarchs, although protected and provided for by God (105:12-22), must wander as strangers in the land. They were **prophets** (105:15; see 105:19, 27; Genesis 20:6-7) because they lived confident in God's Word.

One such "prophet" was **Joseph,** sent by God to prepare the way for His people. Joseph's difficulties (105:17-18) illuminate a truth found elsewhere in this psalm (105:12-13, 25): God keeps His promises, but not always immediately. There may even be a time of **bruised . . . feet** and imprisoned necks (105:18).

319

The scene shifts to Egypt in verse 23, but the theme remains: how God keeps His promise concerning the land. **Moses** and **Aaron** are again cast as prophets (see Deuteronomy 18:18) for they perform miraculous signs.[3] While all but two of the ten plagues (livestock and boils) are mentioned in Psalm 105:28-36, they are not in sequence. They begin with **darkness** (ninth), then return to the Nile waters turned into **blood** (first), **frogs** (second), **flies** (fourth), **gnats** (third), **hail** (seventh), **locusts** (eighth), and the death of **all the firstborn** (tenth). The reason for this order remains unclear.

God not only redeems His people but leads them through the wilderness, protecting them with a cloud, lighting their way with a fire, and giving food and water in abundance (105:40-41). Not a word is said here about Israel's wilderness grumblings, a lack which is abundantly supplied in Psalm 106.

The point of this historical account has been to show how God kept His promise of the land (105:42-44). This is clear from the **for** which begins verse 42, and another mention of the promise to Abraham. Here it is referred to as **his holy promise** (105:42)—that is, a promise guaranteed by **his holy name** (105:3). This is also evident in the psalmist's designation of Israel as God's **chosen ones** (105:43; see 105:6)—that is, those chosen for the Promised Land. The psalmist describes God as a promise keeper in order to produce the praise with which this psalm begins and ends (**Praise the LORD** [105:45b]) and to elicit the obedience to God's **precepts** and **laws** called for at its conclusion (105:45a).

The Israelites were not the only ones who needed to remember that God keeps His promises, even if it does not always happen immediately. We, too, must remember this, especially if we are experiencing a time of **bruised . . . feet** and imprisoned necks (105:18). As the Israelites found—through their worship—reason to hope, so may we.

ENDNOTES

[1] Psalm 105:42a.

[2] Although some prefer to date this psalm during the post-exilic period, it appears to be more at home in the happier days prior to the fall of Jerusalem. Nothing within the psalm rules out a date in David's day.

[3] Paul argues in Galatians 3 and 4 that Christians can now also claim Yahweh as **our God.**

[4] Signs are frequently associated with the work of God's prophets. The connection between 105:27 and a prophetic ministry is strengthened by the

inclusion of *dabar,* usually translated "word." Since "words of his signs" is difficult, many translations either omit *dabar* (as in the New International Version and Today's English Version) or translate it with a less common word such as "acts" (Francis Brown, *The New Brown-Driver-Briggs-Gesenius Hebrew and English Lexicon* [Peabody, Massachusetts: Hendrickson Publishers, 1979], p. 183) or "facts" (F. Delitzsch, *Psalms,* Commentary on the Old Testament, vol. V, translated by James Martin [reprint, Grand Rapids, Michigan: Wm. B. Eerdmans Publishing Co., 1978], p. 139); omission and substitution obscure the connection with the prophetic spoken word. The New Jerusalem Bible avoids this mistake and makes good sense of the Hebrew: "They [Moses and Aaron] worked there the wonders he [God] commanded."

104

"THEY FORGOT THEIR GOD"[1]

Psalm 106:1-48

Israel's history, as recorded in Psalm 106, is a sad affair. When read together with Psalm 105, the effect is doubly sobering: In spite of God's faithfulness, the Israelites continually forgot their God. God, in disgust, ejected them from the Promised Land where **they wasted away in their sin** (106:43). Yet there is hope in these words, for God's **love endures forever** (106:1).

The opening verse presents information about God which can be found elsewhere in the Psalter (see 107:1; 118:1). Their presence in a psalm so consumed with Israel's sin, however, shows that God remains good and loving even when His people are neither. Such a God deserves praise (106:2) and righteousness (106:3) and He can be appealed to in time of need (106:4-5).

Before beginning the litany of disobedience which extends nearly to the end of the psalm, the psalmist makes an important assertion in verse 6: **We have sinned.** Israel's present distress has resulted not merely from the sins of their fathers but from their own sins. What would have been a sobering historical summary becomes reverent confession with implied hopes of restoration.

The sad tale is told in eight scenes which begin just outside Egypt and end in Canaan. In the first, alongside the **Red Sea** (106:7-12; see Exodus 13–15), Israel forgot God's power and love. What telling evidence of His mercy that God should perform one of His greatest miracles against the backdrop of rebellion! Israel's praise on the opposite shore was short-lived (see Psalm 106:12; also verse 2).

"How quickly they forget" might be written across the second scene (106:13-15) where Israel turned from trusting to testing God (see Exodus 16).

He supplied their wants but gave them more than they bargained for, "a deep wasting sickness" (NJB). In the third, they forgot whom God appointed as leaders, murmured against Moses and Aaron (see Psalm 106:16-18; Numbers 16) and paid for it with cataclysmic consequences.

In the fourth scene, Israel forgot God entirely, choosing instead a golden calf (see Psalm 106:19-23; Exodus 32). There is no shortage of irony in these verses, for the scene takes place at the foot of Mount Sinai as Moses was receiving God's law. Even as God was graciously revealing himself more fully than ever before, Israel was replacing Him. The exchange was a bad one, for they gave up **their Glory** (Ps. 106:20)— the only glory they knew—for what ate grass. It would have ended in disaster had not Moses thrown himself into the breach.

Israel's refusal to enter Canaan after hearing the report of the twelve spies (see Numbers 14) is pictured in Psalm 106:24-27; again the emphasis is on their disbelief. Because they remained in their tents rather than entering the Promised Land,[1] God removed their opportunity to enter. While wandering in the wilderness, they became ensnared in **Baal** worship (106:28-31; see Numbers 25); they even sacrificed to **lifeless gods** (Ps. 106:28b) or "to the dead" (RSV). The final wilderness scene actually took place earlier at **Meribah** (Ps. 106:32-33; see Numbers 20). Placed last, it emphasizes Israel's guilt in causing Moses to lose his opportunity to enter Canaan.

Their disobedience did not end after they were given the Promised Land (see Psalm 106:34-43). In fact, their idolatry grew worse, even to the point of child sacrifice (see 2 Kings 21:6). The repetition in Psalm 106:37-38 "expresses emotional shock" at such an outrage.[2] God, in anger, allowed His people to be captured and oppressed by **foes** and **enemies**, the very terms used to describe those from whom He had earlier rescued Israel (106:10).

But then God heard their cries for help and was moved to action by **his great love** (106:45). Since he knew this love was eternal, lasting even to his own day, the psalmist found confidence to turn to God (106:44-47). Israel could again resume its role as those who praise God (106:2), having experienced His holy, promise-keeping love (see 105:3, 42).

No one has reason to boast before God. As for Israel, salvation has come to us because of God's never-ending love. For this reason, we can join Israel in this doxology (originally added to conclude Book 4):

Praise be to the Lord, the God of Israel,
from everlasting to everlasting.

Let all the people say, "Amen!"
Praise the LORD (106:48).

ENDNOTES

[1] See Psalm 106:21.

[2] Leslie C. Allen, *Psalms 101–150,* Word Biblical Commentary, vol. 21, eds. David A. Hubbard and Glenn W. Barker (Waco, Texas: Word Books, 1983), p. 54.

[3] Ibid., p. 49.

Part Five

BOOK 5

Psalms 107:1–150:6

L ike Book 4, the psalms in Book 5 seem to favor referring to God as Yahweh. Unlike Book 4, this one attributes a number of psalms to David (Psalms 108–110, 122, 124, 131, 133, 138–145, and possibly 123) and one to Solomon (Psalm 127). Book 5 contains several smaller collections: the Songs of Ascent are found in Psalms 120 through 134, and two collections of psalms are devoted to praise (Psalms 113–118; 146–150). The longest psalm in the Psalter (Psalm 119)—on the theme of the Law—is found in Book 5. This book has no brief doxology, as had the others. Instead, the final psalm (Psalm 150) reflects the doxology for Book 5 and for the whole Psalter.

105

STORIES OF DELIVERANCE

Psalm 107:1-43

P salm 107 answers the prayer of Psalm 106 and prepares for the praise which pervades Book 5 (Psalms 107–150).[1] It contains four scenes of rescue (107:4-32) and one demonstrating God's authority over the land (107:33-42). Common to all is a sovereign God capable of reversing even the most desperate situation.

Some see in Psalm 107 God's redemption of Israel from the Babylonian exile, in part because of the opening description of God as Redeemer (107:2-3).[2] The nautical narrative (107:23-32), however, has no specific connection with the exile but nicely demonstrates God's sovereignty. Waves which terrified sailors (107:26) would be doubly terrifying to land-loving Israelites; a God in control of the ocean would be doubly comforting. Perhaps these scenes originated prior to the exile, and verses 1 through 3 were added later to reflect the post-exilic context.

The redeemed are summoned to thank God for His eternal love *(chesed)* demonstrated in their rescue from the four points of the compass: **from east and west, from north and south** (107:1-3).[3] As will be true for each of the four scenes, the afflicted (107:4-9) are first described (107:4-5), the refrain follows, and **then they cried out to the LORD in their trouble** (107:6a, 13, 19, 28), followed by deliverance. Here Yahweh leads them to where they find (107:6b-7, 9) precisely what they lacked (107:4-5). They are called to thank Yahweh for **his unfailing love** (107:8; see verses 15, 21, 31).

The prisoners described next (107:10-16) sit in **darkness and the deepest gloom** (107:10),[4] and are doubly bound—literally "prisoners of affliction and iron" (107:10b). This together with the first scene portrays the human plight: lost in a wide world, and constrained in a small prison.[5]

In spite of imprisonment for their own rebellion (107:11-12), they cry to **the LORD** (107:13a) and find freedom (107:13b-16; see Luke 1:79). In the words of Charles Wesley,

> Long my imprisoned spirit lay
> Fast bound in sin and nature's night.
> Thine eye diffused a quickening ray,
> I woke, the dungeon flamed with light.
> My chains fell off, my heart was free,
> I rose, went forth, and followed Thee.

God lifts the oppressed from the pit—even one they dug themselves—when they acknowledge that His way is right (see Psalm 107:17-22). Whereas the first two stanzas follow the call to thanks with reasons (107:9, 16), this one substitutes a call for praise and thank offerings (107:22). Only a portion of this offering was sacrificed; the remainder provided a joyous meal where the delivered could tell of God's **works with songs of joy** (107:22). The person who **loathed all food** (107:18) is now sitting at a banquet!

While the **prisoners** (107:10-16) and **fools** (107:17-22) brought trouble on themselves, this is not said of those traveling by sea (107:23-32). The emphasis is on God's power which can, with a word, stir up a storm so great that their seamanship was useless (107:27). Then, when they cry for help, God can hush that storm to **a whisper** (107:28-29). Their response should be to publicly praise and **exalt** God (107:32).[6]

God's sovereign control over the earth is seen in verses 33 through 42. In what is perhaps an allusion to Sodom and Gomorrah,[7] He turns a garden to a desert **because of the wickedness of those who lived there** (107:34b). Just as easily, He turns a desert into a garden (107:35-38).

The same Hebrew verb in verse 38 (**diminish**) is used again in verse 39 (**decreased**), heightening the reversal described in verses 39 through 42. Jesus' mother sang about such a reversal by the sovereign God who "brought down rulers from their thrones" and "lifted up the humble" (Luke 1:52), bringing joy to the righteous and silence to the wicked (see Psalm 107:42). We, too, can respond to the psalmist's final summons (107:43) to consider how **the great love of the LORD** can turn our desert into a garden.

ENDNOTES

[1]See F. Delitzsch, *Psalms,* Commentary on the Old Testament, vol. V, translated by James Martin (reprint, Grand Rapids, Michigan: Wm. B. Eerdmans Publishing Co., 1978), pp. 162–63.

[2]Derek Kidner (*Psalms 73–150,* Tyndale Old Testament Commentaries, ed. D.J. Wiseman [Downer's Grove, Illinois: InterVarsity Press, 1975], p. 383) points out that such an identification is obscured by modern translations (including the New International Version) which standardize the beginning of all four stanzas ("Some . . ."), although the introductions are not identical in the Hebrew (p. 384).

[3]The final point is, literally, "sea." Some assume a copyist's error (since the Hebrew words for sea and south are very similar), others see a reference to the Red Sea or Mediterranean Sea in the southwest (Delitzsch, p. 165). But see Allen (Leslie C. Allen, *Psalms 101–150,* Word Biblical Commentary, vol. 21, eds. David A. Hubbard and Glenn W. Barker [Waco, Texas: Word Books, 1983], p. 58), who translates it "overseas."

[4]The latter, **deepest gloom,** is the same word used in Psalm 23:4, translated "shadow of death," "deep darkness," or "dark as death."

[5]Kidner, p. 385.

[6]**Exalt** comes from the same verb used for the waves which are **lifted high** in 107:25.

[7]Allen, p. 60.

106

AN OLD SONG FOR A NEW DAY

Psalm 108:1-13

As indicated in the New International Version, this psalm is actually a combination of passages from two psalms. Verses 1 through 5 are taken from Psalm 57:7-11 (with minor variations), while verses 6 through 13 can be found, slightly changed, in Psalm 60:5-12.[1] Such a combination reflects Israel's recognition that God and His promises did not change, and thus, they could be relied upon under any circumstances. By combining earlier material, that material is enriched. In Psalm 60, Moab, Edom and Philistia represent Israel's neighbors, but when combined with 108:5 (see Psalm 57:11) in Psalm 108, these nations symbolize the universal dominion which God will inaugurate.[2]

Although Psalms 57 and 60 reflect times of individual peril, Psalm 108 summons the entire nation to step out in faith. This fits well the post-exilic setting when trust and courage were needed for a reestablished Israel. Also during this time, the hope for a Messiah came to pervade Jewish thought. This hope is right at home with Psalm 108,[3] to one day be fully realized by the One of whom it is said, "He treads the winepress of the fury of the wrath of God Almighty. On his robe and on his thigh he has this name written: KING OF KINGS AND LORD OF LORDS" (Revelation 19:15b-16).

ENDNOTES

[1]For various reasons, scholars believe this psalm borrowed from the other psalms (Derek Kidner, *Psalms 73–150,* Tyndale Old Testament Commentaries, ed. D.J. Wiseman [Downer's Grove, Illinois: InterVarsity Press, 1975], p. 387). See the earlier psalms for discussion of these verses.

[2]J. Becker, *Israel deutet seine Psalmen,* Stuttgarter Bibelstudien 18

(Stuttgart: Verlag Katholisches Bibelwerk, 1966), pp. 65–67, as cited by Leslie C. Allen, *Psalms 101–150,* Word Biblical Commentary, vol. 21, eds. David A. Hubbard and Glenn W. Barker (Waco, Texas: Word Books, 1983), p. 68.

[3]"It seems that the selection and combination here bring a new meaning to the future when the Messiah will deliver Israel from exile and lead them in the conquest over their enemies" (A. Cohen, *The Psalms,* Soncino Books of the Bible, ed. A. Cohen [London: Soncino, 1950], p. 364, citing the medieval Jewish scholar, David Kimchi).

107

HARSH WORDS IN A HARSH WORLD

Psalm 109:1-31

This psalm is not an easy one to read. It appears to grate against the ethic of civility taught in the Sermon on the Mount. The contrast is less striking, however, when compared with Luke's version of the Sermon on the Mount (see Luke 6:20-49) where Jesus utters woes against the rich, well-fed, happy and popular. As with Psalm 69, early Christians saw in the experience of the psalmist the suffering and vindication of Jesus (see Acts 1:20).[1]

The harsh words of the psalmist arise not from agitation or inconvenience but from a deeply wounded heart (see Psalm 109:1-5). In spite of his piety (he gives **praise** [109:1]) and **prayer** (109:4), innocence (109:3) and **friendship** (109:4-5), he has been publicly slandered by ungodly and treacherous deceivers. Without minimizing the emotional trauma of such injustice, its most grievous effect is the challenge it poses to his God.

Convinced that God will not permit this challenge to go unanswered, the psalmist takes his case before the righteous Judge (see 109:6-20). The tone of his appeal is righteous indignation rather than vindictiveness. While it is possible to take all or part of these verses as a quotation of the enemy's curses against the psalmist (see the New International Version's footnote) rather than the psalmist's curses against the enemy, the approach followed by the NIV's text is to be preferred.[2]

The curse in 109:6-15 strikes at what was most meaningful in that society: a loss of standing before God and humanity (109:6-7, 14-15), an early death (109:8-9), the loss of wealth (109:10-12), and the loss of progeny (109:13). **Accuser** (109:6b; forms of the word appear in verses 4, 20, 29) translates the Hebrew from which we get "Satan"; here it lacks any supernatural overtones.

The psalmist asks that all the enemy has accumulated through his malice—wealth, prestige, and a continual **name** through coming generations (109:13-15)—be taken away. Let the enemy be treated as he has treated others (109:16-17), as his very nature requires (109:18-19), and as a righteous God demands (109:20).

Having negated his enemy's curses by placing the matter in God's hands, the psalmist now requests God's help and explains why it is needed (109:21-31). God must act to preserve His reputation as righteous and loving (109:21). A loving God could not overlook the psalmist's great suffering (109:22-25). Although he earnestly and fervently seeks God, he remains as detestable as an insect clinging to a garment and as easily dispatched (109: 23-24). Only his enemies notice his efforts and mock him for it (109:25).

Once again he appeals for vindication (109:26-29). This time, however, he asks that it come in such a way that all can see clearly that God has done it (109:27-28). Verse 29 echoes verses 18 and 19, asking that those who wore cursing as their clothing now be clothed in the very shame they produced. Then he will praise God (109:30) for the clear evidence of His care for the condemned (109:31). **With my mouth** emphasizes the act of praising, while **in the great throng** speaks of restored social relationships (see verses 4-5). The psalmist has had an accuser at his right hand and requested that his enemy experience the same (verses 4, 6). Now he anticipates a time when Yahweh himself will stand at his right hand resulting in complete vindication. For the Christian, anticipation has become reality, for we have One who intercedes for us before God (see Romans 8:27, 34; 1 John 2:1) and enables complete salvation (see Hebrews 7:25).

ENDNOTES

[1] For more on imprecatory psalms, see the introduction to this commentary.

[2] Putting these words into the mouth of the enemy tones down the offensiveness of this psalm and explains the shift to a single enemy (see 109:6-19). But the singular could be used collectively (all alike) or distributively (each one of them) or could be directed to the leader of the hostile forces (see Leslie C. Allen, *Psalms 101–150*, Word Biblical Commentary, vol. 21, eds. David A. Hubbard and Glenn W. Barker [Waco, Texas: Word Books, 1983], pp. 72–73).

108

AT YAHWEH'S RIGHT HAND

Psalm 110:1-7

Psalm 110 is the Old Testament passage most frequently cited by the New Testament authors who found its combination of victorious king and eternal priest a perfect description of the Lord Jesus.[1] The psalm appears to have originally been written as a glowing description of Israel's earthly king, perhaps even to celebrate his enthronement. By the post-exilic period, such a portrayal was taken to refer to the coming King, the Anointed One, the Messiah.

The psalm can be divided into two stanzas (verses 1-3 and 4-7), each beginning with a message from God followed by the psalmist's elaboration. One problem with this approach is that the elaboration in verses 5 through 7 seems to have little to do with the oracle in verse 4. Perhaps more helpful is the outline which identifies three stanzas (verses 1-2, 3-4, and 5-7), describing the king first as absolute ruler, then as eternal priest, and finally as warrior.[2]

The psalm begins with a message from God, introduced forcefully (110:1). The **right hand** was a place of honor where the **Lord** (king) could be seated until the **Lord** (Yahweh) defeated his **enemies.** They will become his **footstool,** an allusion to military triumph (see Joshua 10:24; Psalm 108:9).[3] The king's rule, as an extension of Yahweh's, will be extensive and absolute (see Psalm 110:2).

Although 110:3 is difficult to translate, it appears to describe a holy army, literally, "freewill offerings" **arrayed in holy majesty,** arriving in abundance with the dawn. Over this army of priests stands the priest-king, appointed for eternity by Yahweh himself (110:4).[4] Israel's king was not to function as priest in the Levitical sense (see 2 Chronicles 26:16-21). By virtue of his role as "first citizen" in the theocracy (where Yahweh was the true king), however, he filled a priestly role representing God to the people and the people to God.[5] This is the role which Psalm 110:3-4 emphasizes, a role which took on much deeper significance in light of Calvary.

Verses 5 through 7 bring us to the battle itself. Although many take **Lord** (110:5) to refer to God, it is difficult to see 110:7 as true of Him. Since the king is called **Lord** in 110:1 and is described as being at Yahweh's right hand, verses 5 through 7 are probably the king's words, spoken to God. By faith, he envisions the realization of the promised victory (see 110:2) and sees his rule extending throughout the earth (see 110:6). **Crushing the rulers** (110:6) is, literally, "shattering the head." Unlike those rulers, Israel's king will have his head lifted up in victory (see 110:7). To **drink from a brook beside the way** could refer to the enthronement ritual[6] or could allude to God's continuing provision of strength for the king.

This description is certainly larger than life, even for Israel's greatest kings. In Jesus, however, the perfect fulfillment of this ideal is found. He came in the power and authority of His Father (see John 8:54-58), became the "mediator of a new covenant" (Hebrews 9:15), and remains the warrior who, with justice, "judges and makes war" against wickedness (see Revelation 19:11).

ENDNOTES

[1]Some of the passages where it is quoted or alluded to include Matthew 22:44; 26:64; Mark 12:36; 14:62; 16:19; Luke 20:42-43; 22:69; Acts 2:34-35; 1 Corinthians 15:25; Ephesians 1:20; Colossians 3:1; Hebrews 1:3, 13; 5:6, 10; 6:20; 7:3-28; 8:1; 10:12-13; 12:2; 1 Peter 3:22. Mark 12:35-37 and Acts 2:34 are used to support Davidic authorship.

[2]Derek Kidner (*Psalms 73–150,* Tyndale Old Testament Commentaries, ed. D.J. Wiseman [Downer's Grove, Illinois: InterVarsity Press, 1975], pp. 391–96) comes close to this view as do other commentators (see Leslie C. Allen, *Psalms 101–150,* Word Biblical Commentary, vol. 21, eds. David A. Hubbard and Glenn W. Barker [Waco, Texas: Word Books, 1983], p. 85, for a fuller discussion).

[3]Egyptian art pictures the Pharaoh with his feet resting upon a footstool carved with the likeness of his enemies (Othmar Keel, *The Symbolism of the Biblical World: Ancient Near Eastern Iconography and the Book of Psalms,* translated by Timothy J. Hallett [New York: Seabury Press, 1978], p. 255).

[4]Although only mentioned in the Old Testament here and in Genesis 14:18-20, Melchizedek intrigued the Israelites. Jewish writings from the time between the Old Testament and New Testament present him as a model for the Messiah. Early Christians made much of the similarities between Jesus and this priest-king from Salem (see Hebrews 5–7).

[5]David performed priestly duties in 2 Samuel 6:14-18, and his sons were referred to as "priests" (2 Samuel 8:18; A. Cohen, *The Psalms,* Soncino Books of the Bible, ed. A. Cohen [London: Soncino, 1950], p. 372).

[6]Allen (p. 82), citing 1 Kings 1:38, which refers to Solomon's coronation at the spring at Gihon.

109

A PRIMER OF PRAISE

Psalm 111:1-10

B y more than one definition, Psalm 111 is a primer of praise. As a primer can provide a brief introduction to a subject, so this psalm introduces God's praiseworthy deeds. It is the first of a trilogy of psalms beginning with the declaration, **Praise the LORD** *(Hallelu Yah)*.

A primer is also a device used to teach children to read. Some have suggested that the acrostic style in which this psalm was written[1] was used to help Hebrew children learn their letters. As a primer is also a thing which ignites something else, so Psalm 111 is intended to provoke an explosion of praise in the worshiper.

After the opening verse with its promise of exuberant, public and widespread praise (**I will extol the LORD**), the remainder of the psalm provides reasons for praise (see 111:2-10) which focus on the great works of God. That **they are pondered by all who delight in them** (111:2b) implies that these works are both delightful and worthy of careful study. **Glorious and majestic** (111:3a) translates a Hebrew play on words (also found in Psalms 45:3 and 104:1) while **righteousness** (111:3) refers particularly to God's actions as Vindicator of the righteous. The phrase, **he has caused his wonders to be remembered** (111:4a) probably alludes to God's command that Israel regularly commemorate its deliverance from Egypt,[2] God's greatest demonstration of grace and compassion (see Exodus 34:6). By not specifically mentioning the Exodus, the worshiper is encouraged to consider the full scope of God's wondrous works, as typified in the Exodus.

God not only provided manna and meat for the Israelites in the wilderness, He continues to **provide food for those who fear Him** (Ps. 111:5).[3] He showed His military might by defeating Israel's enemies and granting them the land of Canaan (111:6). He revealed His will through the Law (111:7-8), described as faithful, just, trustworthy and eternal. The creation of Israel as a nation demonstrates that God is holy and to be revered (111:9).

To recognize God's redemption leads to the fear of God, where wisdom begins (**awesome** [111:9c] and **fear** [111:10a] come from the same Hebrew verb). More than knowledge about God, such **wisdom** involves obedience to His law (111:10b). Unlike other types of wisdom, this wisdom produces not pride but praise. In fact, wisdom produces praise which produces wisdom which produces praise . . . and on goes the cycle forever, enabling the psalmist to speak of **eternal praise** (111:10c). The primer has done its work and prompted praise which need not end.

ENDNOTES

[1]There are two letters per verse in 111:1-8 and three per verse in 111:9-10. For more on acrostics, see the discussion on literary elements in Hebrew poetry in the introduction to this commentary.

[2]Passover (see Exodus 13:1-16—Passover is the time when the Jews remember their deliverance from Egypt. The word *Passover* refers to the "passing over" of the angel of death [in the tenth plague upon Egypt], who did not destroy any inhabitants of the Israelite homes under the sign of the blood [see Exodus 12].); the Feasts of Tabernacles (see Leviticus 23:43) and Weeks (see Deuteronomy 16:9-12—The Jewish Feast of Weeks is another name for Pentecost; the day is part of the Jewish observances, and was the beginning of the offering of first fruits. Pentecost primarily refers to the New Testament event when the Holy Spirit was given to the church; this occurred on the day of Pentecost. The Greek term that *Pentecost* comes from means "fiftieth" or "the fiftieth day" and is literally the fiftieth day after the end of the Passover.); and the Sabbath (see Deuteronomy 5:15) all served this purpose (see *Psalms 73–150* by Derek Kidner, Tyndale Old Testament Commentaries, ed. D.J. Wiseman [Downer's Grove, Illinois: InterVarsity Press, 1975], p. 397; *The Psalms* by A. Cohen, Soncino Books of the Bible, ed. A. Cohen [London: Soncino, 1950], p. 374).

[3]This may explain why the psalmist chose a less common word for **food** which is usually translated prey (see Leslie C. Allen, *Psalms 101–150,* Word Biblical Commentary, vol. 21, eds. David A. Hubbard and Glenn W. Barker [Waco, Texas: Word Books, 1983], p. 89). Delitzsch suggests that the **food** could refer to the Passover meal (F. Delitzsch, *Psalms,* Commentary on the Old Testament, vol. V, translated by James Martin [reprint, Grand Rapids, Michigan: Wm. B. Eerdmans Publishing Co., 1978], p. 198).

110

BLESSING ON THE RIGHTEOUS

Psalm 112:1-10

Psalm 112 elaborates the thought with which Psalm 111 concluded: the fear of Yahweh. This is but one link between the two psalms; others include the acrostic style, common opening line (**Praise the LORD,** *Hallelu Yah*) and shared phrases (for example, 111:2 and 112:1). While Psalm 111 exalted God, Psalm 112 celebrates God's person. The psalmist reverences Yahweh by showing great delight in His law (112:1). He is fair (**justice** [112:5b]) and **compassionate** (112:4), even in the use of money (112:5a, 9a). The righteous person not only fears God but trusts Him as well (112:7).

The blessings which come to the righteous read like a Hebrew "wish list." Offspring that are both wealthy and powerful (112:2-3a) mean years of honor for the parent. The phrase, **righteousness endures forever** (112:3b) is found in Psalm 111:3b where it refers to God. In order to imply that God serves as the model for the godly, here the phrase is used to describe the upright.

The **light** which shines in the **darkness** (112:4) could be God's light on the righteous (as the NIV) or it could be the righteous person who shines on the less fortunate.[1] If the latter is correct, this is another example of the righteous person being described in terms used elsewhere for God himself (see 111:3b; Isaiah 60:2).[2] The godly will be rewarded with God's best (**good** [Ps. 112:5]) and with stability (**surely** adds emphasis in 112:6). "There is no need to set up monuments to the righteous," said the rabbis, "their acts are their memorial."[3]

The security promised in 112:7-8a is not freedom from trouble but fearlessness in trouble. Having feared God, the righteous person has nothing else to fear.[4] God will bring victory (112:8b), honor (112:9) and permanence (112:9, 3b, 6b) to the godly, described here as the one who **has scattered abroad his gifts to the poor** (112:9a). Comparison with Psalm 111:5 shows that once again the godly person is described as continuing the work of God.

The blessing of the righteous will infuriate the wicked man but his rage alters nothing, except to diminish what little strength remains to him. **Waste away** (112:10) can be translated "saturated" (Isaiah 34:3), or it can describe weak, unhealthy animals (1 Samuel 15:9). It is used to picture wax melting into liquid in a fire (Psalm 22:14b; 97:5; 2 Samuel 17:10); or disintegration, such as what happened to the ropes on Samson's wrists when the Spirit came upon him (Judges 15:14); or the manna on the ground when the sun rose (Exodus 16:21). **Waste away** can also portray the process of emaciation in a dying person (Isaiah 10:18) which is probably the meaning here. What a contrast to the blessing and permanence of the righteous! To take up the character and duties of God brings with it the smile of God.

ENDNOTES

[1]Derek Kidner, *Psalms 73–150,* Tyndale Old Testament Commentaries, ed. D.J. Wiseman (Downer's Grove, Illinois: InterVarsity Press, 1975), p. 399.

[2]Ibid.

[3]As cited by A. Cohen, *The Psalms,* Soncino Books of the Bible, ed. A. Cohen (London: Soncino, 1950), p. 377.

[4]N. Tate and N. Brady, as cited by Leslie C. Allen, *Psalms 101–150,* Word Biblical Commentary, vol. 21, eds. David A. Hubbard and Glenn W. Barker (Waco, Texas: Word Books, 1983), p. 97.

111

"WHO STOOPS DOWN TO LOOK"[1]

Psalm 113:1-9

Psalm 113 is the last in a triad of praise psalms, each beginning with **Praise the LORD** (*Hallelu Yah*; this psalm ends with it as well). It also stands first in the Egyptian Hallel (Psalms 113–118), a collection of psalms sung at several Jewish holy days to commemorate deliverance from Egypt. Very possibly these psalms were sung by Jesus and the Twelve at the Last Supper. If so, Psalms 113 through 114 probably preceded the meal, and Psalms 115 through 118 followed it.[2]

The opening call to praise (113:1-3) specifies who is to praise—**servants of the LORD** (113:1), making praise more than flattery. The call also identifies the content of the praise—**the name of the LORD** (113:1), preventing praise from becoming guesswork.[3] With the name of Yahweh as subject, praise would never lack for content, for this was the name by which He revealed himself to Israel. The call to praise also identifies when to praise (**both now and forevermore** [113:2]) and where: everywhere, **from the rising of the sun to the place where it sets** (113:3).

Praise must be wholehearted, for it is due to a God who is exalted over all nations and the heavens themselves (113:4). The rhetorical question, **Who is like the LORD our God** (113:5a) is followed by a description of God as so far elevated above earth that He must stoop to see what is happening there (113:5b-6).

But He does stoop to look and thus reveals His concern for the destitute, the theme of the remaining verses (113:7-9). Seeing the poor and needy, He raises them from the **dust** and **ash heap** and from the utter despair which their surroundings represent. The psalmist expresses the exaltation of the poor (113:7) in terms used for God's exaltation of himself (113:4). The latter makes possible the former while the former is one way of demonstrating the latter. Removed from their desperate surroundings, God sets them among princes, a place of great honor. To be seated among **the princes of their people** is even more honorable than among princes of foreign nations.[4] Again the exaltation of the poor is described in terms reflecting God's exaltation (see **seats** in verse 8 with **sits** in verse 5).

In a final picture of God's graciousness, He grants the heart-cry of a childless woman (113:9). To be **barren** was considered a disgrace and left the status of the childless wife in jeopardy.[5] To be granted **children** (literally, "sons") would not only bring overwhelming joy but also security. God reveals His greatness in meeting the needs of one individual.

Perhaps this illustration is meant to bring to mind Samuel's mother, Hannah, whose song is partially reproduced in 113:7-8a (see 1 Samuel 2:8). If so, the worshiper would remember how God's blessing to this woman meant blessing to all Israel through the ministry of her son, the prophet.[6] The use of this psalm on festival days supports the idea that the barren woman may also stand for the nation of Israel (see Isaiah 54:1; 66:8), blessed by God with an abundant population.

God's greatness is evident in His exaltation above the heavens and in His compassion for the neediest of the needy. It is most clearly seen, however, in how He shows compassion in spite of His greatness—**he stoops down to look** (Ps. 113:6).

ENDNOTES

[1]Psalm 113:6a.

[2]Derek Kidner, *Psalms 73–150,* Tyndale Old Testament Commentaries, ed. D.J. Wiseman (Downer's Grove, Illinois: InterVarsity Press, 1975), p. 401; Leslie C. Allen, *Psalms 101–150,* Word Biblical Commentary, vol. 21, eds. David A. Hubbard and Glenn W. Barker (Waco, Texas: Word Books, 1983), p. 100; see Matthew 26:30; Mark 14:26.

[3]Kidner, p. 401.

[4]A. Cohen, *The Psalms,* Soncino Books of the Bible, ed. A. Cohen (London: Soncino, 1950), p. 379.

[5]J.W. Meiklejohn, "Barrenness," *New Bible Dictionary,* rev. ed. (Wheaton, Illinois: Tyndale House Publishers, 1982), p. 125.

[6]Kidner, p. 402.

112

THE PRESENCE OF THE LORD

Psalm 114:1-8

Of the psalms which make up the Egyptian Hallel (see Psalm 113), only Psalm 114 makes explicit mention of the Exodus and does so with striking eloquence. In a sense, it can be understood as elaborating Psalm 113:7-9, supplying "the supreme historical illustration of the claims there made."[1]

Israel did not belong in Egypt among those who did not share the same language (114:1). They belonged in their own country under God's rule and with God's sanctuary in their midst (114:2). As they exited Egypt and moved through the wilderness to the boundary of Canaan, nature grew excited. The parting of the **sea** (see Exodus 13–14) marked the beginning of the journey; the stopping of the Jordan (see Joshua 3), the ending. The skipping of the mountains and hills pictures the shaking of Mount Sinai at the giving of the Law, the most significant event in the wilderness.[2]

Commentator Derek Kidner compares the actions of the Sea, Jordan, mountains and hills to children, "all animated and agog."[3] Psalm 114:5-6 asks the question: Why did they act this way? The answer is given in verse 7: God was there. This point is made more clearly in the Hebrew which translates literally: "before the Lord, tremble O earth, before the God of Jacob." Sea and river saw God and fled; the mountains and hills shook in His presence. Now the psalmist summons the whole earth to do so as well.

God of Jacob (114:7) implies His intention to be faithful to His covenant promises,[4] faithfulness further suggested by the description of God as the One who brought water from rock (114:8; see 78:15-16, 30; Exodus 17:6; Numbers 20:11). Just as Psalm 113 moved from God's majesty to His care for the individual, so this psalm proceeds from God's might (at the sight of which seas flee) to His patient provision of the water of life.[5]

God's ministry in the person of Jesus beautifully illustrates this combination of power and blessing. The One who walked on the water and quieted it with a word promised, "If anyone is thirsty, let him come to me and drink. Whoever believes in me, as the Scripture has said, streams of living water will flow from within him" (John 7:37-38).

ENDNOTES

[1]A. Cohen, *The Psalms,* Soncino Books of the Bible, ed. A. Cohen (London: Soncino, 1950), p. 380.

[2]Ibid.; see Exodus 19:18; 15:14-16; Psalm 68:8; 29:6.

[3]Derek Kidner, *Psalms 73–150,* Tyndale Old Testament Commentaries, ed. D.J. Wiseman (Downer's Grove, Illinois: InterVarsity Press, 1975), p. 403. "With a superb flourish it shows us the scurrying and excitement set up by the Creator's arrival with His earthly court: sea and river falling over themselves, so to speak, to make way for Him; mountains and hills no longer aloof and majestic but all animated and agog."

[4]Kidner.

[5]Ibid.; Delitzsch points out that this psalm ends with a "practical proof of unlimited omnipotence and of the grace which converts death into life" (F. Delitzsch, *Psalms,* Commentary on the Old Testament, vol. V, translated by James Martin [reprint, Grand Rapids, Michigan: Wm. B. Eerdmans Publishing Co., 1978], p. 209).

113

"OUR GOD IS IN HEAVEN"[1]

Psalm 115:1-18

The third of the Egyptian Hallel psalms (Psalms 113–118) was written to express Israel's trust in Yahweh, perhaps in a time of difficulty. That it was intended for public worship is evident; Bible commentator Cohen suggests that verses 1 through 8 and 16 through 18 were sung by a choir of Levites, while each of the intervening verses was sung antiphonally.[2]

As it stands, the opening confession of trust (115:1) could be spoken in either triumph or tribulation. The taunt of the enemy in verse 2 and God's remembrance in verse 12 suggest Israel is in trouble. At such a time, God's **love** *(chesed)* and **faithfulness** are important foundations for appeal.

That Israel, unlike its neighbors, was to have no visible representations of its deity left that nation vulnerable to ridicule, especially in times of national disaster. This explains the mockery of the enemy: **Where is their God?** (115:2). The psalmist turns Yahweh's invisibility into an argument for His superiority (115:3); he argues that God cannot be seen because He is in heaven where He exercises unlimited control.

Then follows a scathing denunciation of idolatry (115:4-8).[3] Some scholars criticize Israel for these immature tirades and explain away such passages as mere propaganda. More likely, Israel lampooned idols because they so perfectly typified the powerlessness of the gods they represented. Israel was laughing at impotence, not idolatry. After all, what characterized Israel's faith was not the absence of idols but the worship of the one, all-powerful God.

Although they were valuable as objects, having been made from precious metal, idols are valueless as objects of worship, because they were **made by the hands of men** (115:4b). (The contrast between the

349

descriptions in verses 3b and 4b is stronger in the Hebrew where **does** and **made** are formed from the same verb root.) They are shaped like humans by humans but cannot do what humans do—speak, see, hear, smell, feel, or walk (115:5-7). They cannot even **utter a sound with their throats** (115:7c), that is, grunt to express basic emotions.[4] Those who make idols and those who trust in them become like the idols, powerless (115:8).

Mention of those who trust in idols leads to a call for faith in the sovereign God (115:9-15). The summons goes out to three groups: the **house of Israel** (verse 9), the **house of Aaron** (verse 10) and **you who fear him** (verse 11) followed by **he is their help and shield.** The first group probably refers to all the lay people of the nation and the second to the priests. The third group could be an all-encompassing description or could refer to non-Israelite worshipers of God.[5]

Israel should trust because God will remember and bless (115:12-13). Blessing is described in the same order as earlier—Israel, Aaron and those who fear God—this time the last phrase is supplemented with **small and great alike.** The pronouncement of impotence in verse 8 contrasts with the pronouncement of increase in verses 14 and 15. Such a promise would be especially meaningful in post-exilic days when Israel's population was depleted.

God made heaven and earth (115:15) but the idols can do nothing. He has chosen to reside in heaven (115:3) but has designated the earth for humanity. How foolish to worship powerless gods while living in the world created by the sovereign God and given to us! How foolish to use earthly and God-given materials to fashion idols to impotent gods! How important that we who claim to worship the one true God use the world and all it contains to support rather than deny our claim.

Such a God deserves praise, something only the living can do (115:17-18). For this reason **it is we who extol the LORD** (115:18; **we** is emphatic in the Hebrew). Even if the final **praise the LORD** was not originally part of the psalm, it illustrates the praise which is to go on **both now and forevermore.**

ENDNOTES

[1]Psalm 115:3a.

[2]See Ezra 3:11; A. Cohen, *The Psalms,* Soncino Books of the Bible, ed. A. Cohen (London: Soncino, 1950), p. 382.

[3]See Isaiah 40:18-20; 44:9-20; and Jeremiah 10:1-16. Psalm 115:4-11 appears in Psalm 135:15-20.

[4]Cohen, p. 383; Leslie C. Allen, *Psalms 101–150,* Word Biblical Commentary, vol. 21, eds. David A. Hubbard and Glenn W. Barker (Waco, Texas: Word Books, 1983), p. 108.

[5]Allen (p. 108) chooses the first option, while Kidner (*Psalms 73–150,* Tyndale Old Testament Commentaries, ed. D.J. Wiseman [Downer's Grove, Illinois: InterVarsity Press, 1975], p. 406) and the medieval rabbi Shlomo ben Isaac (cited by Cohen, p. 383) choose the second.

114

CALL UPON THE LORD

Psalm 116:1-19

At a particularly difficult time, perhaps during a serious illness, the psalmist cried out to God and promised public praise if delivered. His prayer was answered; Psalm 116 records the fulfillment of that vow. After the sacrifice of a thank offering in the Temple, a communal meal would be held during which this psalm was recited to the assembled guests.[1] Psalm 116 became part of the Egyptian Hallel when the psalmist's experience was taken over by the nation to express its deliverance from Egypt.

The first stanza (116:1-7) contains an account of the psalmist's difficulty (116:3-4) flanked by expressions of confidence (116:1-2, 5-6). Verse 2b fits better in this context when translated "and all my life I will proclaim."[2] With Death pursuing him like a hunter after game, the psalmist cries out (the verb tense implies repeated crying) for deliverance in the name of Yahweh (115:4; see Psalm 18:4-5). The answer to that prayer shaped the description of God in 115:5-6: **gracious,** willing to vindicate the upright (**righteous**), and full of **compassion.** His love extends even to those who do not deserve it, the **simplehearted** who create their own problems. Having such a God, the **soul** can be perfectly composed (115:7).[3]

The second stanza (115:8-14) celebrates the psalmist's complete deliverance—from **death, tears,** even **stumbling** (115:8). Now he can walk about freely in broad, spacious lands (see 116:9; 56:13). According to 115:10-11, the psalmist's faith was not extinguished by his dire circumstances, God's delay (115:4) or the faithlessness of others. These only increased the intensity of his faith and drove him to pray to the God of verses 5 and 6. The stanza concludes with his promise to publicly express thanks (115:13-14). As he prayed (115:4), so he will proclaim (115:13).

The verse which opens the final stanza (115:15-19) has likely brought comfort to many in their final hour. While God does not always prevent the death of those He loves, each loss costs Him dearly. Since this time the psalmist has been spared, he strongly reaffirms his allegiance to God saying, **truly, I am your servant** (**truly** is emphatic). He is not only a servant, but the son of God's **maidservant**—that is, a lifelong member of the master's household.[4] The promise of a **sacrifice** and public testimony reappears (115:17-19). **The cup of salvation** (115:13) is replaced by the sacrifice of a **thank offering** (115:17) **in the courts of the house of the LORD** (115:19).

Much has changed from the psalmist's day to this. We no longer have a Temple or altar. We no longer have a communal meal to publicly thank God for deliverance (although the idea has merit). But God has not changed. He still allows His children to call upon His name and still honors the faith that holds firm in spite of difficulties. And He remains delighted with the public proclamation of His power by His people.

ENDNOTES

[1] For more on such songs of thanksgiving, see the discussion on psalm types in the introduction to the commentary.

[2] Leslie C. Allen, *Psalms 101–150,* Word Biblical Commentary, vol. 21, eds. David A. Hubbard and Glenn W. Barker (Waco, Texas: Word Books, 1983), pp. 111–12.

[3] The Hebrew word translated **rest** in 116:7 indicates a perfect rest (A. Cohen, *The Psalms,* Soncino Books of the Bible, ed. A. Cohen [London: Soncino, 1950], p. 386).

[4] Allen (p. 113), citing R. de Vaux.

115

ALL PEOPLES ON EARTH WILL BE BLESSED THROUGH YOU

Psalm 117:1-2

For all its brevity, Psalm 117, addressed to all the **nations** and all the **peoples** of the world, offers a perspective of universal proportions.[1] The topic to be taken up by all earth's inhabitants is God's **love** and **faithfulness** to Israel (117:2a). Given the place of this psalm in the Egyptian Hallel (Psalms 113–118), the psalmist probably has the Exodus in mind. God redeemed Israel because He was faithful to His people. He cared about their suffering and remembered the promise he made to their forefathers (see Exodus 6:4-5). In the Exodus, God showed that "His faithful love is strong" (Exod. 6:2 TEV), strong enough to defeat the Egyptians, control nature, and tolerate Israel's complaints.

The call for foreigners to praise God for His love and faithfulness to Israel was more than just nationalistic bluster on the part of Israel. Universal recognition of the greatness of God has been a part of Israel's mission from the beginning. When God called Abram to be the father of the Jewish nation, it was so that "all peoples on earth will be blessed through you" (Genesis 12:3). In the words of the Jewish scholar, Abraham Cohen, "the mission of Israel remains unfulfilled until the hope voiced in this Psalm becomes a reality."[2]

Christians contend that this psalm has already begun to become a reality, thanks to the Messiah's death on the cross.[3] So Paul understood it. In his letter to the Romans, he quoted Psalm 117:1 to defend the spread of the gospel among the Gentiles (see Romans 15:11). Now, through Jesus, all nations can know and praise the God who is revealing himself to them. We would do well to consider the reminder of Bible commentator Derek Kidner that the use of this psalm obligates the user to make known the love and faithfulness of God to all the world.[4]

ENDNOTES

[1]This is the shortest psalm in the Psalter and the shortest chapter in the Bible.

[2]A. Cohen, *The Psalms,* Soncino Books of the Bible, ed. A. Cohen (London: Soncino, 1950), p. 388.

[3]Significantly, this may have been one of the last psalms sung by Jesus and the disciples before His arrest and crucifixion (for more, see comments on Psalm 113).

[4]Derek Kidner, *Psalms 73–150,* Tyndale Old Testament Commentaries, ed. D.J. Wiseman (Downer's Grove, Illinois: InterVarsity Press, 1975), p. 412.

116

A PROCESSION OF PRAISE

Psalm 118:1-29

The Old Testament reveals Israel's worship to be rich in ritual. With its description of a procession of worshipers passing through the gates of the Temple in Jerusalem (see Psalm 118:19-20) and approaching the altar (118:27), Psalm 118 clearly sounds a liturgical tone. The Egyptian Hallel psalms (Psalms 113–118) were used at many of Israel's festivals, but Psalm 118 seems most at home at the Feast of Tabernacles.[1] By the post-exilic period, the psalm had assumed Messianic overtones. The early church found Psalm 118 a rich source of allusions to Jesus (see Mark 12:10-11; Acts 4:11; Ephesians 2:20-21; 1 Peter 2:4-8 and all accounts of Jesus' triumphal entry).

Psalm 118 begins and ends with an important Old Testament statement of faith which celebrates God's goodness and eternal **love** *(chesed)*. Verses 2 through 4, which were probably read antiphonally, identify the same groups encountered in Psalm 115:9-13. Twice in 118:5-18, there is an account of God's deliverance followed by a statement of the confidence which resulted. The first cycle (118:5-9) tells, in the briefest of terms, of the psalmist's distress, cry, and rescue (118:5). The deliverance reinforced his sense of Yahweh's presence. His presence eliminated all need for fear (118:6-7) and provided greater security than what could be found in even the most powerful of men (118:8-9).

The second cycle (118:10-18) describes the psalmist's plight in greater detail. He was surrounded by his enemies on all sides and besieged by an inescapable and painful foe. Although he is more active in his deliverance than in verse 5 by cutting off his enemies quickly (118:10-13), the battle still belonged to Yahweh. Three times the psalmist emphatically asserts that victory came **in the name of the LORD** (118:10b, 11b, 12c).

The confidence resulting from this deliverance is extolled in language borrowed from the song sung after the Egyptians were drowned in the sea (118:14-18). Psalm 118:14 quotes Exodus 15:2a exactly, while Psalm 118:15-16 allude to Exodus 15:6. Because God has spared him, the psalmist promises to publicly proclaim God's goodness (see Psalm 118:17-18), a promise he carries out in 118:19-28.

The procession (including the psalmist) appears at **the gates** to the Temple, seeking entrance (118:19). The gatekeepers grant access with a word affirming the vindication of the psalmist (118:20), and the psalmist responds by asserting his desire to publicly thank God (118:21). The psalmist and his companions (note the plural pronouns) rejoice in God's deliverance (118:22-24). God chose to manifest His power on what appeared undeserving when He selected Israel as His covenant people.[2] The early church saw in this a reference to Jesus: despised by humanity but chosen by God (see 1 Peter 2:7). The appeal for help in Psalm 118:25 reflects Israel's continuing recognition of their need for God.

The procession continues with an exchange of blessings (118:26) and a summons to approach God's **altar** (118:27). Although the simplest reading of the Hebrew text invites the worshiper to tie his sacrifice to **the horns of the altar,** this never seems to have been Israel's practice. The New International Version's rendering makes good sense but takes some liberties in translating the Hebrew. Bible commentator Derek Kidner's translation, "bring the sacrifice, bound, to the horns of the altar," is preferred.[3] As the psalmist completes his vow of public thanksgiving in verses 28 and 29, he expresses truths about God which are as rich in meaning as when spoken in the Temple courts. God is our God, worthy of thanks and adoration. He is the source of all that is good and His love is eternal.

ENDNOTES

[1]This feast commemorated Israel's wilderness wanderings (Leviticus 23:33-43). Other links with Tabernacles can be found in the phrases **tents of the righteous** (Ps. 118:15) and **boughs in hand** (118:27; see Leviticus 23:40). The seventh day of this festival was called the Great Hosanna (see Psalm 118:25) and later Jewish interpretation of the Old Testament specifically associated this psalm with Tabernacles (Leslie C. Allen, *Psalms 101–150,* Word Biblical Commentary, vol. 21, eds. David A. Hubbard and Glenn W. Barker [Waco, Texas: Word Books, 1983], p. 123). For more on the Egyptian Hallel, see comments on Psalm 113.

[2]**Builders** is only a proverbial way of saying that God has chosen to use a very ordinary object for extraordinary purposes.

[3]Derek Kidner, *Psalms 73–150,* Tyndale Old Testament Commentaries, ed. D.J. Wiseman (Downer's Grove, Illinois: InterVarsity Press, 1975), p. 416.

IN PRAISE OF THE LAW

Psalm 119:1-176

salm 119 is monumental not only in length but in artistic skill and the breadth to which it develops its theme, the Law. It is composed of 22 stanzas, one stanza for each letter of the Hebrew alphabet, which it follows in order. Each stanza is eight lines long, with each of those lines beginning with the same letter of the Hebrew alphabet. Eight words are used to describe the Law, all roughly synonymous (and found in Psalm 19).[1] Within this rigid structure, the psalmist has freely and creatively woven the threads of his thought into a work of great skill.[2] The effect is like a kaleidoscope; the ever-changing pattern enriches without obscuring its theme, God's law.[3]

Described by any of the eight terms, the Law is God's revelation of His will, whether given through the prophets or through the greatest of the prophets, Moses. Not surprisingly, much of what this psalm says about the Law is also true of the Bible. Both are precious, both provide illumination, and both reveal God. The New Testament surpasses the Old Testament because it contains the record of God's most complete revelation in Jesus. The Christian reader must be careful, however, not to read this psalm as if "Law" were simply a synonym for the Bible. To do so is to miss the insight this psalm (and the rest of the Old Testament) offers into the faith of Israel, the foundation of Christianity.

Throughout these 176 verses, the psalmist reveals his delight for God's Law (see verses 14, 16, 47, 72, 77, 103, 111, 127, 131, 161-162, 174). Far from a burden, it was a source of hope (119:81), peace (119:165a), security (119:165b), freedom (119:45, 96), illumination (119:34, 73, 105, 125, 130, 144, 169) and life (119:144, 159).[4] The psalmist knew that the source of all these blessings was not the Law but the Giver of the Law. Nor is there a hint of legalism in this psalm. God's people knew they must do more than **keep his statutes** (119:2a); they must **seek him with all their heart** (119:2b).

One blessing especially dear to the psalmist was the Law's ability to assist in difficulty. The author appears to have been a young man (119:9, 99-100), facing powerful opponents (119:23, 61, 69, 87, 141, 143, 157, 161), and waiting for an answer from God (119:81-88). Because he knew that obedience to God does not bring freedom from difficulty but does provide a place to go for help, the psalmist prays for two things: to more clearly understand God's Law and to know its full effects (rescue and vindication).

The *Aleph* stanza, after an introduction which summons the reader to experience the blessings of wisdom (119:1-3), expresses the psalmist's desire to obey the Law (119:4-8), not only for the blessings but because of God's command (119:4). He asserts his obedience to the Law in the *Beth* stanza (119:9-16).

When opposing forces begin to emerge in the *Gimel* stanza (119:17-24), instead of turning away from the Law, the psalmist resolves to find relief in a better understanding of it. He knows that the Law will put wings on His weary feet and set Him free (*Daleth;* 119:25-32), so for this Law he pleads in earnest (*He;* 119:33-40). In answer to His prayer, he promises public testimony to God's faithfulness, even in the very presence of the king (*Waw;* 119:41-48).

The *Zayin* stanza (119:49-56) speaks to the suffering saint of the sustaining power of God's revelation: **My comfort in my suffering is this:/Your promise preserves my life** (119:50). Because God—not His blessings or even His law—is the psalmist's portion, God will be obeyed (*Heth;* 119:57-64). Through suffering, the Law becomes more clearly understood (*Teth;* 119:65-72) and stands out as a source of strength (*Yodh;* 119:73-80).

In the *Kaph* stanza (119:81-88), the psalmist's distress comes most clearly to the forefront. God's delay has left him hanging—**like a wineskin in the smoke** (119:83)—a metaphor of harmful neglect. Because he still trusts in God's **love** (*chesed;* 119:88), he retains his hope in God's word (119:81). Against such a dark backdrop, his praise of the Law in the *Lamedh* stanza (119:89-96) shines brighter still. Both in the heavens and on the earth, God's Word stands secure.

> **To all perfection I see a limit;**
> **but your commands are boundless** (119:96).

Next follows a quiet interlude *(Mem;* 119:97-104) asking nothing from God; it only extols the effects of instruction from God himself (**you** is emphatic in verse 102). For this reason, the psalmist will walk in the light of God's Law even though the night becomes very dark around him *(Nun;* 119:105-112).

In the *Samekh* stanza (119:113-120), the Law is revealed as a two-edged sword, protecting the righteous but judging the wicked. Even the psalmist stands in awe of God's Laws (119:120). His conscience clear, the psalmist appeals for rescue based on his status as God's servant *(Ayin;* 119:121-128). Like a good servant, he strongly desires the will of his master and feels pain when others disobey that will *(Pe;* 119:129-136).

The *Tsadhe* stanza (119:137-144) asserts that, in spite of the rebellion of others, God's Law remains right because God is righteous. God's righteousness refers to His vindication of the righteous. It is for such vindication that the psalmist appeals in the *Qoph* stanza (119:145-152). This stanza is rich in contrasts: The psalmist rises **before dawn** and continues crying **through the watches of the night** (119:147-148). Though the enemy is **near** him and **far** from God's Law, God is **near** to the psalmist (119:150-151). "The threat is not glossed over; it is put in perspective by a bigger fact."[5]

Once again the psalmist pleads for rescue *(Resh;* 119:153-160) based on his faithfulness to God and God's faithfulness to His eternal Word. The permanence of the Law "which implicitly reflects Yahweh's own permanence, gives hope to the sufferer that his life will not be cut short."[6] The psalmist's protest of innocence and loyalty in the *Sin/Shin* stanza (119:161-168) supports his appeal in the previous verses. He obeys both because God is watching (119:168b) and for love of His commands (119:167). The final stanza *(Taw;* 119:169-176) repeats what has been the dual goal of this prayer: a clearer understanding of God's law and the vindication it should bring.

An alphabet acrostic emphasizes the totality of a subject; it covers everything from *A* to *Z* (or *Aleph* to *Taw* in Hebrew). To the Israelite, the Law represented the fullness of God's revelation to humanity. To the Christian, that fullness is represented in Christ, "the Word [become] flesh" (John 1:14). God's revelation in the Law and His fullest revelation in Christ are both recorded for us in the authoritative, written record which we know as the Bible.

ENDNOTES

[1]David Noel Freedman, "The Structure of Psalm 119: Part II," *Hebrew Annual Review* 14 (1994), pp. 55–88.

[2]Freedman, p. 81. Cohen calls it a "verbal fugue" (A. Cohen, *The Psalms,* Soncino Books of the Bible, ed. A. Cohen [London: Soncino, 1950], p. 394).

[3]Leslie C. Allen, *Psalms 101–150,* Word Biblical Commentary, vol. 21, eds. David A. Hubbard and Glenn W. Barker (Waco, Texas: Word Books, 1983), p. 139.

[4]Freedman (p. 78) suggests that the eight-lined stanzas and eight synonyms for the Law were meant to "reflect the perfection of the universe as created by God, and the resulting correspondence between the law as the perfect expression and the universe as the perfect creation of the same God."

[5]Derek Kidner, *Psalms 73–150,* Tyndale Old Testament Commentaries, ed. D.J. Wiseman (Downer's Grove, Illinois: InterVarsity Press, 1975), p. 428.

[6]Allen, p. 144.

118

EAGER TO RETURN HOME

Psalm 120:1-7

The title **"A song of ascents"** appears before each of Psalms 120 through 134. Although not necessarily written for this purpose, these psalms were collected (probably in the post-exilic period) for use during those festivals when all Jewish men were required to come to Jerusalem. Some envision pilgrims from the surrounding territories singing these songs as they traveled toward Jerusalem. Supporting this view, the psalms progress from remote lands (Psalm 120), to Jerusalem (Psalm 122), and into the Temple (Psalm 134). Others imagine pilgrims singing these 15 songs in the Temple as they climbed the steps that separated the Court of Women from the Court of the Men.[1] Considered apart from its setting as a pilgrim song, Psalm 120 is a cry for help by one alienated from those around him. When incorporated into the Songs of Ascent, God's festival in Jerusalem became a source of relief from his alienation.

Although the New International Version translates the calling in verse 1 as a present occurrence, it probably refers to an earlier difficulty when the psalmist called to Yahweh and was promptly answered.[2] Judging by his call (recorded in verse 2), he had been slandered by **lying lips** and **deceitful tongues.**

Emboldened by God's encouraging answer, the psalmist threatens the enemy (120:3-4) with judgment. **Sharp arrows** fired by a warrior would put an end to slanderous barbs. The **broom tree** (120:4) is a hard wood which burns well and yields notable coals. Coals are spoken of in 140:10 as fitting punishment for slanderers.[3]

The psalmist's past deliverance prompts his prayer in the present (120:5-7). He laments having to live among a barbarian and warlike

365

people in a location described as **Meshech** and the **tents of Kedar.** Since there was no location inhabited by both Meshech (a region well north of Israel) and Kedar (Arab tribes living in the southeast), some have tried to change the Hebrew. More likely, the psalmist is using these terms symbolically to describe his enemies as "hostile barbarians."[4] The metaphor would be particularly appropriate for Israel's opponents during the post-exilic period (see Ezra 4:1-5; Nehemiah 4:1-3; 6:1-14).

Like the psalmist, Christians are to be people of peace, aliens and strangers in hostile territory (see 1 Peter 1:1-2; 2:11-12). Along with him, we must leave our vindication in God's hands (see Psalm 120:1-3). Relief is found, as the pilgrim Israelites knew, in God's presence with His people.

ENDNOTES

[1]Cohen cites later Jewish tradition (A. Cohen, *The Psalms,* Soncino Books of the Bible, ed. A. Cohen [London: Soncino, 1950], p. 417).

[2]Hebrew word order emphasizes the object of the psalmist's prayer (**on the LORD**) and the prompt response (**call** and **answer** are placed side by side).

[3]Derek Kidner, *Psalms 73–150,* Tyndale Old Testament Commentaries, ed. D.J. Wiseman (Downer's Grove, Illinois: InterVarsity Press, 1975), p. 430, note 3; see Leslie C. Allen, *Psalms 101–150,* Word Biblical Commentary, vol. 21, eds. David A. Hubbard and Glenn W. Barker (Waco, Texas: Word Books, 1983), p. 146.

[4]Allen points out that both Meshech (see Ezekiel 32:26; 38:2-4; 39:1-3) and Kedar (Isaiah 21:16, 17) are warlike peoples.

119

ISRAEL'S WATCHMAN

Psalm 121:1-8

There is no more secure place than under the watchful eye of Israel's Guardian. Six times in this, the second of the Songs of Ascent (Psalms 120–134), Yahweh is described as the one who **watches over** His people (121:3, 4, 5, 7 [twice], 8).[1] The Hebrew word can mean sentry (Judges 7:19), city watchman (Psalm 127:1), or doorkeeper in the Temple (2 Kings 12:9) or palace (2 Chronicles 12:10). It can also refer to a shepherd (1 Samuel 17:20), the meaning that fits best here.

Although the psalm does not mention a pilgrimage, its language makes it easy to envision a group of travelers on the way to Jerusalem who imagine themselves as a flock with Yahweh as their shepherd.[2] The **hills** they encounter can be understood positively to represent God's power and strength.[3] More likely, they signify a threatening place from which the "flock" can be assaulted. Writer Othmar Keel agrees, for "when the psalms speak of mountains, they emphasize Yahweh's superiority over them" (see Psalm 89:12; 90:2; 97:4-5; 104:32).[4] Since in the ancient Near East it was common to identify the mountains as homes of the gods, the psalmist could also be comparing Yahweh with the gods of other nations. The comparison favors the Lord for He is **the Maker of heaven and earth** (121:2) which includes the mountains. Therefore, He can be trusted to look out for the pilgrim.

Yahweh, the watchful shepherd, dominates the scene in verses 3 through 8. Ever alert, He will lead in such a way that the flock is preserved from stumbling. Perhaps verse 3 should be read as a negative wish, responded to in verse 4:

> May he save your foot from stumbling;
> may he, your guardian, not fall asleep!

> You see—he neither sleeps nor slumbers,
> the guardian of Israel (NJB).

This shepherd provides a shady place where one finds protection from the heat of the sun (121:5-6; see Numbers 14:9; Jeremiah 48:45; Lamentations 4:20). Sun and moon could be used here to represent the total picture, like our expression "day and night."[5] They might instead be mentioned here because of their harmful effects. The Middle Eastern sun can produce a blazing and injurious heat (see Jonah 4:8; 2 Kings 4:19; Isaiah 49:10; Psalm 102:5). Then, as now, the moon was thought to have an ominous effect on people.[6] Because both sun and moon were worshiped as deities, here again the psalmist may be asserting Yahweh's superiority over these gods.[7]

Coming and going (Ps. 121:8) fits the picture of sheep or pilgrims going to or from worship.[8] Perhaps the psalmist refers to the daily activity of the Israelites going out to their fields in the morning and returning to their homes in the city at night, or some combination of these three possibilities.[9]

Your is singular rather than plural, reminding each of us that no matter where our comings and goings might take us, the Maker of heaven and earth watches over us continually, **now and forevermore**—a faithful Shepherd.

ENDNOTES

[1] The first use in 121:7 is translated **will keep you.**

[2] Others place the psalm in Jerusalem, after the festival, where the pilgrims receive an encouraging word before setting out for home (Leslie C. Allen, *Psalms 101–150,* Word Biblical Commentary, vol. 21, eds. David A. Hubbard and Glenn W. Barker [Waco, Texas: Word Books, 1983], p. 153).

[3] King James Version; Allen, pp. 150–51.

[4] Othmar Keel, *The Symbolism of the Biblical World: Ancient Near Eastern Iconography and the Book of Psalms,* translated by Timothy J. Hallett [New York: Seabury Press, 1978], p. 20.

[5] Derek Kidner, *Psalms 73–150,* Tyndale Old Testament Commentaries, ed. D.J. Wiseman (Downer's Grove, Illinois: InterVarsity Press, 1975), p. 432, note 1.

[6] Allen, p. 152.

[7] Keel (p. 208) includes a drawing showing the Mesopotamian sun-god seated on mountains (see Psalm 121:1); see T.C. Mitchell, "Moon," *New Bible Dictionary,* rev. ed. (Wheaton, Illinois: Tyndale House Publishers, 1982), p. 793.

[8] Allen, p. 152.

[9] See Kidner, p. 432; Allen, p. 152.

120

COMING HOME

Psalm 122:1-9

With the third of the Songs of Ascent (Psalms 120–134), the pilgrims have reached Jerusalem. Joyously anticipated, the journey has now ended in a euphoria nothing short of exuberant. The immediate object of the psalmist's delight is this city which stands at the center of Israelite society and the Temple which stands (symbolically) at the center of the city. Ultimately, the psalmist rejoices in Israel's covenant relationship with Yahweh, symbolized in His selection of Jerusalem, His giving of the Law (122:4), and His choice of David's lineage (122:5).[1] By returning to Jerusalem, Israel returned home, to the heart of what it meant to be an Israelite.

The journey to Jerusalem is described in verses 1 and 2, from the invitation to participate (122:1), greeted with joy, to the arrival in Jerusalem (122:2), greeted with awe. In the description of the city which follows (122:3-5), Jerusalem is said to be **closely compacted together** (122:3), not what we consider a commendable quality. For commentator F. Delitzsch, who assumes a post-exilic origin for this psalm, this refers to the city rebuilt without gaps in the walls.[2] If this refers to pre-exilic Jerusalem, its compactness could refer to its solid and impregnable buildings.[3] People rather than buildings could be in view, and closeness could refer to its unity, even in the presence of many tribes (122:4).[4] The psalmist could be rejoicing because the crowds indicated that many of his people were willing to obey God, even though it meant traveling far from home.

By rearranging the lines in verse 4, the New International Version has smoothed the flow but sacrificed the psalmist's emphasis. **According to the statute given to Israel** should come between **that is where the tribes go up, the tribes of the LORD** and **to praise the name of the LORD.** The psalmist is emphasizing God's revelation of His law to Israel (specifically Exodus 23:17; Deuteronomy 16:16) and Israel's obedience to that Law. People gathered to praise God (more precisely, to thank God)—that is, they came to acknowledge their dependence upon Him for the blessings He had given. One such blessing was Israel's justice system (see Psalm 122:5), designed to foster fairness and equity along standards established by God's law.

In the remaining verses, the psalmist prays for the prosperity of Jerusalem (122:6-9). The word translated **peace** means more than the absence of conflict; it means the absence of want and the presence of all that is good. The psalmist's delight in his subject emerges with a playful alliteration in verses 6 and 7 between the *sh* sound in the Hebrew words for **pray, peace, Jerusalem,** and **security.** He seeks a blessing on the city (122:7), on its inhabitants (122:8), and especially on the **house of the LORD our God** (122:9). A blessing on Jerusalem meant a blessing for the nation and clear evidence that all was well between Israel and its God.

The psalmist reveled in the city of God and the house of God because they represented God's relationship with Israel. This relationship has entered a new dimension in Christ. "The Word became flesh and made his dwelling among us. We have seen his glory, the glory of the One and Only, who came from the Father, full of grace and truth" (John 1:14).

ENDNOTES

[1]**Of David** in the title here cannot mean "written by David," for these are the words of a visitor to Jerusalem at a time when the Temple was standing. "Concerning David" or "on behalf of the Davidic dynasty" is probably the best way to understand the phrase (Leslie C. Allen, *Psalms 101–150,* Word Biblical Commentary, vol. 21, eds. David A. Hubbard and Glenn W. Barker [Waco, Texas: Word Books, 1983], p. 155).

[2]F. Delitzsch, *Psalms,* Commentary on the Old Testament, vol. V, translated by James Martin (reprint, Grand Rapids, Michigan: Wm. B. Eerdmans Publishing Co., 1978), p. 277.

[3]Allen, p. 156.

[4]Derek Kidner, *Psalms 73–150,* Tyndale Old Testament Commentaries, ed. D.J. Wiseman (Downer's Grove, Illinois: InterVarsity Press, 1975), p. 433.

121

AN APPEAL TO THE JUDGE

Psalm 123:1-4

P salm 123 fits best in the post-exilic period as the Jews returned to rebuild Jerusalem. During this time, Israel mourned the contrast between the city before and after the exile (Ezra 3:12) and felt the sting of their neighbors' scorn (compare Psalm 123:3b-4 with Ezra 4:1-5; see also Nehemiah 4:1-3; 6:1-14). Perhaps those responsible for compiling the Songs of Ascent (Psalms 120–134) in the post-exilic period added Psalm 123 to express their grief over the devastation of the holy city. Their earlier cry of delight (Psalm 122) fills this cry for mercy with misery.

From the opening verses (123:1-2), the psalmist lays his need before God. "To you" begins the psalm in the Hebrew; it is to God and no other that the psalmist looks for help. **I lift up** might better be translated "I have lifted up" (see 121:1), emphasizing the ongoing appeal as implied in 123:2. If Psalm 123 was written with Psalm 122 in mind, mention of God's **throne** (123:1) calls to mind the thrones of the princes in 122:5. Jerusalem's disgrace was the greatest travesty of justice; therefore, appeal must be made to the highest court in the universe.

As the metaphor changes from judicial to household (see 123:2), the appeal becomes more personal. First in general terms (slaves to master), then in more specific terms (maid to mistress), the servant's absolute dependence on the master is pressed home. Awaited from the master's hand is not direction but provision. They craved mercy as passionately as their own food and knew they could find it nowhere else but in God's hand.

A passionate plea for **mercy** in 123:3a is followed by the reason for that appeal (123:3b-4). **Endured** might better be rendered "we have had more than our fill."[1] They could tolerate no more **contempt** and **ridicule,** terms chosen to emphasize how far Israel had fallen. Mockery is more painful when spoken by the **proud,** or more accurately, "those that are at ease" (NJPS). What galled the psalmist was that Israel's critics had the resources to assist in the rebuilding but refused to do so. They were unimpressed by the noble task to which the Jews had been called; they chose instead to mock their efforts.

Here the prayer ends without resolution. Here too is where we sometimes find ourselves: suffering unjustly under a silent heaven. Because he remembered that God is righteous (123:1) and merciful (123:2), the psalmist continued to wait at the feet of his Master (123:2). This is still the path to faithfulness under fire.

ENDNOTE

[1]Leslie C. Allen, *Psalms 101–150,* Word Biblical Commentary, vol. 21, eds. David A. Hubbard and Glenn W. Barker (Waco, Texas: Word Books, 1983), p. 159.

122

WE HAVE ESCAPED

Psalm 124:1-8

An important part of Israel's worship was the backward glance, remembering God's faithfulness to His people. This Song of Ascent (see Psalms 120–134) celebrates their deliverance from an unnamed enemy, brought about because Yahweh was on Israel's side. Placed next to Psalm 123, it affirms that God does answer prayer.

Although many commentators doubt this psalm was written by David,[1] its optimism fits his day. Bible commentator Derek Kidner points specifically to when the kingdom passed from Saul to David. The Philistines, seeking to take advantage of the situation, would have annihilated Israel but for God's intervention (see 2 Samuel 5:17-25). The comparison of the enemy to a flood in 2 Samuel 5:20 is similar to what is found in Psalm 124:4-5.[2]

The threat against Israel is described in Psalm 124:1-5 first as a monster with gaping jaws, capable of swallowing the nation in a single gulp (124:3b). Next the enemy is pictured as a flood capable of sweeping Israel to destruction. The Israelites had ample opportunity to witness the devastating effects of flash floods. Within the space of an hour, a wadi can be transformed from a dry roadway to a rushing torrent several feet deep. Othmar Keel relates how just such a transformation claimed the lives of twenty-two tourists in 1963.[3]

Let Israel say (124:1) indicates this psalm's role in the nation's corporate liturgy and reminds the people that the blessings of subsequent generations can be traced to God's past victories. Verses 3 through 5 each begin with the word *azi,* usually translated "then." Bible commentator Leslie Allen reproduces the parallel structure:

> Were it not for Yahweh,
> who took our side
> when men attacked us,
> then they would have swallowed us alive,

> so furious was their anger against us.
> Then the waters would have overwhelmed us,
> the torrent would have gone above our necks,
> then it would have gone above our necks—
> those raging waters.[4]

Yahweh did intervene and is to be praised for it (124:6-8). Israel was spared from the vicious jaws of the enemy (124:6b) and released from the hunter's snare (124:7).[5] Israel's helplessness is pictured in the comparison to birds who could not escape unless someone else broke the trap.[6]

The danger of the snare was its deceptiveness. Well-hidden and attractive, who could know whether the path ahead meant safety or disaster? Perhaps this is why Israel looked for help to the **name of the LORD** (124:8). Because **LORD** (Yahweh) was Israel's covenant name for God, they could be sure of His love for them. Because this name emphasizes God's eternal nature, He would know the path ahead. Power was in abundant supply for Yahweh, the God of the Exodus and **Maker of heaven and earth** (124:8). All the metaphors used in this psalm to describe Israel's enemy are chosen from the natural world, the same world which Israel's God created. Our path may be uncertain, but if we proceed with the Lord at our side, we too will experience help from the Maker of heaven and earth.

ENDNOTES

[1]Some early versions do not refer to David and the language is from a later period (see *Psalms* by F. Delitzsch, Commentary on the Old Testament, vol. V, translated by James Martin [reprint, Grand Rapids, Michigan: Wm. B. Eerdmans Publishing Co., 1978], p. 282; Leslie C. Allen, *Psalms 101–150,* Word Biblical Commentary, vol. 21, eds. David A. Hubbard and Glenn W. Barker [Waco, Texas: Word Books, 1983], p. 162).

[2]Baal Perazim means "Lord who breaks out," referring to an outburst of water (see 1 Chronicles 14:11; Derek Kidner, *Psalms 73–150,* Tyndale Old Testament Commentaries, ed. D.J. Wiseman [Downer's Grove, Illinois: InterVarsity Press, 1975], pp. 436–37).

[3]Othmar Keel, *The Symbolism of the Biblical World: Ancient Near Eastern Iconography and the Book of Psalms,* translated by Timothy J. Hallett (New York: Seabury Press, 1978), pp. 73–74.

[4]Allen.

[5]Keel includes a description and drawings of the various types of nets and snares used in the ancient Near East (pp. 91–94).

[6]Delitzsch renders Psalm 124:7d "and we, we escaped."

123

AS SOLID AS JERUSALEM

Psalm 125:1-5

Jerusalem appears frequently in the Songs of Ascent (Psalms 120–134); this time it is an example of permanent security. The psalmist calls God's people to a righteousness characterized by **trust in the LORD.** Those who trust become like **Mount Zion, which cannot be shaken** (125:1), a strong statement in a land where earthquakes are not infrequent. Jerusalem is located on a hill (just over 2400 feet) surrounded by other, higher hills. In the same way, Yahweh himself surrounds His people. The Hebrew word for eternity appears twice in 125:1-2 (**forever** [125:1]; **forevermore** [125:2]). This emphasizes Jerusalem's security but, more to the psalmist's purposes, the security of the righteous. Because this security is based not on Jerusalem but on Jerusalem's God, it lasts forever.

Many commentators date this psalm to the post-exilic period because of the picture of foreign domination which they find in the phrase, **scepter of the wicked** (125:3).[1] This view falters on two counts. First, Jerusalem is used in verses 1 and 2 as a metaphor for permanent security. Post-exilic Jerusalem, which was destroyed by the Babylonians and did not recover its former glory until long after this psalm was written, is not a good example of permanent security. Second, the Hebrew for **scepter** could also be translated as rod, such as one uses to inflict discipline (89:32; Proverbs 13:24), shepherd sheep (Psalm 23:4; Ezekiel 20:37), or wield as a weapon (2 Samuel 18:14; 23:21). "Rod of the wicked" could describe the oppressive influence of evil in Israelite society. God, says the psalmist, will not allow evil to finally triumph, for this would eliminate the incentive of the righteous to remain so. If they cease to trust in Yahweh, the righteous and that society will cease to be secure (see Psalm 125:1-2).

So that this does not occur, God is asked to distribute the rewards of righteousness and wickedness (125:4-5). May the righteous—the **good** and **upright in heart**—know God's goodness, but may the unrighteous be banished (125:5).[2] To refer to the unrighteous as **those who turn to crooked ways** (125:5) brings to mind the desperate state of society in Judges 5:6 where the same word is used. The sense differs slightly here since the **evildoers** foster anarchy by choosing to deviate from the straight and narrow (Ps. 125:3).

Given that the goal is to preserve society, banishment is the appropriate punishment for the unrighteous (125:5). Whether or not the final line was originally part of the psalm,[3] peace will result when the unrighteous are banished. "The final words of the psalm have arrived at *peace,* not by compromise but by the only road that leads to it: the way of righteousness."[4]

ENDNOTES

[1]A. Cohen, *The Psalms,* Soncino Books of the Bible, ed. A. Cohen (London: Soncino, 1950), p. 426; F. Delitzsch, *Psalms,* Commentary on the Old Testament, vol. V, translated by James Martin (reprint, Grand Rapids, Michigan: Wm. B. Eerdmans Publishing Co., 1978), pp. 285-286; Leslie C. Allen, *Psalms 101–150,* Word Biblical Commentary, vol. 21, eds. David A. Hubbard and Glenn W. Barker (Waco, Texas: Word Books, 1983), p. 167.

[2]The Hebrew can be read as a prediction (NIV) or as a wish, parallel to 125:4.

[3]See Allen.

[4]Derek Kidner, *Psalms 73–150,* Tyndale Old Testament Commentaries, ed. D.J. Wiseman (Downer's Grove, Illinois: InterVarsity Press, 1975), p. 438.

124

A SONG OF RESTORATION

Psalm 126:1-6

The delirium seen in the opening stanza of Psalm 126 resulted from the restoration of Zion's fortunes. Most would agree that this Song of Ascent (see Psalms 120–134) celebrates the return of the Jews to Palestine after the Babylonian exile.[1] Drawing confidence from this answered prayer, the psalmist appeals to God to complete the restoration He began (126:4-6).

Nothing short of restoration from exile could account for the picture of joy in 126:1-3. "It was like a dream" (TEV), that is, "the redemption that broke upon us so suddenly seemed to us at first not to be a reality but a beautiful dream."[2] Even the surrounding nations realized that **the LORD has done great things for them** (126:2). For centuries, God had challenged Israel to live up to its calling as a source of blessing to the nations (see Genesis 12:3; Psalms 72:17; 117; Isaiah 19:19-25; 56:6-7). At least some of their joy on this occasion arose from the recognition that God was being glorified among the nations. Psalm 126:3 summarizes the first stanza and prepares us for the prayer which follows.

The psalmist consciously crafted the opening line of the second stanza (126:4-6) to closely resemble that of verse 1; he wants God to finish what He started. The assurance of past action made possible his prayer for future help and his confidence that a favorable answer would come. "Hope lends wings to their prayer, and both are grounded in Yahweh's historical revelation of his character as faithful to his covenant people."[3] To recognize what God has done—for us and for others—enables us to pray with confidence (see Philippians 1:6).

Restoration from exile was a slow process. There must have been times when rebuilding a population, a city, and a livelihood seemed as overwhelming as being released from Babylonian control. Thus there is no contradiction when the psalmist rejoices in restoration and prays for it in the same psalm.

Having made his request in Psalm 126:4a, the psalmist displays his confidence through two metaphors. God could restore His people as quickly and easily as **the Negev** wadis flood after a rain (126:4b; see 124:4-5). On the other hand, the answer may come slowly and laboriously, like the growing of a crop (126:5-6). Even if slow, the result will be no less certain. The Hebrew of 126:6 places great emphasis on the contrast between going out **weeping** (tearfully) to sow and returning **with songs of joy** with the harvest.[4]

> Weeping may remain for a night,
> but rejoicing comes in the morning (Psalm 30:5b).

The psalmist was able to pray confidently for God's intervention, in part, because he knew of God's action in the past. The backward look, not to the pleasures of "Egypt" but to how God has been faithful in our wilderness experiences, will help us to move forward in faith. This way, whether He chooses to act suddenly, like a flash flood, or slowly, like a ripening crop, we will not be surprised when He answers our prayers.

ENDNOTES

[1]The language of 126:1a may refer to a lesser restoration, as some contend, but it would need to be sufficiently staggering to cause the surrounding nations to acknowledge Yahweh's work (see 126:2c). Cohen sees a completely different purpose: "The Psalm prophesies the feelings and thoughts of the people during the final redemption" (A. Cohen, *The Psalms,* Soncino Books of the Bible, ed. A. Cohen [London: Soncino, 1950], p. 427).

[2]F. Delitzsch, *Psalms,* Commentary on the Old Testament, vol. V, translated by James Martin (reprint, Grand Rapids, Michigan: Wm. B. Eerdmans Publishing Co., 1978), p. 289. Medieval Jewish rabbi David Kimchi suggests "past events will seem as if they never happened" (as cited by Cohen).

[3]Leslie C. Allen, *Psalms 101–150,* Word Biblical Commentary, vol. 21, eds. David A. Hubbard and Glenn W. Barker (Waco, Texas: Word Books, 1983), p. 175.

[4]Emphasis is accomplished in several ways, including the contrast between a small amount of seed (**seed to sow** refers to "the handful of seed taken from the rest for casting out" [Delitzsch, p. 290]) and sheaves of grain, the contrast between weeping and shouting for joy, and by repeating the Hebrew word for **carrying.**

125

"UNLESS THE LORD BUILDS THE HOUSE"[1]

Psalm 127:1-5

C enturies ago on a plain in Mesopotamia, people sought to make a name for themselves by their accomplishments, specifically by building a city and tower (see Genesis 11). To establish permanence with human hands continues to be the goal of many. In Psalm 127, the psalmist traces a different route, identifying permanence as the result of trusting in God.

It is ironic that Solomon should be mentioned in connection with this psalm. If he wrote it, the record of his life shows he did not follow his own advice (see 1 Kings 11:1-11; 12:4). For the same reason, it seems strange to dedicate the psalm to him.[2] It may have been chosen as a Song of Ascent (see Psalms 120–134) because it spoke of permanent prosperity, a quality admired in pre-exilic Jerusalem and desired for that city after the Exile.

The opening stanza (127:1-2) insists that blessings come, not from human effort, but from Yahweh. A house can be well-built, but unless its occupants put their trust in God, the household—like the building it occupies—will not last (127:1a). A city can post its watchmen, but true security comes when its residents make God the Watchman (127:1b).

Exhausting physical labor can put bread on the table (127:2), but only God can provide true and lasting blessings. There is some question what the psalmist meant at the end of verse 2. The New International Version takes **sleep** as God's gift and contrasts the frenetic activity of the laborer with the sweet slumber that heaven sends. **Sleep** might instead refer to the time when God grants His blessings (when we are doing nothing to obtain them).[3] Some avoid the question by retranslating the Hebrew as "honor."[4]

The second stanza (see 127:3-5) reaffirms that the household is built by the Lord, but it places greater emphasis on the human role. It is God who gives sons and daughters (127:3) as an inheritance. **Sons born in one's youth** (127:4) are given to the father. Born in his youth they can protect his interests when he is older. **Like arrows in the hands of a warrior,** he can put them to immediate use in battle. Human responsibility is essential; children no more raise themselves than arrows shoot themselves. In fact, "the greater their promise, the more likely that these sons will be a handful before they are a quiverful."[5]

God's promise of permanence does not rule out the possibility of enemies and accusations. The **gate** (127:5) was where the city elders would sit to decide civil cases and where father and sons might need to come to their own defense. God's blessing insured that, through the litigation, they would not be **put to shame.**

By joining these stanzas into one psalm, the psalmist shows that although God's work is essential, He designed blessings to accompany our wholehearted effort. The opening stanza does not criticize the human builder, watchman or laborer but only points out that permanence requires the work of God.

Contrast the Tower of Babel with another event in the same chapter (see Genesis 11), the birth of Abraham to Terah. Both required human involvement. Because the Tower lacked God's blessing, it amounted only to confusion. From Terah's son God produced the Jewish nation; from that nation He brought Jesus; and through Jesus He revealed himself to the entire world.[6] When God builds the house, its builders do not labor in vain.

ENDNOTES

[1]Psalm 127:1a.

[2]Links with Solomon include the fact that the word for **house** is sometimes translated "Temple" (A. Cohen, *The Psalms,* Soncino Books of the Bible, ed. A. Cohen [London: Soncino, 1950], p. 428; Leslie C. Allen, *Psalms 101–150,* Word Biblical Commentary, vol. 21, eds. David A. Hubbard and Glenn W. Barker [Waco, Texas: Word Books, 1983], p. 178); the word for **those he loves** sounds like one of Solomon's names (Jedidiah) and the psalm's proverbial character (F. Delitzsch, *Psalms,* Commentary on the Old Testament, vol. V, translated by James Martin [reprint, Grand Rapids, Michigan: Wm. B. Eerdmans Publishing Co., 1978], pp. 291–92).

³Delitzsch, p. 293.

⁴See Allen, p. 177 ("he confers honor on those he loves" [Ps. 127:2d]), who cites what he calls similar uses in Proverbs 5:9; 14:17; and 24:21.

⁵Derek Kidner, *Psalms 73–150,* Tyndale Old Testament Commentaries, ed. D.J. Wiseman (Downer's Grove, Illinois: InterVarsity Press, 1975), p. 442.

⁶Kidner (p. 441) makes this point.

126

A BLESSING ON THE PILGRIMS

Psalm 128:1-6

Having made the pilgrimage to Jerusalem to worship, this Song of Ascent (see Psalms 120–134) may have been spoken as a word of blessing to those gathered in the Temple courts.[1] "The quiet blessings of an ordered life are traced from the centre outwards in this psalm, as the eye travels from the godly man to his family and finally to Israel."[2]

The blessing is specifically addressed to **all who fear the LORD.** Reverence requires obedience, as revealed in the parallel description of those **who walk in his ways** (128:1). Verses 2 through 4 describe the blessing, beginning with the privilege of enjoying what one has worked for (128:2). It brings great satisfaction to see the fruit of one's labors and be nourished by it. The Hebrew asserts emphatically that this satisfaction will most certainly be enjoyed by the righteous.[3] Of course, labor is required (see 127:3-5); this was "a favorite text of the rabbis when teaching the dignity of honest work."[4]

Blessing is next described in domestic terms. The **wife** of the righteous man will be like a fruitful vine within the house (128:3a). This metaphor speaks of a large family—something highly prized among the Israelites—but also of sexual charm (Song of Songs 7:8-13) and festive joy (Judges 9:13). The Hebrew emphasizes that this wife is **within** the house, unlike the wayward woman whose "feet never stay at home" (see Proverbs 7:11). The wife of the righteous man is firmly committed to the well-being of her husband and children.

The righteous man will also know the blessing of **sons,** described as **olive shoots** (Ps. 128:3b). The olive was one of the most valuable trees to the Israelite, for it lasted a long time and produced an important cash crop. The way olive shoots spring up from the ground around the base of the parent tree reminded the psalmist of the righteous man surrounded by his sons. That each of these shoots would become a fruit-producing tree meant great prosperity for the family. Verse 4 acts as a hinge between the stanzas. It summarizes the blessing and sets the stage for the pronouncement of blessing which follows in verses 5 and 6.

For some reason, the New International Version reverses the order of lines in the Hebrew in verse 5. It should read,

> May Yahweh bless you from Zion!
> May you see Jerusalem prosper
> all the days of your life (NJB).

Since these words were probably spoken to the pilgrims by a priest in the Temple area, it is appropriate to speak of the blessing as from the Lord and from Zion (128:5a).

There is a direct connection between God's blessing on Zion (**Jerusalem** [128:5b NIV]) and His blessing on each family (128:1-4, 5a), for as Zion prospered so would each family in Israel. To "see Jerusalem prosper all the days of your life" (NJB) meant a stable and prosperous society. It also implies the privilege of attending festivals in Jerusalem for years to come.

To live to enjoy one's grandchildren has always been a tremendous delight (128:6a). One who reached old age (a position of honor in that society) assured that the family name would be perpetuated. The continuation of families, generation after generation, meant solidity for the nation. Solidity meant **peace** (*shalom;* that is, prosperity) would be **upon Israel** (128:6b).

God's blessing may no longer fall from the mouth of a Temple priest, but it continues to come to those **who fear the LORD** (128:1) for God has not changed. His blessing brings a life of wholeness *(shalom)* both for families and society; God's ways can bring no less.

ENDNOTES

[1]Leslie C. Allen, *Psalms 101–150,* Word Biblical Commentary, vol. 21, eds. David A. Hubbard and Glenn W. Barker (Waco, Texas: Word Books, 1983), p. 184.

[2]Derek Kidner, *Psalms 73–150,* Tyndale Old Testament Commentaries, ed. D.J. Wiseman (Downer's Grove, Illinois: InterVarsity Press, 1975), p. 443.

[3]Allen, p. 182.

[4]A. Cohen, *The Psalms,* Soncino Books of the Bible, ed. A. Cohen (London: Soncino, 1950), p. 430.

127

BOWED BUT NOT BROKEN

Psalm 129:1-8

P salm 129 rings with resilience. It reveals a spirit which, in spite of
suffering, has not surrendered in despair. As with many of the
Songs of Ascent (Psalms 120–134), its focus is on Jerusalem; it
probably originated in the post-exilic period.[1] Throughout their history,
the Israelites were no strangers to oppression, whether from Egypt,
Philistia, Midian, Assyria, Babylon or Persia. The psalmist has all of this
in mind, especially slavery in Egypt.[2] Although the oppression has been
great and long-standing, Israel remains unbroken (see 129:2b).

The psalmist illustrates this with an agricultural metaphor. Israel has
been like a field, its back plowed long by the enemy. Some commentators
see in the **furrows** a second metaphor referring to the welts left by a whip.[3]
The **cords** cut (129:4) could be the whip, the traces which hold the draft
animal to the plow[4] or the ropes which bind the prisoner.[5] More important
than what the cords represent is who cut them; it was Yahweh (see 129:4).
The LORD is righteous refers to His reputation as Vindicator of His people.

The psalmist has such strong words for Zion's enemies (see 129:5-8)
because they are not just enemies of Israel, they are enemies of God.
When they oppose Israel and Jerusalem, they oppose the people and city
of God's choosing, those with whom He linked himself by covenant.
These enemies will be **turned back in shame** (129:5) when they realize
how futile their efforts have been and how blessed is the object of their
scorn. The psalmist requests that the enemies' existence be brief and
unproductive (see 129:6-7). Relying on another agricultural metaphor, he
asks that they be like **grass** on the housetop. Before amounting to
anything, it **withers** and dies (129:6). The harvest will be too little even
to hold (see 129:7).

The picture in verse 8 is almost comical: reapers on the roof, empty-handed. It was customary to greet the harvesters in the field with a blessing from God (see Ruth 2:4), but what could one say when passing a scene which clearly held no evidence of **the blessing of the Lord** (Ps. 129:8)? It is unclear whether to take Psalm 129:8b as additional words of the passersby, the return blessing from the harvesters,[6] or a final pronouncement of blessing upon the worshipers.[7] By any reading, God's blessing on Zion is clear enough. This blessing was experienced not because of Israel's strength but because of its relationship with a righteous God. God remains the Vindicator of His people; resilience belongs to those who will remember this.

ENDNOTES

[1]Both the language and mood of the psalm—resilient but not exuberant—fit the post-exilic period (Leslie C. Allen, *Psalms 101–150,* Word Biblical Commentary, vol. 21, eds. David A. Hubbard and Glenn W. Barker [Waco, Texas: Word Books, 1983], p. 189).

[2]The Exodus is commemorated by two of the three pilgrim feasts at which the Songs of Ascent were sung (Derek Kidner, *Psalms 73–150,* Tyndale Old Testament Commentaries, ed. D.J. Wiseman [Downer's Grove, Illinois: InterVarsity Press, 1975], p. 444).

[3]Kidner; Allen, p. 187.

[4]See Job 39:10; A. Cohen, *The Psalms,* Soncino Books of the Bible, ed. A. Cohen (London: Soncino, 1950), p. 431; Allen, p. 187.

[5]See the New International Version, which adds **me free from** after **cuts**). Keel suggests Israel is compared to an ox whose back is scarred by the harness (or whip) as a result of plowing long furrows. Although a little forced, it provides a close link to the cutting of the cords in 129:4 (Othmar Keel, *The Symbolism of the Biblical World: Ancient Near Eastern Iconography and the Book of Psalms,* translated by Timothy J. Hallett [New York: Seabury Press, 1978], p. 98).

[6]F. Delitzsch, *Psalms,* Commentary on the Old Testament, vol. V, translated by James Martin (reprint, Grand Rapids, Michigan: Wm. B. Eerdmans Publishing Co., 1978), p. 301.

[7]Allen, pp. 187–88.

128

A PRAYER FROM THE DEPTHS

Psalm 130:1-8

The feeling of being so far down that one must look up to see bottom is nothing new. Most assume from Psalm 130:3-4 that the psalmist was in the depths due to his sin.[1] That Israel took it up as a Song of Ascent (see Psalms 120–134) indicates that the pilgrim festivals were also times for repentance.

Elsewhere, **depths** (130:1) refers to the bottom of the sea or a place associated with calamity, chaos, and death.[2] Down here, the psalmist feels alienated from God. His faith is strong enough, however, to believe that God can hear him and to claim a relationship with God as servant to master (see 130:2).

In the second stanza (130:3-4), the psalmist not only reveals the cause for his predicament but also the basis for his appeal. He acknowledges that all humans are sinful and unable to stand before a holy God (130:3; see 76:7). God, however, is more than willing to forgive sins. He does not desire the sinner's destruction; He would much rather see that sinner repent and be forgiven. God's tendency is to forgive.

This agrees with Jesus' depiction of God in parables such as the Prodigal son (Luke 15:11-32) and the forgiven debtors (Luke 7:41-42).[3] Just as the Pharisees reacted strongly to Jesus' words and actions, some think such a view of God brings the Almighty into disrepute. On the contrary, says the psalmist. The exercise of God's free grace increases, rather than decreases, the reverence He receives (see Psalm 130:4b).[4] In any case, as Jesus shows, God is willing to take this risk.

Knowing God's character and having repented of his sins, the psalmist resolves to wait for God (see 130:5-6). The change from **I wait** to **my soul waits** (130:5) "denotes the intentness and complete concentration of the act of waiting."[5] The **word** of God in which he has put his hope is a promise of salvation (see 119:81).

Watchmen would wait anxiously for the morning when the daylight made their duties less difficult. The psalmist would wait still more eagerly for God's light in his darkness. The Hebrew for **watchmen** could instead be translated "temple workers" (see Numbers 3:38). More eagerly than the Levites waited for dawn when they could again offer morning sacrifice,[6] did the psalmist wait for God. Repetition adds urgency and conveys the sense of long delay.[7] A night through which one must stay awake seems to last forever, but morning does come, every time.

Psalm 130 concludes with a summons to wait and reasons to do so (see verses 7-8). Redemption was assured because of the **unfailing love** of God *(chesed)* and because of His **full redemption.** The latter term, elaborated in verse 8, refers to God's "unlimited power to deliver" from the tangible effects of sin.[8] His love and power leave no doubt that **he himself will redeem Israel** (130:8; **he** is emphatic).

As the New Testament presents a more comprehensive view of sin and its effects than the Old Testament, it also presents a more comprehensive view of God's power to deal with it. His forgiveness touches individuals (Romans 3:23-26) and affects the universe (Romans 8:19-25). It brings the possibility of salvation, even full salvation, for anyone (1 John 1:8–2:2).

ENDNOTES

[1] For this reason, the church has long considered this one of the seven penitential psalms. The others are Psalms 6, 32, 38, 51, 102, and 143.

[2] See *The Psalms* by A. Cohen, Soncino Books of the Bible, ed. A. Cohen (London: Soncino, 1950), p. 433; Leslie C. Allen, *Psalms 101–150,* Word Biblical Commentary, vol. 21, eds. David A. Hubbard and Glenn W. Barker (Waco, Texas: Word Books, 1983), p. 191; Othmar Keel, *The Symbolism of the Biblical World: Ancient Near Eastern Iconography and the Book of Psalms,* translated by Timothy J. Hallett (New York: Seabury Press, 1978), p. 64.

[3] There is thus no contradiction between 130:3a and passages which speak of God's keeping track of sins (see Deuteronomy 32:34; Hosea 13:12). Those speak of God's absolute knowledge and holiness; this of the inclination of His heart.

[4] See 1 Kings 8:38-40; Allen, p. 192.

[5] Cohen.

[6] Targum (early Jewish translations of the Old Testament), as cited by Cohen, p. 434.

[7]F. Delitzsch, *Psalms,* Commentary on the Old Testament, vol. V, translated by James Martin (reprint, Grand Rapids, Michigan: Wm. B. Eerdmans Publishing Co., 1978), p. 304; Cohen, p. 434.

[8]Cohen, p. 434. One tangible effect of Israel's sin was the destruction of Jerusalem. **Full redemption** here refers to God's power to fully deliver a person not from the power of sin but from its effects.

129

CONTENT IN HIS ARMS

Psalm 131:1-3

A beautiful picture of contentment and trust emerges from the three verses of Psalm 131. If the psalm was written by David (and there is nothing in the psalm to dictate otherwise), it sounds more like David in his early years. Later it was included with the Songs of Ascent (Psalms 120–134) to guide Israel in the difficult post-exilic days.

The psalmist begins with three denials: his **heart is not proud;** his **eyes are not haughty;** and he does not concern himself **with great matters . . . things too wonderful for me**—that is, his mind does not overreach its proper boundaries. A proud heart and exalted eyes describe a person who looks down on others, treating them as less important.

The third denial strikes us as strange since our culture accepts no boundaries to the free movement of the human mind. Without question, this insistence has brought tremendous advances in learning. Some things, however, God has withheld for himself (see Deuteronomy 29:29). He rarely tells us why things happen as they do or what our future holds. While it is not sinful to ask God why or what next, it is presumptuous to demand an answer. This is what the psalmist refuses to do in Psalm 131:1c.

He follows the three denials with an emphatic assertion (**But** here indicates emphasis).[1] Like the calm surface of a lake, he has **stilled and quieted** his soul.[2] He compares himself to a **weaned child with its mother** (131:2). Because this child is no longer breast feeding, it can lie contentedly in its mother's arms, desiring less what the mother can give than the mother herself. An end to self-centered demands means the child can enjoy the mother's comfort.[3] To approach God, not for what He can do for me but because He is my God and Father, is to enjoy a deeper, more satisfying level of contentment.

In language quite similar to Psalm 130:7, the psalmist turns his attention outward (see 131:3). The rewards of trust prompt him to summon **Israel**—and us—to do the same, **both now and forevermore** (131:3b).

ENDNOTES

[1]Leslie C. Allen, *Psalms 101–150,* Word Biblical Commentary, vol. 21, eds. David A. Hubbard and Glenn W. Barker (Waco, Texas: Word Books, 1983), p. 197; F. Delitzsch, *Psalms,* Commentary on the Old Testament, vol. V, translated by James Martin (reprint, Grand Rapids, Michigan: Wm. B. Eerdmans Publishing Co., 1978), p. 306.

[2]Delitzsch.

[3]Weaning probably occurred around age three (Allen; see Delitzsch, p. 307).

130

REMEMBERING DAVID

Psalm 132:1-18

E ven beyond its opening summons, Psalm 132 remembers David. Drawing from important episodes in David's life, a later generation found reason to hope in Yahweh. Commentator Derek Kidner may be correct to date it to Solomon's reign, since verses 8 through 10 appear in 2 Chronicles 6:41-42 at the dedication of the Temple.[1]

Psalm 132 fits with the other Songs of Ascent (Psalms 120–134), for it celebrates Jerusalem and the Temple as Yahweh's dwelling (132:5, 7, 13), resting place (132:8, 14), the place of His throne (132:14), and footstool (132:7). Israel may have celebrated God's choice of David and Jerusalem on an annual basis with a pilgrimage, perhaps even reenacting the arrival of the ark. If so, this song may have been sung to accompany the procession.[2]

The psalm is comprised of two stanzas. In each, a request is followed by reasons why God should answer. The first appeal is for God to **remember David** for the **hardships he endured** (132:1) on God's behalf. Mention of his **hardships** recalls David's words to Solomon: "I have taken great pains to provide for the temple of the LORD," followed by an accounting of the staggering wealth he set aside for this purpose (1 Chronicles 22:14). "Great pains" translates the same Hebrew word as **hardships he endured.**

Several reasons why God should remember David are then given in Psalm 132:2-9. David had firmly resolved to find a **place** (132:2-5) for Yahweh. This was first a temporary home for the ark of the covenant (see 2 Samuel 6, especially verse 17 where the same word for **place** appears), then a permanent Temple. The **Mighty One of Jacob** (Ps. 132:2, 5) may refer to how God fulfilled His promises to the Patriarchs.[3]

David fulfilled his promise and brought the ark (**it** in 132:6) from **Jaar** (Kiriath Jearim) to Jerusalem (132:6-9) with great celebration. Mention of **Ephrathah** (associated with Bethlehem) is puzzling since the ark was apparently never there. No shortage of explanations exist, but most likely the two place names refer to the same general locale.[4]

The procession in Psalm 132:7-9 could refer either to David's procession or a later reenactment or both. Verse 8 refers to **the ark** (the only explicit mention in the Psalter) and contains the words spoken whenever the ark was lifted up for travel in the wilderness (see Numbers 10:35). Priests are **clothed with righteousness** while the **saints** (Ps. 132:9)—probably the Levites—**sing for joy.**

The request which begins the second stanza (132:10-18) is more specific: **Do not reject your anointed one**, or king (132:10). Judah's history provides many examples of threatening times; the Exile need not be in view. The basis for this request is first God's own promise regarding David's dynasty (132:11-12). In language meant to echo David's oath in verse 2, God promises that David would always have an heir on the throne, so long as his descendants obeyed the covenant (132:12; see 2 Kings 11:12).

Second, God should help the king because He had accepted David's invitation and had taken up residence in **Zion** (132:13-18). God can be expected to look after the affairs of His hometown; therefore, the Davidic dynasty will be secure eternally (note the **for** which begins verse 13).

God himself answers Israel's requests in verses 14 through 18. He will rule henceforth from Jerusalem, showering abundant blessings on His people (see 132:14-15). His presence means that the priests now wear **salvation,** while the Levites shout more exuberantly than before (see 132:9, 16). David will be remembered with a **horn,** symbolizing growing strength, and a light which symbolizes joy and a perpetual reign (see 2 Samuel 21:17). The enemies will wear **shame** (not righteousness or salvation) while the king wears a **crown.**

The Jews of the post-exilic period knew such a description could only be fulfilled by the Messiah. His arrival meant God had "raised up a horn of salvation for us in the house of his servant David" (Luke 1:69). Jesus fulfilled all the promises of Psalm 132:14-18: abundant spiritual blessings, garments of salvation, and joy in an eternal kingdom. The psalmist rejoiced in God's inhabiting the Temple; Christians know His presence in the heart.

ENDNOTES

[1]Derek Kidner, *Psalms 73–150,* Tyndale Old Testament Commentaries, ed. D.J. Wiseman (Downer's Grove, Illinois: InterVarsity Press, 1975), pp. 448–49.

[2]Kidner thinks it likely (p. 451), as does Allen (Leslie C. Allen, *Psalms 101–150,* Word Biblical Commentary, vol. 21, eds. David A. Hubbard and Glenn W. Barker [Waco, Texas: Word Books, 1983], p. 207), who cites Psalm 24:7-10. See Psalm 68 for another procession psalm.

[3]Cohen suggests it is because Jacob illustrated how God had raised another lowly shepherd to great honor (A. Cohen, *The Psalms,* Soncino Books of the Bible, ed. A. Cohen [London: Soncino, 1950], p. 436).

[4]F. Delitzsch, *Psalms,* Commentary on the Old Testament, vol. V, translated by James Martin (reprint, Grand Rapids, Michigan: Wm. B. Eerdmans Publishing Co., 1978), p. 310. See Allen (p. 202) for a helpful discussion of the possibilities.

131

LIFE FOREVERMORE

Psalm 133:1-3

Although Jerusalem is an important theme for the Songs of Ascent (Psalms 120–134), some of the most eloquent praise of the city is found in one of the collection's briefest psalms.[1] The opening verse, usually taken to refer to Jerusalem's **unity,** may speak primarily of the beauty of a crowded city (literally, "brothers dwelling also together"). This song is for a festival, a time when all Israelite males were to come to Jerusalem. Therefore, a crowded city is a good sign indicating a nation intent on the worship of God (see 122:3).

Two illustrations of this harmonious convocation follow in 133:2-3a. First, it is like **precious oil** on **Aaron's beard** (133:2; **precious** is from the same word translated **good** in 133:1b). **Aaron** represents the high priest whose anointing symbolized his consecration. The high priest's work brought about the sanctification and blessing of the nation (see Exodus 29:21).

The second illustration concerns Mount **Hermon,** about 200 miles north of Jerusalem. The **dew** from that mountain is legendary, although a literal fulfillment of Psalm 133:3a seems out of the question. It would appear that Hermon, with its superior size and power to moisturize, now serves the smaller and less fertile, but much more important **Mount Zion.**[2] Since Hermon was widely associated with Canaanite gods, the psalmist might also be pronouncing Yahweh's superiority to these gods.

The question remains: Where lie the similarities between the crowds in Jerusalem, oil on Aaron's beard, and Hermon's dew on Zion? One can begin with the three uses of the verb for "to go down," twice in reference to the oil **running down** from Aaron's head (133:2) and once to the dew **falling on** Jerusalem (133:3a). All three—the crowd, the oil and the dew—proceed from God. The people came to Jerusalem at God's bidding; He established the priesthood; and, as Creator, He sends the dew.

The similarity extends still further in that all three reveal God's greatness. The crowds gather to worship Him, the priesthood reflects His desire for reconciliation, while Mount Hermon (and its occupants) humbles itself before Him. Not only God's greatness, but Jerusalem's greatness is revealed by these three. It was only to Jerusalem that the crowds came and, in coming, revealed the glory of the city. Only in Jerusalem did the pilgrims find the Temple with an anointed priesthood offering atonement. Even the great Hermon was forced to pay its tribute of dew to the greater mountain.

Finally, all three are capable of conveying God's blessing. Through its worship, the crowd attracts God's blessing and distributes it to others (see 1 Kings 8:55-61, 66; Psalm 134). The anointing oil enables the priesthood to reconcile humanity with God. The ground is made fertile because of the dew.

All this becomes explicit in the psalm's final line: God has commanded (rather than **bestows**) that Jerusalem be blessed with **life forevermore** (Ps. 133:3b). The promise is not that Jerusalem will always exist but that where God is enthroned blessings of the highest quality can be found. This is as true for the individual believer (see John 10:10) as it is for the New Jerusalem (see Revelation 21:22-23; 22:1-5).

ENDNOTES

[1]Davidic authorship is usually challenged although the evidence against it is weak. Some doubt it because the psalm uses a relative pronoun generally regarded as post-exilic in origin, and because "of David" is missing in some early versions (see F. Delitzsch, *Psalms,* Commentary on the Old Testament, vol. V, translated by James Martin [reprint, Grand Rapids, Michigan: Wm. B. Eerdmans Publishing Co., 1978], p. 317; Leslie C. Allen, *Psalms 101–150,* Word Biblical Commentary, vol. 21, eds. David A. Hubbard and Glenn W. Barker [Waco, Texas: Word Books, 1983], p. 214). Kidner accepts Davidic authorship (Derek Kidner, *Psalms 73–150,* Tyndale Old Testament Commentaries, ed. D.J. Wiseman [Downer's Grove, Illinois: InterVarsity Press, 1975], p. 452).

[2]**Mount** in the Hebrew is plural, one way the Hebrew language expresses the majesty of an object (Othmar Keel, *The Symbolism of the Biblical World: Ancient Near Eastern Iconography and the Book of Psalms,* translated by Timothy J. Hallett [New York: Seabury Press, 1978], p. 114).

132

A FAREWELL BLESSING

Psalm 134:1-3

The final Song of Ascent (see Psalms 120–134) concludes, appropriately, with a farewell blessing.[1] The last evening of the festival (see 1 Chronicles 9:33; Isaiah 30:29) has come, and the pilgrims are gathered for the final time in the Temple courts before returning home in the morning. With a word, they summon the priests and Levites to "come" [left out in the New International Version] and **praise the LORD** (134:1-2). Those who lift their hands do so in prayer either for supplication or, as 134:2b indicates, for blessing.[2] The ministers respond to this call to bless Yahweh by blessing the people (see 134:3) who issued the call. They pray that the Lord will, from His holy city, bless the congregation.

God is described in the psalm's final phrase (in Hebrew)[3] as **Maker of heaven and earth** (134:3). Up to this point, the emphasis has been on Zion—**house of the LORD** (134:1b), **sanctuary** (134:2a), **Zion** (134:3b in Hebrew). This last line turns the focus outward to the whole universe. Pilgrims soon to depart Jerusalem would find comfort in knowing that God was not restricted to any one place (see 121:2). The end of the festivities meant the resumption of everyday struggles, struggles made more manageable with the help of the all-powerful Creator. The **Maker of heaven and earth** surely has the power to bless.[4]

Bless *(barak)* is the key word in Psalm 134. The Hebrew verb appears in all three verses, translated in verses 1 and 2 as **praise** and in verse 3 as **bless**. When blessing God (see 134:1-2), one only does what ought to be done; one only gives Him what He deserves. To be able to ask God to bless humanity (see 134:3), however, assumes grace has been at work. It was grace that made Him voluntarily initiate a relationship with Israel and commit himself to their well-being. It was grace which privileged Israel to seek God's blessing. In His greatest demonstration of grace, God sent Jesus to reconcile the world to himself. The Cross provides both ample reason to bless God and the confidence to seek His blessing.

ENDNOTES

[1]See Allen for other interpretive possibilities (Leslie C. Allen, *Psalms 101–150,* Word Biblical Commentary, vol. 21, eds. David A. Hubbard and Glenn W. Barker [Waco, Texas: Word Books, 1983], pp. 216–18).

[2]Othmar Keel, *The Symbolism of the Biblical World: Ancient Near Eastern Iconography and the Book of Psalms,* translated by Timothy J. Hallett [New York: Seabury Press, 1978], p. 313.

[3]For clarity, the New International Version has altered the Hebrew order of the clauses in Psalm 134:3. More literally it reads, "May Yahweh bless you from Zion, maker of heaven and earth."

[4]A. Cohen, *The Psalms,* Soncino Books of the Bible, ed. A. Cohen (London: Soncino, 1950), p. 384.

133

THE EVER-POWERFUL NAME OF ISRAEL'S GOD

Psalm 135:1-21

P salm 135 is a carefully crafted mosaic, with phrases chosen from throughout the Old Testament.[1] The resulting hymn praises God for His praiseworthy and powerful name (see 135:1, 3, 13) as it has been revealed in nature and history. This name represents the eternal and gracious nature of God. It also calls to mind His past actions, for it was by this name that He revealed himself to His people (see Exodus 3:15).

The call to **praise** continues in Psalm 135:3-4 with continued emphasis on the name of Yahweh; it is repeated twice in one phrase (135:3a). The **pleasant** task (135:3b) of recounting God's praise occupies much of the rest of the psalm. That which is most precious—God's choice of Israel—is singled out for special mention (135:4).[2]

Yahweh's greatness is demonstrated in both nature and history (verses 5-18, with a pause in verses 13-14 for praise directed to God). Those who have been **chosen** (135:4) know firsthand that Yahweh is supreme (**I** is emphatic in 135:5). He is **greater than all gods** who are not really gods at all. In verses 6 and 7, the psalmist points to God's supremacy over nature and, therefore, over the deities associated with nature by Israel's neighbors. Yahweh does whatever He wants, wherever He wants, even on the turf of the Canaanite gods of **the seas** (Yam), death (Mot, associated with **depths**), and storm (Baal).

Israel's history also reveals the Lord's power over the gods of the Egyptians (see 135:8-9) and Canaanites (see 135:10-12). Because the Egyptians viewed the Pharaoh as divine, the death of his son in the

Exodus reflected defeat for Egypt's gods. Yahweh then repossessed the land of the Canaanite gods and gave it to His people as their **inheritance** (135:12).

Because all this, especially the giving of the land, has demonstrated the greatness of the name of the Lord, the psalmist stops to sing His praise (see 135:13-14) in borrowed words (see Exodus 3:15; Deuteronomy 32:36). Yahweh has proven that He is true to the meaning of His name—eternal. He has always been faithful and merciful to the people He chose.

Most of the rest of Psalm 135 (verses 15-20) is taken, with slight modification, from 115:4-11 (see comments on Psalm 115). Psalm 135:15-18 reiterates the theme of 135:5-14: the supremacy of Yahweh. The impotence of other gods and their worshipers was illustrated in verses 6 through 12; here their powerlessness is specifically described.

The final call to **praise the LORD** (Yahweh; 135:19-21) is intended to echo the opening call to praise (see 135:1-4). All of Israel is summoned, including both professional praisers and foreigners who embraced Yahweh (see 115:11-13). The closing description of the Lord, **him who dwells in Jerusalem** (135:21), again emphasizes His covenant relationship with Israel.

God's name has not changed nor has the nature it represents (see 135:13). Although supreme over all the natural and supernatural world, He continues to show compassion to His servants (see 135:14), those in whom He dwells through His Holy Spirit.

ENDNOTES

[1]See Allen for a listing of borrowed passages (Leslie C. Allen, *Psalms 101–150,* Word Biblical Commentary, vol. 21, eds. David A. Hubbard and Glenn W. Barker [Waco, Texas: Word Books, 1983], p. 224).

[2]**Jacob** is emphasized in the Hebrew.

134

HIS LOVE ENDURES FOREVER

Psalm 136:1-26

When reading Psalm 136, one is struck by the repetition of the same words in every other line: **His love endures forever.** This refrain indicates that this psalm was used in Israel's worship. It is called the Great Hallel (or Great Psalm of Praise), and was probably sung antiphonally (responsively, alternating between groups of singers).

Because of the repetition, one is tempted to overlook these words as extraneous. To do so, however, is to miss something important. The refrain indicates the purpose of the psalm: to celebrate God's eternal love. Like the warp threads on a loom, it served as the framework into which Israel wove its history. The finished tapestry reveals the nation's firm faith in a loving God.

Modern versions find it difficult to render the refrain with the same force and brevity of the original. Even a very literal translation of the three Hebrew words takes six in English: "for to eternity [is] his love." God's **love** *(chesed)* is based on the relationship He established with His people. He voluntarily obligated himself to meet their needs and to do so **forever.** His love is the reason why God should be praised, as indicated by the **for** in the refrain.

The opening call to **give thanks** (136:1-3) is followed by the reasons for that thanks (136:4-25). The psalmist turns first to creation (136:4-9). With consummate wisdom, the Master Craftsman, working alone, fashioned the world as an expression of His eternal love.

His love was also expressed in the events surrounding the Exodus (136:10-15). God is described as a Warrior with **mighty hand and outstretched arm** (136:12). He strikes down the **firstborn of Egypt** (136:10; see 135:8), cuts apart the **Red Sea** (Sea of Reeds; 136:13), and

403

shakes off **Pharaoh and his army** like crumbs from the lap of a robe (136:15; see Nehemiah 5:13). All this fury, however, was an expression of the Warrior's eternal love. Israel's passage through the wilderness and into Canaan (see Psalm 136:16-22), described in language very similar to Psalm 135:8-12, demonstrates God's love.

Psalm 136:23-25 expresses, in general terms, God's loving care for His people. In the Exodus, and many times since, God remembered Israel in its **low estate** (136:23) and delivered the nation from its **enemies** (136:24). To describe God as the One who feeds **every creature** (136:25) unites His supernatural provision (manna, for example) with the very natural processes He began in creation. The psalm ends with another call for thanks to the **God of heaven** (136:26).

Psalm 136 gave Israel hope that what God had done before, He could still do. Still more encouraging was the emphatic truth that God's motive in past actions was love. Like Israel, we can look back on evidence of God's love in creation, in sacred history—especially to the Cross—and in our own history. Our recollections can weave a tapestry which reflects the eternal love of God.

135

BY THE RIVERS OF BABYLON

Psalm 137:1-9

Psalm 137 reveals something of the heartache of Judah in exile. Written in the exilic or post-exilic period, it was later appointed to be read on the ninth of Ab (July-August) to commemorate the destruction of Jerusalem.[1] Its placement alongside Psalm 136 demonstrates that God's love does not automatically prevent such disasters (but see Psalm 138).

The poignant scene opens **by the rivers in Babylon** (137:1-3). There sit captives from Judah, weeping as they remembered their homeland. In despair, they hung their lyres on the poplars. Even the Jews, known for their music, were too grief-stricken to sing. Hanging their harps was also an act of defiance, for their captors had asked for joyous music (see 137:3).

The captives question how they can sing **the songs of the LORD** (137:4; **of Zion** [137:3]). This may refer to an earlier collection of psalms associated with Jerusalem and the Temple (thought to include Psalms 46, 48, 76, 84, 87, and others). To sing such songs would remind them of their homeland where the Temple lay in ruins because of their sins. Although they could not *sing* of Jerusalem, they *think* of her (**you** clearly refers to the city) and promise never to forget her. If they do forget the theme of their songs, they promise never to play or sing again.

Israel knew that Jerusalem was destroyed because God is just and must punish sin. They also knew that God's justice meant punishment for all sin, including the sins of Israel's enemies such as **the Edomites** and **Babylon** (137:7-9). **Remember** is a term at home in court[2]; the psalmist appeals to the righteous Judge for judgment (see 137:7) against the guilty. Edom, although distantly related to Israel (through Jacob's brother,

Esau), took great delight in the fall of Jerusalem (see Obadiah 1, 8-14), ransacking its ruins and cutting off survivors.

Babylon also stood under the threat of divine judgment which the psalmist describes with defiant irony. One of the literary features of the Songs of Zion—the songs requested by the tormentors—was the beatitude ("Blessed be . . ."; see Psalm 84:4). The captives borrow this beatitude formula and turn it against the captors.[3] They envision judgment in graphic terms (see Jeremiah 51:56) by asking God to do to the Babylonians what they did to Jerusalem. The brutality of Psalm 137:9 was not uncommon in the warfare of the ancient Near East (see 2 Kings 8:12; Isaiah 13:16; Hosea 10:14; Nahum 3:10) and may well have been inflicted on Judah.[4]

The Babylonian exile and resulting grief and harsh words of Psalm 137 reveal the consequences of sin. Because God remains holy and just, sin remains serious. But God's justice is also reason for hope, for it guarantees that His way will triumph in the end.

ENDNOTES

[1]Leslie C. Allen, *Psalms 101–150,* Word Biblical Commentary, vol. 21, eds. David A. Hubbard and Glenn W. Barker (Waco, Texas: Word Books, 1983), p. 239.

[2]Ibid., p. 236.

[3]Ibid., p. 242.

[4]The imagery is less vicious if we follow Keel in seeing Mother Babylon (see Psalm 137:8) with her babies, the kings. He argues that, in the ancient Near East, the king was sometimes pictured as a child in the lap of a wet nurse. To destroy these "babies" would be to break that kingdom's destructive power. Verse 9 means "happy is he who puts an end to your self-renewing domination" (Othmar Keel, *The Symbolism of the Biblical World: Ancient Near Eastern Iconography and the Book of Psalms,* translated by Timothy J. Hallett [New York: Seabury Press, 1978], p. 230). For more on imprecatory psalms, see the introduction to this commentary.

136

BETTER THAN PROMISED

Psalm 138:1-8

I n a crisis, what a delight to find a friend who is "as good as his word" and treats our concerns like his own. The psalmist, having found such a friend in God, expresses his thanks in Psalm 138.[1]   The wholeheartedness of his praise (see 138:1) reveals the extent of his gratitude. His willingness to praise Yahweh **before the "gods"** indicates the measure of his commitment (138:1b).   The deities of Israel's neighbors, though a constant source of temptation, meant nothing to the psalmist whose loyalties belonged to Yahweh.   He would not be intimidated by these "gods," for his God, alone, was God.

The psalmist promises to come into the Temple courts and praise God's name, a name characterized by God's **love** *(chesed)* and **faithfulness** (138:2b).   The New Jerusalem Bible has captured the intent of the last line of verse 2: "your promises surpass even your fame."   "God's name, His revealed nature as the perfection of truth and other such qualities, gave us confidence that He would honor His plighted word to us; but what He has actually done for us exceeds what we anticipated."[2]   God is even better than His promises.

The deliverance itself is described in verse 3, although briefly and in general terms.   The psalmist called, and God answered.   Courage or "new strength" (NJB) could be the result of his deliverance or the deliverance itself.   "It is not always the situation which most needs changing; it is, as often as not, the man involved in it."[3]   Because God is even better than His promises, His praise deserves to be sung universally, by **all the kings of the earth** (138:4), not just by Israel.   His great glory should be praised even by those at the highest echelons of human society (see 138:4-5).

Still more reasons to praise this great God follow in verses 6 through 8. Although He is exalted, He still can see each person on earth (see 138:6). On the humble He looks with loving eye (see 113:5-6), but on the proud He looks with a penetrating and critical gaze. The path of the psalmist may pass through the valley dark as death (see 23:4), but even there, God preserves his life (see 138:7). The furious foe cannot penetrate the protection provided by God's hand. His **right hand,** a "symbol of overwhelming might," brings salvation, just as it did at the Sea of Reeds (Exodus 15:6).[4]

The New International Version must supply **his purpose** to Psalm 138:8a since the Hebrew does not mention the object of the verb **fulfill.** Without this addition, the psalmist's statement of confidence is bolder: "Yahweh acts as avenger on my behalf."[5] He bases this solid conviction on the still more solid **love** of God (*chesed;* 138:8b). The psalm's closing appeal (138:8c) refers back to the safety provided by God's hands (138:7). As Bible commentator Artur Weiser points out, the psalmist's protection has become "God's work."[6] Here is a God who can be counted on in difficulty, for not only is He better than His promise, He has made our concerns His own.

ENDNOTES

[1]"Of David" in the title could mean David wrote this psalm (Derek Kidner, *Psalms 73–150,* Tyndale Old Testament Commentaries, ed. D.J. Wiseman [Downer's Grove, Illinois: InterVarsity Press, 1975], p. 461) or that it was written about him (F. Delitzsch, *Psalms,* Commentary on the Old Testament, vol. V, translated by James Martin [reprint, Grand Rapids, Michigan: Wm. B. Eerdmans Publishing Co., 1978], p. 338). Those who accept David's authorship must explain the reference to bowing toward the temple (see Psalm 138:2) since it had not yet been built.

[2]Cohen's paraphrase (A. Cohen, *The Psalms,* Soncino Books of the Bible, ed. A. Cohen [London: Soncino, 1950], p. 449).

[3]Kidner, p. 462.

[4]Cohen, p. 41.

[5]Leslie C. Allen, *Psalms 101–150,* Word Biblical Commentary, vol. 21, eds. David A. Hubbard and Glenn W. Barker (Waco, Texas: Word Books, 1983), p. 243.

[6]Artur Weiser, *The Psalms—A Commentary,* translated by Herbert Hartwell, The Old Testament Library, gen. eds. G. Ernest Wright, John Bright, James Barr and Peter Ackroyd (Philadelphia: Westminster Press, 1962), p. 799.

137

"YOU KNOW ME"[1]

Psalm 139:1-24

Although Psalm 139 presents some of the most profound theology in the Bible, it is "applied theology, the meaning of God for the believer in a particular situation of stress."[2] Although the nature of his difficulty remains obscure, the psalmist is convinced that because God knew Him, He would help Him.[3]

The psalm opens with a hymn of praise (see 139:1-18) which first exalts God's omniscience (see 139:1-6). God has absolute knowledge of humanity in its full range of activity: sitting, rising, traveling, lying down, thinking, speaking. He knows more than *what* is being done, He understands and evaluates the *motives* behind those actions. The word translated **perceive** implies insight, while **discern** suggests the winnowing or sifting of grain (139:2-3). Like a besieging army,[4] God's knowledge surrounds the psalmist. He confesses that God knows him better than he knows himself (see 139:5-6).

The psalmist turns next to God's omnipresence (see 139:7-12). **Heavens** and **depths** (literally, "Sheol")[5] includes these and everything in between (139:8). **Wings of the dawn** represents the sunrise and, since **sea** can mean west, **the far side of the sea** is probably the sunset (139:9).[6] From height to depths and from the extremes of east and west, God is there. Why? To guide, protect, and hold the psalmist securely in His strong right hand (see 139:10; 138:7). What if it becomes dark? Even then there is no need to worry, for God is never in the dark (see 139:11-12).[7]

The third stanza (139:13-18) presents God as personal Creator and Custodian. The marvel of the human body testifies to the wisdom of its Creator. Perfect knowledge at work in hidden places created a beautiful tapestry, **woven** (literally, embroidered) with skill upon a **frame** (that is, a skeleton; 139:15).

He not only created the psalmist but carefully planned the psalmist's life and continued to give loving thought to his well-being (see 139:16-18).

When I awake (139:18) implies that counting God's thoughts is a process that cannot end. All hours—both waking and sleeping—would need to be spent to accomplish this task.[8]

The hymn of praise has prepared us for the prayer for deliverance in verses 19 through 22. In spite of God's loving thoughts (see 139:17), the psalmist found himself attacked by **wicked** and **bloodthirsty men** (139:19). Adding to his injury was the fact that they failed to acknowledge the omniscient, omnipresent, personal God; they even mocked His name (see 139:20). The psalmist, by contrast, was on God's side, faithful to His covenant and loyal to the end (see 139:21-22).

The closing verses reveal the truth of the psalmist's words. God had already searched and known him (see 139:1), but He could do so again (see 139:23; the verbs are the same). He could even **test** the psalmist's inmost thoughts (139:23; **anxious** may not be the implication here). The psalmist's chief desire was to avoid the wrong path and to be led in **the way everlasting** (139:24). An omniscient, omnipotent, and personal God—a God who knows us—deserves nothing less.

ENDNOTES

[1]Psalm 139:1b.

[2]Leslie C. Allen, *Psalms 101–150,* Word Biblical Commentary, vol. 21, eds. David A. Hubbard and Glenn W. Barker (Waco, Texas: Word Books, 1983), p. 263.

[3]Because this psalm contains several words which did not enter the Hebrew language until after the Exile, some rule out Davidic authorship (but see Derek Kidner, *Psalms 73–150,* Tyndale Old Testament Commentaries, ed. D.J. Wiseman [Downer's Grove, Illinois: InterVarsity Press, 1975], p. 464).

[4]Elsewhere, **hem . . . in** has this meaning (A. Cohen, *The Psalms,* Soncino Books of the Bible, ed. A. Cohen [London: Soncino, 1950], p. 452).

[5]Elsewhere in the Psalms, Sheol means separation from God. These views can be reconciled by realizing that Sheol "is not within Yahweh's sphere of blessing" but "is within his sphere of sovereignty" (Allen, p. 251).

[6]Kidner, p. 465.

[7]Kidner suggests that the psalmist may want to flee God's presence (139:7b, 11a) because he is frightened by God's omniscience (p. 464; see 139:1-6).

[8]This is the thought of Cohen (p. 454) and Delitzsch: "He has not done; waking and dreaming and waking up, he is carried away by that endless, and yet also endlessly attractive, pursuit, the most fitting occupation of one who is awake, and the sweetest . . . of one who is asleep and dreaming" (F. Delitzsch, *Psalms,* Commentary on the Old Testament, vol. V, translated by James Martin

[reprint, Grand Rapids, Michigan: Wm. B. Eerdmans Publishing Co., 1978], p. 352). Allen prefers to modify the vowels and translate "come to an end" (p. 252), while Kidner suggests a reference to resurrection (p. 467).

138

THE FAITHFUL AND RIGHTEOUS GOD

Psalm 140:1-13

This carefully crafted psalm sets solid confidence against a backdrop of malicious slander. Little wonder the psalmist cries for rescue and protection in the face of the foe described in 140:2-3. Their premeditated (**in their hearts**), habitual (**every day**), and violent evil inflicts wounds with words. They have ground their **tongues** razor sharp, as the warrior did with his sword before battle (see 64:3). The tongue of the serpent, sharp and quick, precedes its fangs, full of deadly venom. Again in 140:4-5, the psalmist cries out for protection but now describes the enemy as hunters. Deceitful as well as violent, they try to trip him with traps of every description.

In the center of the psalm (see 140:6-7), the psalmist acknowledges his dependence upon God (**you are my God** [140:6a]) and again appeals **for mercy** (140:6b). He exchanges his identity as hunted animal to protected warrior (140:7b) with the **Sovereign LORD** as his **strong deliverer** (140:7a). With renewed confidence, he asks God to deny the wishes of the wicked (see 140:8)—in particular, their wish to destroy the psalmist. If allowed to triumph, the already proud evil ones (see 140:5) would become more certain that they lie beyond the reach of God's judgment.

The psalmist prays not only for personal deliverance but for a permanent end to the wicked (**never to rise** [140:10]) so that no one else need suffer (see 140:9-11). He calls for the shameful effects of their slander to rain down on their heads as **burning coals** (see 18:8). **Fire** probably modifies coals rather than **pits,** which are usually associated with muck and mire (140:10).

Slanderers (literally, "man of tongue"), referring back to the sharp-tongued serpents of 140:3, will "find no rest anywhere" (140:11a NJB).

Hardly a clearer picture of the "boomerang" effects of evil could be found than in 140:11b, where **disaster** (same word as **evil** in 140:1-2) becomes the hunter (see 140:4c-5) pursuing the men of violence to a violent end.

The psalmist anticipates a better end because he knows the character of Yahweh (see 140:12-13). The faithfulness and righteousness of the Lord insure justice for the afflicted and the poor. By knowing the character of God one finds all that is necessary in times of difficulty. The righteous will most **surely** have cause to praise God as they live before Him.

AN ASCENDING APPEAL

Psalm 141:1-10

Like its neighbors (Psalms 140–143), Psalm 141 records a prayer for deliverance from enemies. As the smoke from the altar of incense or the evening sacrifice, prayer ascends to God (see 141:1-2). This comparison of prayer to the ritual acts of burning reveals the psalmist's conviction of God's grace. God is no machine that waits to hear a prayer only after the right amount of money has been deposited. Rituals were intended to foster the right attitude in the worshiper, not to appease a distant God.

In 141:3-7, it appears that David is praying for strength to resist the temptation to disobey. More likely these verses provide reasons why God should answer the prayer he offered in verses 1 and 2. He asks God to help him avoid evil in word, thought or association (see 141:3-4). Although he recognizes sin's **delicacies,** he asks God to remove the temptation. The psalmist is teachable and prepared to accept rebuke as joyously as anointing oil (see 141:5).

God should answer his prayer and **come quickly** because David hates wickedness (141:5b-7). These verses, although difficult to translate, find the wicked admitting the righteous were right (their confession appears in verse 7). The wicked lack David's teachability and only learn their lesson at the bottom of the cliff. His trust in God (see 141:8a) presents David's last basis for appeal and leads to the request itself in verses 8b through 10.

Do not give me over to death (141:8b) reflects his fear of falling into one of the snares or traps the enemy has set for him (see 141:9). Because the enemy has hidden the trap, leaving visible only the bait, God needed to help. Confident that He would, David contrasts the fates of the wicked and the righteous in verse 10. Ironically, the former will experience the effects of their own evil and become entangled in their own nets. Even more ironically, while they are trying to extricate themselves, the psalmist himself, the very object of their designs, will **pass by in safety.**

God remains willing and able to assist us and hear the cry of a righteous heart, however unorthodox that cry may sound. As verses 3 through 7 reveal, however, He also places responsibility on our shoulders. We must avoid evil, be willing to accept rebuke, and maintain our confidence in God, in spite of the prosperity of the wicked. We may not solve our problems by being righteous, but we certainly can prevent some.

140

FRIEND TO THE FRIENDLESS

Psalm 142:1-7

Created for fellowship, humanity cannot endure loneliness. Psalm 142 expresses the cry of a lonely, isolated, forsaken, and forgotten man. The historical note in the title, the first since Book Two, identifies this as David's prayer from **in the cave.** Those who accept Davidic authorship locate this cave as the one at En Gedi where David hid from Saul (see 1 Samuel 24; also Psalm 57).

David reveals his desperation in the opening two verses as he piles up phrases of appeal. Twice in Psalm 142:1 he mentions **my voice** (not translated in verse 1a), and **before him** in verse 2. **Complaint** is too petty; "worries" more closely reflects the psalmist's meaning.[1]

Although this desperate tone continues through the next two verses, hope still flickers. The harsh realities of isolation drained strength from his spirit, but somehow David retained the conviction that God knew about him (**you** is emphatic in verse 3). This knowledge sustains him to the end.

In this certainty he found courage to travel dangerous paths. Without a guide who knew the way, hidden and baited snares spelled disaster. Again, desperation rises (see 142:4) when the psalmist, looking around, sees no one to help him. No defender stands at his right hand (see 109:31; 110:5; 121:5). He has no place to hide and is haunted by the thought, "no one cares whether I live or die" (NJB).

At this darkest point, hope begins to burn more brightly. David acknowledges that, although abandoned by humanity, Yahweh remains his refuge and **portion in the land of the living** (142:5). For provision, God gave each tribe in Israel its **portion** of land, except for the Levites who received their portion from the Temple sacrifices (see Numbers 18:21). With Yahweh as his portion, David could claim God's provision even when prevented from enjoying his tribal inheritance (see Psalm 16:5-6; 73:26; 119:57). Such a strong confession of faith surely would not escape God's notice.

Three more times the psalmist calls for God's help (see 142:6-8). Each call seeks a greater measure of assistance: **Listen to my cry . . . rescue me. . . . Set me free . . .** (142:6-7). God should listen because of the psalmist's **desperate need** (142:6). God must rescue or else the pursuers will overtake and destroy David. If released from prison, the psalmist would publicly praise God's name, probably with a thanksgiving offering and communal meal.

His circumstances had not changed, and David remained alone; yet he anticipated a joyous celebration surrounded by friends and family. What gave him such hope even in desperate straits? He knew that God knew all about Him (see 142:3). Even when we are utterly alone, our God is the Friend to the friendless.

ENDNOTE

¹Leslie C. Allen, *Psalms 101–150,* Word Biblical Commentary, vol. 21, eds. David A. Hubbard and Glenn W. Barker (Waco, Texas: Word Books, 1983), p. 275.

141

A LOYAL SERVANT IN NEED

Psalm 143:1-12

The covenant God made with His people pervades Israel's self-identity. They delighted in prosperity as evidence of God's pleasure. In adversity, they appealed for mercy based on that covenant alliance, as Gibeah pleaded with Israel when attacked by the Amorites (see Joshua 10:6-7). Psalm 143 presents such an appeal from one of God's servants in difficulty (see 143:2, 12).[1]

The opening call for help (see 143:1-2) focuses on God's **faithfulness and righteousness.** Both terms speak of His commitment to covenant obligations: He keeps His promises and defends His covenant partner. While not reflected in the New International Version, the psalmist couched his request for **relief** in between these attributes: literally, "faithfulness," "righteousness." Although verse 2 can be read as acknowledging guilt,[2] it primarily reveals the psalmist's conviction that this covenant relationship must not be trifled with.

To insure a hearing for his prayer, David describes his difficulty (see 143:3-4). His description, while general enough to apply to many circumstances, nevertheless reveals his fear and pain. Before him looms a brutal and imminent death, followed by anonymity—completely forgotten **like those long dead** (143:3). No wonder his spirit faints and his heart is dismayed.

Formerly, God demonstrated faithfulness and righteousness to His covenant partners with miracles like the parting of the Sea of Reeds. In verses 5 and 6, David asks God to once again manifest this power on his behalf. He extends his hands in prayer, asking that God will extend His hands in power. Like **parched land** yearning for rain, the servant awaits his master.

The cry for help which follows in verses 7 through 12 is interspersed with reasons why God should grant David's appeal. God should reveal himself and His love once again or else the psalmist will die (**go down to the pit** [143:7]). As with the dawn, God should show the light of His face once more. Although containing a plea to **rescue me** (143:9), verses 8b through 10 primarily reflect David's desire for God's instruction. He has assumed the posture of a pupil, having lifted his soul in worship and acknowledged God as his own.

Finally, he asks God to deliver him from his enemies (**preserve my life . . . destroy all my foes** [143:11-12]). The order of his requests reveals his priorities: revelation of God (143:7-8a), instruction from God (143:8b-10), then deliverance from enemies (143:11-12). To remind God that His reputation as loving and righteous would suffer if He did not rescue the psalmist took the courage that came from knowing he was God's **servant** (143:12).

As Christians, God has called us to a relationship with Him. This relationship makes us responsible to obey our Master, but it also provides tremendous privileges. We can expect God to hear our prayers, take seriously our concerns, and provide for our needs. Recognizing these privileges without forgetting our obligations provides this same kind of "covenant confidence."

ENDNOTES

[1]Except that Psalm 143 makes significant use of other psalms (see *Psalms* by F. Delitzsch, Commentary on the Old Testament, vol. V, translated by James Martin [reprint, Grand Rapids, Michigan: Wm. B. Eerdmans Publishing Co., 1978], pp. 373-78), there is no strong argument against Davidic authorship.

[2]By reading verse 2 as such an acknowledgment, Psalm 143 has been identified as one of the seven penitential psalms (see Psalm 6, 32, 38, 51, 102, 130, and 143).

142

"BLESSED ARE THE PEOPLE WHOSE GOD IS THE LORD"[1]

Psalm 144:1-15

P salm 144 celebrates the blessing on the nation whose God was Yahweh, the Lord. He had delivered Israel from difficulty and poured out prosperity on His people. The royal language (see 144:10) and communal response (see 144:12-15) suggests the king and his subjects sang this psalm as part of worship in Jerusalem.[2]

The opening words of confidence (see 144:1-2) borrow heavily from Psalm 18 (which is also attributed to David). God protects the psalmist (God is referred to as **rock, fortress, stronghold,** and **shield**), delivers him from enemies, and grants him victory (**subdues peoples**). That the psalmist shares responsibility for his own deliverance is clear from the training described in 144:1. **My loving God** reflects an uncommon term for God (from *chesed*); it is translated by the New English Bible as "my help that never fails." **Peoples** (144:2b) should be "my peoples" (as noted in the New International Version's footnote), here understood to encompass foreign nations who have become the king's subjects after a military victory.

Against the background of God's power, humanity appears frail and powerless. The psalmist, borrowing from Psalm 8:4, contemplates the brevity of life; this prepares one for his impassioned appeal (see 144:5-8). Only Yahweh could come in such cataclysmic style: **heavens** opened, **mountains** smoking, **lightning** shooting out like arrows (144:5-6). The long arm of the Lord would rescue and deliver the psalmist, even from ominous mighty waters and the **hands of foreigners** (144:7). Verse

8 suggests that other nations had broken treaties they had sworn (**right hands**) with Israel and had left national security in jeopardy.

If delivered, the psalmist promised praise (see 144:9-10). A new song marked an especially noteworthy occasion; to play on a **ten-stringed lyre** apparently meant "pulling out all the stops." Then, in terms almost identical to verse 7, the psalmist repeats his appeal for **rescue** (144:11). With Yahweh as its God, Israel could know deliverance from difficulty.

The remaining verses (144:12-15) show that the Lord also brings material blessings. Foremost among these is the blessing of children (see 144:12). He makes **sons** grow into **well-nurtured plants**—fruitful and stable; **daughters**—like carved corner **pillars**—beautify and support the home. The blessings of the field also reveal God's pleasure. Full **barns,** increasing flocks (**sheep**), healthy **oxen** (144:13-14a)—few things meant more to a society dependant on the soil. Finally, Yahweh blesses His people with security (see 144:14b), the very thing endangered by foreign deception.[3]

Having a God like Yahweh marked a people as **blessed** (144:15). This remains as true for the Christian as it was for Israel. To belong to a God to whom we can turn in difficulty and who showers us with "every good and perfect gift" (James 1:17), makes us truly a **blessed** people.

ENDNOTES

[1]Psalm 144:15b.

[2]Some assume Davidic authorship based on the title and Psalm 144:10. Others, arguing from the psalm's late language and its use of older material, suggest an author writing about David or one of the kings in his dynasty.

[3]Leslie Allen sees the agricultural metaphor continuing, translating verse 14 as

> Our cattle are in fine fettle.
> There is no plague nor abortion,
> nor bellowing in our broad meadows.

(Leslie C. Allen, *Psalms 101–150,* Word Biblical Commentary, vol. 21, eds. David A. Hubbard and Glenn W. Barker [Waco, Texas: Word Books, 1983], p. 287.)

143

LET THE EARTH HEAR HIS VOICE

Psalm 145:1-21

Ironically, the title **A psalm of praise** appears only here in all the Psalter (called the Book of Praises in Hebrew). It may be ironic, but it is not surprising that Psalm 145 should receive this title. Written as an alphabet acrostic, it finds in its survey of God's character more than enough reasons to praise.

David begins with a promise to praise God each day, **for ever and ever** (145:1-2). Twice he promises to **praise your name,** the name by which God revealed himself in all His greatness. To praise God's name means responding to His revealed character; in this psalm (see 145:1, 11-13), God's nature as King predominates.

Even praising daily and forever, the psalmist cannot hope to fathom, let alone exhaust, the **greatness** God has revealed (145:3). Therefore, he describes this process continuing from generation to generation (see 145:4). Because God revealed His greatness to individuals as well as nations, he alternates between corporate and personal praise (see 145:5-6). No doubt the psalmist envisions Israel in public assembly, remembering God's past goodness to Israel and celebrating in song (see 145:7).

Any survey of God's treatment of Israel reveals Him as **gracious, compassionate, slow to anger,** and **rich in love** (145:8). That these words, found often in the Old Testament, would portray the character of the Heavenly King should surprise no one, for God used these same words to describe himself to Moses (see Exodus 34:6-7).

Such a king, **good to all** and showing **compassion on all he has made** (Ps. 145:9), deserves the praise of all He has made (see 145:10). His subjects will tell of the greatness of His kingdom so that **all men** will glorify God (145:12). In this way, Israel can fulfill its mission to be a source of blessing for the nations (see Genesis 12:3). Psalm 145:13a finds its echo and fulfillment in Revelation 11:15: "The kingdom of the world has become the kingdom of our Lord and of his Christ, and he will reign for ever and ever."

In Psalm 145:13b-20, David provides a closer look at the character of the divine King, a character which embodies the kingly ideal.[1] This King is faithful to His promises and **loving toward all he has made** (145:13b). He manifests that integrity and compassion by providing for His subjects on an ongoing basis (**give, open,** and **satisfy** here imply continual action) and according to their **desires** (145:15-16).

As a good king should, God vindicates the cause of the needy (see 145:17-20). Motivated by love *(chesed),* He stands by those who fear Him, listening for their cries and fulfilling their desires. This King desires not only reverence, but **love** from His subjects (145:20a). Over these He watches protectively, while **all the wicked he will destroy** (145:20b).

Once again the psalmist commits himself to praise, then summons **every creature** to join him in praising God's **holy name** forever (145:21). From what we have learned of our divine King, what response could be more appropriate?

ENDNOTE

[1]Psalm 145:13b is not found in most Hebrew manuscripts but does appear in the Dead Sea Scrolls and in some early versions. Most modern versions include it, partly because it completes the alphabet acrostic by adding the missing Hebrew letter *nun.*

144

"THE LORD REIGNS FOREVER"[1]

Psalm 146:1-10

The final five psalms in the Psalter form a collection in which each begins and ends with a call to praise and each takes praise as its theme. Like Psalm 145, Psalm 146 sings praise for Yahweh's kingship; the former lifts its praise heavenward while the latter addresses God's people in Jerusalem.

The opening verses can be read as call and response. The summons to **praise the LORD** in 146:1 is answered with the psalmist's determination to make praise a lifelong habit (see 146:2). Before giving reasons for praise (see 146:5-10), he offers advice: **Do not put your trust in** (do not depend on) human beings, even powerful ones such as **princes** (146:3-4). If this psalm originated after the Exile, a warning against faith in **princes** could allude to the failure of Judah's monarchy or a general distrust of human leadership. God's people still need this warning lest they find they have put their trust in dust. After the spirit of **mortal men** (literally, "Son of *Adam*") departs, they **return to the ground** *(adamah)*. With this play on words, the psalmist illustrates the folly of putting trust in people.

The description of God which follows (see 146:5-9) first addresses God's role in history and creation (see 146:5-6). By calling Yahweh **the God of Jacob** (146:5), the psalmist emphasizes God's covenant with Jacob (Israel) and his descendants. The psalmist also praises the Lord as **Maker of heaven and earth** and all they contain (146:6a). The God of Jacob governs more than Israel; He rules over everything by virtue of having created everything. How could Israel be certain that this almighty Creator was not merely raw power, like a bolt of lightning that destroys what it touches? Because **he remains faithful forever** (146:6b). He has made promises to Israel and marshals His omnipotence and eternal nature to fulfill each one.

In verse 3a, the psalmist warned, **Do not put your trust in princes.** Instead, put your trust in the God of Jacob, the all-powerful and promise-keeping God, who perfectly fulfills the role of King (see 146:7-9). The description in these verses highlights God's ongoing activity, rather than what He did or will do. He vindicates **the oppressed,** insuring that justice is served (146:7a). By describing vindication using the word translated **Maker** in verse 6, the psalmist emphasizes that the God who created the universe is also concerned about the needs of the oppressed.

This King also provides for the needs of His subjects, whether the need is **food** (146:7b), freedom (146:7c), **sight** for the blind (146:8a), or assistance for those **bowed down** under life's load (146:8b). Clearly, this King loves His people, especially the needy. The three groups singled out in verse 9 (**alien, fatherless,** and **widow**) are society's most vulnerable. As a necessary corollary to His care for the needy, God **frustrates** the work of **the wicked** (146:9b).

Human kings are undependable because they are temporary, but this perfect King reigns forever. The psalmist summons the Israelites to praise because—blessing of blessings—they have been chosen by this King to be His subjects forever! When we remember that this same God has chosen to rule over us, in Christ, we can join ancient Israel in a heartfelt **Praise the LORD** (146:10).

ENDNOTE

[1]Psalm 146:10a.

145

HIS POWERFUL WORD

Psalm 147:1-20

Like voices in conversation, Psalm 147 presents two alternating portraits of God. Sometimes He appears as Israel's covenant Lord; at other times He is the God over nature. Both portraits offer post-exilic Israel ample reason for praise.[1]

There are three stanzas, each containing a call to praise followed by reasons for praise. The opening statements strongly affirm **how good it is to sing praises to our God** (147:1). Praise is **pleasant** because it represents what humanity was created to do.[2] Praise is **fitting,** entirely appropriate to what God deserves.

The reasons for praise begin in Jerusalem where the covenant God is at work rebuilding both the city and the broken hearts of its citizens (see 147:2-3). Then the psalmist looks beyond Jerusalem to the realm of nature where God, like a celestial Shepherd, **determines the number of the stars and calls them each by name** (147:4). This verse reminds us of God's promise that Abraham would have descendants as numerous as the stars (see Genesis 15:5), a welcome word to the depleted population of post-exilic Jerusalem. Yahweh, the covenant God, incomparably powerful and wise, is also merciful, defending the afflicted and defeating the wicked (see 147:5-6).

The same two themes—God of covenant and God of nature—appear in the second stanza (see 147:7-11). The psalmist begins in nature, describing the natural process God uses to supernaturally provide (see 147:8-9). He brings the **clouds,** which produce the **rain** that **makes grass grow,** and **grass** feeds the creatures (see Job 38:41).

The focus then shifts to what pleases the God of the covenant (see Psalm 147:10-11). Because horses carried soldiers and pulled chariots, they were valuable war machines, worth five times the price of a male slave.³ Any king would have desired strong soldiers capable of long marches and fierce fighting. To God, however, these mean nothing. He desires those who revere Him and trust in His covenant **love** (*chesed;* see 33:16-18).

The third stanza (147:12-20) begins with a call to praise addressed to **Jerusalem** (147:12) and with a view to the prosperity of God's chosen city (see 147:13-14). Security comes not from horse and warrior but from Yahweh, who grants the nation peaceful borders and bountiful harvests. In verse 15, the psalmist turns again to God's power over nature—specifically, how He produces the precious commodity, water, by unusual means. He starts by sowing **snow, frost,** and **hail** with an **icy blast.**⁴ Then, at His **word** (*dabar;* 147:15, 18) the ice melts, yielding a harvest of flowing waters. God the Covenant-Keeper returns in the description of God's law (see 147:19-20a). That Israel alone has received this gift is no reason for pride but for gratitude and a renewed commitment to be a light to the nations (see Isaiah 49:6).

The two portraits of God converge in His **word,** which has the authority to command both nature (147:15, 18) and humanity (see 147:19). If the Law was reason for Israel to praise (see 147:20b), how much more fitting is it that we, to whom God has spoken by His Son (see Hebrews 1:2), should **Praise the LORD** (Ps. 147:20).

ENDNOTES

¹This date is based on 147:2 and on the psalm's use of biblical material from late in the pre-exilic period (see Leslie C. Allen, *Psalms 101–150,* Word Biblical Commentary, vol. 21, eds. David A. Hubbard and Glenn W. Barker [Waco, Texas: Word Books, 1983], p. 309).

²"The chief end of man is to glorify God, and to enjoy him forever," according to the Westminster Shorter Catechism (cited in *The Creeds of the Evangelical Protestant Churches* by Schaff [New York: Harper, 1877], p. 676).

³Othmar Keel, *The Symbolism of the Biblical World: Ancient Near Eastern Iconography and the Book of Psalms,* translated by Timothy J. Hallett (New York: Seabury Press, 1978), p. 238.

⁴What the New International Version renders as a rhetorical question in 147:17b (**Who can withstand his icy blast?**) can also be translated as a statement ("No one can endure the cold he sends!" [TEV]) or, with a slight change in the Hebrew, "water standing frozen before his cold" (Allen, p. 305).

146

PRAISE FROM HEAVEN AND EARTH

Psalm 148:1-14

salm 148 elicits praise for Yahweh that is truly universal in scope. Invitations extend first to heaven, then earth, and all the inhabitants of each. Strikingly, only a few of the psalm's fourteen verses express reasons for praise; the rest simply call for praise. A call to praise, however, is just another form of adoration. Identifying those who should praise implies their debt to God, and a debt assumes something has been given.[1] The psalmist designed the two stanzas (148:1-6 and 148:7-14) as a pair; both contain extended invitations followed by reasons to praise.

He directs the first stanza to **the heavens** and their occupants. The **angels** and **heavenly hosts** (148:2) would be expected to give praise as God's messengers and heavenly army. But so, too, must the celestial bodies (see 148:3) which were worshiped by Israel's neighbors. That which occupies the highest part of heaven, including the reservoirs of rain (**waters above the skies**), must praise **the name of the LORD** (148:4-5). All these must praise Him because they have been created by Him, and Him alone (**he** is emphatic in verse 5b). It only took a word for infinite power to form the universe and sustain it forever (see 148:6a). The permanent **decree** (148:6) refers to the "laws of nature," which, though referring to nature, had their origin in God.

In the second stanza (148:7-14), the focus shifts to the earth and its occupants. Many of these summoned in verses 7 through 12 were feared or worshiped in the ancient Near East. The **great sea creatures** (148:7) were considered supernatural forces (74:13),[2] and the Canaanites often worshiped their gods, including the storm god (148:8), Baal, on the mountains (148:9). By summoning them to worship Yahweh, the psalmist demonstrates that He alone is worthy of adoration. From the sea to the storm, from the hills and trees to the animals and birds (see 148:7-10), all nature was called to worship God. Humans as well, from kings to children, Israel and foreigners, all people must worship Yahweh.

These verses praise Yahweh for the salvation He accomplished by raising a **horn** for His people (148:13b-14c). Horn here could refer to a national restoration like the return from exile. It could also mean strong one, that is, the king (see the New International Version's footnote). Since Israel did not have its own king during the post-exilic period (when this psalm was probably written), perhaps this refers to the coming Messiah.[3]

The God who created the universe and deserves its praise cares enough to stoop down and take Israel **close to His heart** (148:14c). In this, God demonstrates the love that will eventually stoop to the level of a servant and give up His life for humanity (see Philippians 2:6-11).

ENDNOTES

[1]Leslie C. Allen, *Psalms 101–150,* Word Biblical Commentary, vol. 21, eds. David A. Hubbard and Glenn W. Barker (Waco, Texas: Word Books, 1983), p. 316.

[2]Othmar Keel, *The Symbolism of the Biblical World: Ancient Near Eastern Iconography and the Book of Psalms,* translated by Timothy J. Hallett (New York: Seabury Press, 1978), pp. 47–56.

[3]**Has raised** (148:14) would then refer to God's future intervention, which was so certain that it could be described in the past tense.

147

A SONG OF FINAL VICTORY

Psalm 149:1-9

In militant terms, Psalm 149 describes the victory to which Psalm 148:14 alludes. Israel, knowing God would one day have universal dominion, envisions the role it will play in bringing that about. Such a forward glance belongs in the closing pages of Israel's hymnal. Early Christians also worshiped with one eye on God's ultimate victory as they anticipated Christ's return. A call for judgment, similar in tone to Psalm 149, appears at the end of the New Testament in the Book of Revelation.

Because of the horrible uses to which this psalm has been put in the name of God,[1] one may be reluctant to take seriously its message of conquest. Israel cannot triumph, however, unless Israel's enemies are defeated. "Why Israel?" someone asks, "Isn't this unfair?" Israel's victory is really God's victory. They execute the judgments He decrees (see Psalm 149:9) as their king (149:2), judgments which He inflicts because of His covenant with Israel.[2] He must keep these promises (including punishment of Israel's enemies) or be found unreliable. He must preserve the covenant or see the dissolution of His redemptive plan.

The victory to which this psalm refers could be something in Israel's distant past, such as the conquest of Canaan[3] or in Israel's future.[4] Most likely, the psalm takes Israel's recent return from Babylonian exile as evidence that final victory was coming soon, and it sings in anticipation.

The festive scene of the opening stanza (149:1-5) bears all the marks of a victory celebration with singing (the **new song** marked a special occasion), **dancing,** and the music of **tambourine and harp** (see Exodus 15; 1 Samuel 18:6-7; Psalm 68:25-26). Psalm 149:4 pictures this victory as the expression of God's **delight in His people.** The King elevates His **humble** subjects to the level of royalty, crowning them with **salvation.**

Such an honor brings **joy,** even **on their beds** (149:5). Since the word for "bed" can also mean "couch," Bible commentator Derek Kidner suggests a reference to reclining at a celebratory banquet, while Leslie Allen tentatively proposes a meaning of lying prostrate in humility before God. Most likely, the phrase implies that a joy-induced insomnia has replaced an anxious sleeplessness.[5]

The second stanza (149:6-9b) contains a call for **praise** (149:6a) followed by a call for justice (see 149:6b-9), implying that both express the will of God. The Law forbids revenge against a fellow Israelite (see Leviticus 19:18), but, for those nations which have oppressed and imprisoned Israel, punishment in kind must follow. **The sentence written against** these enemies (Ps. 149:9a) refers to God's covenant promise of protection and justice. To be the means of divine justice meant **glory** for Israel (149:9b).

The world has not yet seen the judgment envisioned in this psalm. Instead, God came in the person of Jesus to endure divine justice on the Cross. The church—God's new covenant people—now awaits His return when, finally and forever, righteousness will prevail.

ENDNOTES

[1]See F. Delitzsch, *Psalms,* Commentary on the Old Testament, vol. V, translated by James Martin (reprint, Grand Rapids, Michigan: Wm. B. Eerdmans Publishing Co., 1978), p. 411; Artur Weiser, *The Psalms—A Commentary,* translated by Herbert Hartwell, The Old Testament Library, gen. eds. G. Ernest Wright, John Bright, James Barr and Peter Ackroyd (Philadelphia: Westminster Press, 1962), p. 839.

[2]Allusions to the covenant include God as Israel's **Maker** (149:2) and the threefold use of **saints,** once each in the first and last verses and once in the middle.

[3]See Weiser.

[4]See A. Cohen, *The Psalms,* Soncino Books of the Bible, ed. A. Cohen (London: Soncino, 1950).

[5]Derek Kidner, *Psalms 73–150,* Tyndale Old Testament Commentaries, ed. D.J. Wiseman (Downer's Grove, Illinois: InterVarsity Press, 1975), p. 489; Leslie C. Allen, *Psalms 101–150,* Word Biblical Commentary, vol. 21, eds. David A. Hubbard and Glenn W. Barker (Waco, Texas: Word Books, 1983), p. 317.

148

HALLELUJAH

Psalm 150:1-6

J ust as each of the four preceding books of the Psalter closed with a doxology, so the fifth book and the Psalter itself conclude with a summons to praise. Considered another way, however, the Psalter does not close with Psalm 150. Its repeated and widely scattered calls to praise summon each reader—ancient and modern—to add his or her own praise.

The psalmist begins by locating two places where Yahweh's praise is most appropriate (see 150:1b). **His sanctuary** identifies a specific place on earth where God chose to make His presence known. **His mighty heavens** refers, not to a specific location, but to that vast expanse which is still too small to contain Him (see 2 Chronicles 6:18). The reason for praise, according to Psalm 150:2, is both for what God has done (**his acts of power**) and who He is (**his surpassing greatness**).

Dancing and every type of instrument—strings, percussion and winds—are needed to express the greatness of this God. The **trumpet** (*shofar*) begins the list, perhaps because it often signaled the start of a special occasion. **Harp and lyre** appear frequently in liturgical settings. **Dancing** and the **tambourine** are found together at victory celebrations (see 149:3). **Strings** may refer to instruments more commonly used in a secular setting (45:8). The quiet **flute** and noisy cymbals are also summoned to join this exuberant song of praise to Yahweh.

The call extends to **everything that has breath** (150:6a). With this concluding invitation, "the Psalmist sums up the aspiration and aim of Israel's mission and the purpose of its existence as God's appointed messenger to mankind."[1] From Israel's hymnal we have learned why God deserves our worship. Now we have heard the summons to praise. The time has come to add our own voices to the timeless song.

ENDNOTE

[1]A. Cohen, *The Psalms,* Soncino Books of the Bible, ed. A. Cohen (London: Soncino, 1950), p. 479.

SELECT BIBLIOGRAPHY

This commentary has been written with the purpose of enabling the Christian in the pew to understand God's message in the book of Psalms. Below is a list of resources that may help the reader who wishes to do further study.

Alter, Robert. "The Psalms: Beauty Heightened Through Poetic Structure." *Bible Review* 2 (1986), pp. 29–41.

Ashburn, Daniel G. "Creation and Torah in Psalm 19." *Jewish Bible Quarterly* 22 (1994), pp. 241–48.

Bandstra, Barry L. *Reading the Old Testament: An Introduction to the Hebrew Bible.* Belmont, California: Wadsworth Publishing Company, 1995.

Booij, Th. "Psalm LXXXIV, A Prayer of the Anointed." *Vetus Testamentum.* Vol. XLIV (1994), pp. 433–41.

Brown, Francis. *The New Brown-Driver-Briggs-Gesenius Hebrew and English Lexicon.* Peabody, Massachusetts: Hendrickson Publishers, 1979.

Cohen, A., ed. Soncino Books of the Bible. *The Psalms* by A. Cohen. London: Soncino, 1950.

Freedman, David Noel. "The Structure of Psalm 119: Part II." *Hebrew Annual Review* 14 (1994), pp. 55–88.

Freeman, D. "Tabernacles, Feast of." *New Bible Dictionary,* rev. ed. Gen. ed. J.D. Douglas. Wheaton, Illinois: Tyndale House, 1982.

Good, Robert M. "Baal." *Harper's Bible Dictionary.* Gen. ed. Paul J. Achtemeier. San Francisco: Harper, 1985.

Gordon, R.P. "Hagrites." *New Bible Dictionary,* rev. ed. Gen. ed. J.D. Douglas. Wheaton, Illnois: Tyndale House, 1982.

Hubbard, David A. and Barker, Glenn W., eds. Word Biblical Commentary. Vol. 19, *Psalms 1–50,* by Peter C. Craigie. Waco, Texas: Word Books, 1983.

Hubbard, David A. and Barker, Glenn W., eds. Word Biblical Commentary. Vol. 20, *Psalms 51–100,* by Marvin E. Tate. Waco, Texas: Word Books, 1990.

Hubbard, David A. and Barker, Glenn W., eds. Word Biblical Commentary. Vol. 21, *Psalms 101–150,* by Leslie C. Allen. Waco, Texas: Word Books, 1983.

Keel, Othmar. *The Symbolism of the Biblical World: Ancient Near Eastern Iconography and the Book of Psalms.* Translated by Timothy J. Hallett. New York: Seabury Press, 1978.

Keil, C.F. and Delitzsch, F. Commentary on the Old Testament. Vol. V, *Psalms,* by F. Delitzsch. Translated by James Martin. Reprint, Grand Rapids, Michigan: Wm. B. Eerdmans Publishing Company, 1978.

Kirkpatrick, A.F. The Cambridge Bible for Schools and Colleges. *The Book of Psalms* by A.F. Kirkpatrick, 1902. Reprint, Cambridge: Cambridge University Press, 1910.

Kraus, Hans-Joachim. *Theology of the Psalms.* Translated by Keith Crim. Minneapolis: Augsburg Press, 1986.

Lewis, C.S. *Reflections on the Psalms.* New York: Harcourt, Brace and World, 1958.

Longman, Tremper, III. *How to Read the Psalms.* Downers Grove, Illinois: InterVarsity Press, 1988.

Luther, Martin. *Works.* Eds. E. Helmut Lehmann and Theodore Bachmann. 55 vols. St. Louis: Concordia; and Philadelphia: Muhlenberg Press, 1958–86.

Meiklejohn, J.W. "Barrenness." *New Bible Dictionary,* rev. ed. Gen. ed. J.D. Douglas. Wheaton, Illinois: Tyndale House, 1982.

Mitchell, T.C. "Moon." *New Bible Dictionary,* rev. ed. Gen. ed. J.D. Douglas. Wheaton, Illinois: Tyndale House, 1982.

Perowne, John J.S. *The Book of Psalms.* 2 vols. Andover, Massachusetts: Warren F. Draper, 1885.

Rattray, Susan. "Worship." *Harper's Bible Dictionary.* Gen. ed. Paul J. Achtemeier. San Francisco: Harper, 1985.

Spurgeon, Charles H. *The Treasury of David.* 7 vols. New York: Funk and Wagnalls, 1882.

Weinstein, James M. "Zoan." *Harper's Bible Dictionary.* Gen. ed. Paul J. Achtemeier. San Francisco: Harper, 1985.

Weiser, Artur. *The Psalms—A Commentary.* Translated by Herbert Hartwell. The Old Testament Library. Gen. eds. G. Ernest Wright, John Bright, James Barr, and Peter Ackroyd. Philadelphia: Westminster Press, 1962.

Wiseman, D.J., ed. Tyndale Old Testament Commentaries. *Psalms 1–72* and *Psalms 73–150* by Derek Kidner. Downer's Grove, Illinois: InterVarsity Press, 1973, 1975.